DON'T GIVE UP ON AN AGING PARENT

OTHER BOOKS BY THE SAME AUTHOR

The Silent Disease: Hypertension

The Laboratory of the Body

The Family Book of Preventive Medicine
with Benjamin F. Miller, M.D.

How Long Will You Live?

Freedom from Heart Attacks
with Benjamin F. Miller, M.D.

Your Heart: Complete Information for the Family
with William Likoff, M.D., *and* Bernard Segal, M.D.

Adult Physical Fitness Manual, President's Council on Physical Fitness

DON'T GIVE UP ON AN AGING PARENT

Lawrence Galton

Crown Publishers, Inc., New York

Inquiries should be addressed to
Crown Publishers, Inc., 419 Park Avenue South, New York, N.Y. 10016
Library of Congress Catalog Card Number: 74–80309
Printed in the United States of America
Published simultaneously in Canada by
General Publishing Company Limited

Design by Leonard Telesca
Second Printing, February, 1975

To my mother –
and to my sister Lorna who understands so well
the meaning of the title of this book

CONTENTS

1

BUT ARE THEY REALLY BEYOND HELP? NOW? TODAY?

In the previous year he had gradually lost his memory, could not remember what day it was nor the names of doctors he had seen. His judgment and insight had deteriorated, his conversation became confused, his habits untidy; he had difficulty in walking; and he had become incontinent.

He was old and, it seemed, senile—a victim of senile dementia, a typical "old-man-with-gravy-on-his-vest" victim, doddering, witless, and beyond help.

But was he? It turned out later, with persistent investigation, that he was, in reality, suffering from hydrocephalus—"water on the brain." Once the effort was made to detect it, the condition was relieved and he recovered completely.

A rare problem? On the contrary, occult hydrocephalus, as the condition is called, may be quite common. Nobody knows the true incidence, but there is evidence that many such patients may be vegetating in both mental institutions and homes for the aged. Occult hydrocephalus, now detectable and treatable, may afflict millions in view of the increased life expectancy of the general population. "For the first time, we can look over those patients who have been abandoned to a life of dependency and pluck them back from oblivion," says a leading neurosurgeon.

Old Age and "Therapeutic Futility"

Many of the so-called senile aren't really senile, aren't really suffering because of incurable artery hardening or chronic brain disease, aren't at all beyond help.

And of those who are truly senile, who do have chronic brain disease and incurable artery hardening, many still are not beyond help.

Moreover, many of the severe physical illnesses of the aged—chronic, incapacitating arthritis and other aches and pains, crippling heart and lung disease, and others—are now treatable. Medicine and surgery—applied as matters of course to the young with the same problems—have been shown to be no less applicable to many of the aged.

A seventy-five-year-old woman suffers through years of increasing arthritic pain and disability; hip, knee, both hands, are affected. Finally, she receives sixteen days of expert and intensive treatment in the hospital. It includes physical as well as medical therapy and instruction for self-therapy at home. At discharge, she isn't capable of dancing but she can get about and function without pain and maintain her independence.

A whole series of patients, more than two hundred, disabled by lung disease, turn wheels by hand, walk on motor-driven treadmills, ride stationary bicycles. They have to be given oxygen to get them started. They have been unable to walk slowly on the level for two city blocks; many have been unable to exert themselves slightly, even cross a room, without running short of breath. When they finish the rehabilitation program, and a year later as well, they can walk for half an hour on the treadmill and have an increased tolerance for activities of daily living. Life is once more enjoyable.

An elderly man, confined to a wheelchair because of crippling muscular pain, weakness, and low-grade fever, has made a fruitless round of doctors; hundreds of dollars have been spent for laboratory studies looking for evidence of arthritis or cancer, and finding none. He is one of a whole group of patients whose condition is finally recognized to be a common, overlooked, easily remediable disease of the elderly. Within forty-eight hours after simple treatment he is out of his wheelchair.

The "Too-Little-in-Contact" Myth

In Wheeling, West Virginia, a seventy-eight-year-old woman is withdrawn, apathetic, not interested in anything. Her family reports that she has reached the point of not wanting to see relatives or friends, spends most of her time sitting, has to be told to eat and to go to bed. And the family is led to think that she must be suffering from progressive hardening of the arteries.

Yet, after two weeks of treatment, she is alert and active and feels better than she has felt in many years.

Medical Misadventure

An eighty-year-old woman is admitted, in coma, to an Albany, New York, hospital from a nearby nursing home. For six months before going into coma, she had been increasingly lethargic.

After seventy-two hours of intensive care, she is brought out of coma but she speaks in a Marlene Dietrich voice. It suggests to an alert physician the possibility of thyroid deficiency. The woman had been under routine treatment for heart disease, high blood pressure, and chronic bronchitis. Among her drugs was potassium iodide for the bronchitis but she was extremely sensitive to it and it had depressed her thyroid gland. When, thanks to that physician, the iodide was stopped and she was given a thyroid preparation to make up for the gland depression, she became active and enjoyed better health than ever before in her latter years. As a happy sequel, her own thyroid began to function normally again and she requires no further thyroid medication.

Drugs must be watched carefully. Some of the aged, including the seemingly senile aged, are victims not so much of disease as of toxic psychosis from poor treatment of disease. They may take excessive amounts of medication or may even be sensitive to small amounts. The fault may lie in remedies taken without medical advice or even in prescribed medications.

For example, often the elderly require digitalis for heart problems. It is one of the oldest, most widely used, most valuable drugs in medicine. But proper dosage—proper on an individualized basis—is crucial. An excess can produce toxicity, with confusion, weakness, and deterioration simulating brain disease. The symptoms quickly disappear when the drug is stopped and may remain absent when it is reinstituted in the right dosage.

Confusion, excitement, and even hallucinations sometimes can be traced to excessive amounts of atropine and atropine-like drugs used for gastrointestinal complaints. Correctable mental symptoms also develop in some elderly people treated for cardiovascular problems with restricted salt diets and diuretic drugs that may lead to body chemical imbalances unless compensations are made.

Item: But It Isn't Impossible to Improve Brain Nutrition

In Pittsburgh, an experimental treatment is employed for a series of elderly patients, most of them with symptoms of organic brain disease: impaired memory, poor judgment, disorientation. They receive an anticoagulant drug often used to help thin the blood in younger patients. The hope is that if the blood is thinned, more of it can squeeze through hardened, narrowed brain arteries, improving nutrition of deprived brain cells and thereby helping to restore normal function.

Among the patients is a retired executive who, after seven weeks of treatment, can recognize his wife, remember his physician's name, dress himself, get up, and walk about unescorted. Another patient, a woman, was so confused she gave the population of the United States as ten million and, despite a long career in nursing, couldn't name correctly even the three types of blood vessels in the body. She has begun to recover and, with further recovery, may return to nursing.

Supposedly, for the elderly with "chronic brain syndrome," brain nutrition cannot be improved and the picture must be grim. Yet it's increasingly apparent that impaired blood flow in the brain can stem from problems having nothing to do with brain arteries.

Treat a weakening heart adequately and as it pumps out more blood circulation to the brain may improve. Correct a vitamin or other dietary deficiency and the patient not only improves physically but often at least partially recoups mental function.

A seventy-two-year-old woman finally is hospitalized because of mental confusion and failing physical health after her doctor's prescriptions do no good. She is found to have previously unsuspected pellagra, caused by deficiency of a vitamin, niacin. In a few weeks after niacin treatment is begun, her physical symptoms vanish and her confusion clears.

Mental function may improve, too, when a mild, smoldering infection is found and overcome or an anemia is uncovered and treated. Anemia in an elderly person may stem from a bleeding polyp or other benign and readily curable gastrointestinal problem; and especially now, when the aged, thanks to improved surgical and anesthetic techniques, can come through surgery safely, they deserve complete investigation just as much as do younger people.

Item: Not Necessarily Too Late for Surgery

The patient is an elderly man with a peptic ulcer that has refused to yield to medical treatment. An operation is needed. But an operation is also needed for gallstones. Both of the surgical procedures are carried out in one sitting. He comes through well.

An eighty-two-year-old man develops paralysis of the right side of his body, has difficulty talking and understanding speech. Studies indicate a hematoma, a clotted blood mass in the brain. Brushing aside objections that the patient is far too old for anything to be attempted, surgeons operate, remove the hematoma. The patient recovers promptly, completely.

These are not isolated cases. There is now considerable evidence that surgery often can help the aged and that when necessary some of the most complex operations can be carried out with remarkable success.

Although there are still some physicians as well as many lay people who think surgery for the aged is excessively risky and not likely to be worthwhile, the fact is that many of the aged now can benefit greatly from surgery to repair dropped wombs, bladders, and rectal tissue; surgery to treat peptic ulcers, diverticular disease, benign tumors, and malignant growths; surgery to treat glaucoma and cataract; and surgery for many other conditions.

Operations considered essential in younger people are hardly impossible now when needed in the elderly.

One particularly dramatic example of what is now possible is hip joint replacement. The removal of a whole hip joint and its replacement with an artificial substitute is an extensive procedure. Too grueling for an elderly person? Yet, currently, more than ten thousand Americans are walking around on artificial hips and most of them are elderly, some of them in their late seventies and eighties. Among them are some notables, including former Senator Margaret Chase Smith of Maine and conductor Eugene Ormandy, joyous over rescue from a crippling state.

Elderly patients, as we will see later, also have benefited from another major surgical procedure, heart revascularization, which involves use of a vein from the leg to bypass clogged portions of arteries feeding the heart muscle. They have come well through five and six hours and more on the operating table to show significant improvement.

It is true that not many years ago age in itself was a contraindication to surgery. The surgical and anesthetic techniques of the time could not prevent an unacceptable mortality rate.

Now age in itself is no longer a bar to necessary surgery, but attitudes may be—as they may be to much else that can be done for the aged.

Astonishing Results? Yes . . . and No

With considerable pride, a group of physicians reported not long ago that they had implanted a heart pacemaker in a ninety-two-year-old woman. Automatically, whenever her heart began to slow down dangerously, the pacemaker took over and kept it beating properly until her heart resumed beating normally on its own.

It seemed remarkable. But it wasn't. Very shortly, reports from other physicians came in. One reported implanting a pacemaker in a 96-year-old woman four years earlier, and she is doing well. Another told of implanting a pacemaker in a 101-year-old man who went home in less than a week and informed his daughter, aged 77 years, that he was seriously considering getting married again. Still another physician reported implantation of a pacemaker in a 103-year-old man who then returned home to his usual level of activity, happily puttering around the house and grounds.

When a curious investigator checked back on the records at one medical center covering 292 patients who had suffered cardiac arrest—actual stoppage of the heart—and had been resuscitated, it turned out that the survival rates after cardiac arrest were identical in the over-sixty and under-sixty age groups.

Recently, the Veterans Administration had among its patients 108,500 aged persons. Many suffered from confusion, hostility, disorientation, and withdrawal from reality. They were seemingly beyond help, doomed to just "fade away."

Yet the results of a simple, pioneering program at one VA hospital suggest strongly that they are not beyond help. Such "fading away" often begins with a medical crisis—such as pneumonia, heart disease, or stroke—or a psychosocial crisis—an economic, social, or emotional stress. The elderly patient becomes dependent on family care and the family reacts by providing care even in areas where the patient can function. The elderly person feels and acts more helpless and the family, without any guidance, understandably begins to see the situation as hopeless. The usual end result is permanent institutionalization and fading away.

In the belief that dependency and loneliness lie behind the "fading," the hospital initiated a program, modest in nature, to keep the aged constantly in touch with the surrounding environment. Instead of ignoring the rambling or forgetfulness of patients, attendants return them to reality matter-of-factly, repeatedly telling them who they are, where they are, what is going on. There are brief class periods oriented to time, place, and person; to current events, socialization, trips of interest into the community.

One-third of the 125 patients in the program have shown significant improvement; two-thirds have become stabilized; only a single patient has sunk deeper into the dim world of senility. Striking results for an ailment conventionally looked upon as progressive and irreversible!

Medical Failings and Social Failings

The ranks of people over sixty-five are swelling at an accelerated rate. By 1980, there should be 24.5 million; by the year 2000, 40 million—too many to hide or forget. The problem is urgent.

The aged have been a deprived minority group that most of us are likely to join. They have been deprived when it comes to medical care, to receiving all the benefits that medicine could, if it would, confer. But they have been deprived, too, by society, gravely so. And while the emphasis of this book is on what medicine can do for the aged, it would be foolish to do other than recognize the extreme importance of social attitudes and their impact on older people.

Ours is a society guilty of emphasizing youth and downgrading the aged, of failure to realize the contributions the aged can make, and of making them feel unwanted, unneeded, without dignity.

On the one hand, we have a value system that degrades nonworkers; on the other hand, we force older people to stop working. The elderly find it more difficult to be meaningful to others because they are not permitted to work; because their children no longer need them in ways they once did; because their experience and acquired wisdom are looked upon as outmoded and without relevance. Without influence, they are unable to command consideration.

Americans, it has been observed, like best to invest money, time, effort, and emotional involvement in people who will pay off, and society is contrived so that older people are unlikely to pay off, at least in the accepted values of society, through future "achievements."

What we need is a new set of "ground rules." Is the proposal of one behavioral scientist startling? Why not stop focusing on those most likely to pay off in the future? We have no shortage of people eager to knock themselves out as producers and achievers. Why shouldn't our major responsibility be to the elderly who will be here a relatively brief period? Having devoted their energies to work in and for society, they need their reward now, not in a future to which younger people can look forward. Moreover, what better way to maintain worthwhile values and ideas than to reward the aged, thus serving to encourage the young to continue traditional values so that in turn, when they are old, they can be rewarded.

Ironically, one of the worst by-products of the youth cult, as a perceptive young (twenty-eight-year-old) observer points out, is that it in effect dooms the young to a life sentence of "getting old" even beginning at twenty. Not only the old are disemboweled; so are the young, fearful of and fighting the coming of age and glumly mourning rather than celebrating each birthday.

It is not the purpose of this book to dwell on society's failings for they have been the focus of many other books. Our emphasis, rather, is on what can be done, even despite unhealthy social attitudes, to help the elderly. Unhealthy social attitudes have played no small part in fostering an unhealthy medical attitude of condescension toward the elderly.

But our hope is to demonstrate—with particulars—that when the elderly are looked upon as problems for diagnosis, not disposal, and when they are given active, vigorous, optimistic medical treatment, they respond. They are not hopeless cases.

Such treatment is not always easily found. But the chances of finding it are greatly increased if older people and their families and friends realize that treatment does exist and are aware of its results.

If you have an aging parent who might possibly benefit from a whole new look at his or her problem and from more hopeful and aggressive care, hopefully this book will increase the chances of finding a physician willing and able to provide that look and that care.

It is possible, too, that in the slowly but progressively changing medical climate, you can encourage a present physician to consider what might now be done, even if he hasn't thought of trying it before.

Such treatment, too, is likely to increase in availability as people demand and seek it. The stirrings are there within the medical profession: recognition of failings and old attitudes of condescension; increasing concern with changing the interactions between physicians and older patients and with tearing down old myths and misconceptions and replacing them with new knowledge and insights.

2

CONDESCENSION MEDICINE

A British medical officer created a furor in England and the United States when he declared his belief that to treat people over the age of sixty-five is a waste of medical resources. He was, he announced, all for automatically labeling "Let die" any aged person entering a hospital.

To which Dr. Alex Comfort, a distinguished British gerontologist, responded: "If this physician is amazed by the outcry his comment caused and the mischief it may have done to the profession's credit with old people (who already suspect that many doctors think like this), I am sorry for him.

"But the suspicious older patients are right," Dr. Comfort

went on. "The attitude of that outspoken physician is supported by the profession's total unawareness of the progress made in geriatric medicine in the last fifteen years; by the consoling belief that we die when Allah wills and that it is hubristic as well as uneconomic to waste medicine on the old."

That same year, 1969, an American Medical Association committee on aging reported that after fifteen years of study it had been unable to find a single disease entity or mental condition that is necessarily related to the passage of time.

Too long and too often had the terms "aging" and "degeneration" been used interchangeably by medical men and in the medical literature. The terms, the committee declared, needed to be clearly distinguished. If degeneration occurred with age, it wasn't because of age per se.

Age should be no bar to good medical or surgical treatment, the committee declared firmly, and gave a name to the kind of medical practice that barred such treatment: "condescension medicine."

"Clinical Undertakers"

Among many of the thoughtful in the medical profession, there has been growing recognition of the failure to do all that can be done for the aged, of condescending attitudes, and even of aversion to dealing with the aged.

A deplorable avoidance of the problems of the aged, they are frank enough to admit, has characterized both the teaching and the practice of medicine.

"We often act as though the passing of a sixty-fifth birthday automatically relegates a person to a mothball existence," one physician remarks bluntly. "Too many of us still throw up our hands when faced with the problems of our aged patients."

Only recently have many physicians given any real thought to the idea that elderly patients can be rehabilitated. And still strange to many is the concept that it is desirable, possible, and often remarkably effective to deal with the emotional difficulties as well as physical illnesses of the aged.

Too many physicians have been "clinical undertakers" for the aged, merely tolerating but not adequately treating elderly patients, disregarding their emotional reactions to long-term illnesses, looking upon them as basically untreatable. "There are," says one physician sharply, "no untreatable patients, but there are physicians who, for various reasons, are having difficulty in treating this group of patients."

Some Examples of Condescension Medicine

Attitudes of condescension or of aversion—and the two often coexist—can be manifested in many ways.

They may be at work when a physician tut-tuts an elderly patient's physical complaints with a "There, there, this is what we all must expect as we grow old."

They may be at work when a physician nods wisely when the family of an elderly patient worries over failing memory, growing apathy and confusion, and explains, seemingly so kindly but without making any real investigation, that "This is senility . . . you know, hardening of the brain arteries that comes with age."

They may be at work when a physician vetoes out of hand any suggestion that an elderly person who may have several ailments but is especially bothered by one might benefit from surgery for that particularly troublesome disorder. "Too old, you know . . . it would be far too risky . . . and, with the other problems too, why bother?"

They may be at work when an elderly patient has physical problems but suffers unduly from them, suffers out of all proportion to the extent of the physical problems, and so may be suffering in no small part because of emotional disturbance—and yet the physician long delays or never gets around to referring the patient for possible psychiatric help, perhaps because, consciously or unconsciously, he classifies the patient as simply "an old crock."

They may be at work when an elderly patient seems psychotic because his actions appear to be strange—and he *is* elderly. Physicians, if they have preconceptions, can be fooled by the preconceptions. Dr. Theodore Linz of Yale tells the story of a man of seventy-six who was hospitalized in heart failure and was completely disoriented. But after the heart failure was brought under control and, as a result, his brain again could get enough oxygen, he appeared to be oriented and rational.

However, because this man of seventy-six kept saying that as soon as he was ready to go home, his mother would drive over and pick him up, his physicians decided they had better keep him hospitalized a few weeks more to see if they could get any further improvement in his mental state. "Then," says Linz, "one day, somewhat to their chagrin, his mother of ninety-five drove over from a town some hundred miles away, accompanied by her ninety-seven-year-old sister, and took their little boy home."

Preconceptions can lead to potentially tragic neglect. The chief medical director of The Metropolitan Life Insurance Company told of a visit to one of New York City's major hospitals. "One of the internists there told me the story of an elderly person who came into the hospital because of a coronary attack—or at least a pain in the chest. In listing the history, the resident found that the patient also had Hodgkin's disease, so he threw up his hands and said, 'There is really no use in taking an electrocardiogram.' This attitude possibly was the result of a fault in his medical school training. However, he did proceed with the ECG. The patient survived for about fourteen years."

The late Dr. Edward Henderson told the story of a sixty-eight-year-old friend who had a heart attack and was put into the hospital. "He was a personal friend of the doctor who was taking care of him. The next morning I asked how the patient was and the doctor said, 'The situation is pretty bad. He has anuria [suppression of urine excretion] and I'm afraid he is going out.' "

Dr. Henderson wanted to know if there had been any urological examination, any attempt to catheterize and drain urine. No, there hadn't been, possibly because of a defeatist attitude: the man was old and, with a heart attack, doomed; nothing else mattered.

Yet, when Dr. Henderson pointed out that he knew that the man had an enlarged prostate and prostatitis, and that urological examination might be in order, the examination got under way at once and 1,000 cc of urine was removed. With proper treatment, the patient recovered and went home.

Some Sources of Condescension Medicine

What medical men often forget, as some of the leaders among them are the first to admit, is that though they are used to seeing elderly people in hospitals and clinics—and these are people with pressing health problems—most older Americans are healthy and energetic.

It is a serious error, to begin with, to consider the aged

invalid as "normal" and a healthy, vigorous eighty-year-old as "exceptional." It is an error that colors thinking, that makes it seem that all but the "exceptional" over age sixty-five must be ready for and doomed by nature to a mothball life. If invalidism is taken to be normal, it is only a short step to the notion that little or nothing can be done to prevent or overcome what is "normal."

The fact is that fewer than 5 percent of those over sixty-five need to be hospitalized or institutionalized. The remaining 95 percent are capable of living productive, self-fulfilling lives.

Even far-advanced age need not inevitably mean invalidism. The number of people over age 100 who are drawing social security benefits now has risen to well above four thousand. The biographies of 218 of them appear in volumes IX and X of *America's Centenarians* issued by the Social Security Administration.

Among them is Thomas Anderson, 101, who has outlived the name of his home town, Ninety-Six, North Carolina. A licensed surveyor who still runs a line occasionally when the weather is good, Anderson taught Sunday school until two years ago. Another of those profiled is 128-year-old Charlie Smith of Bartow, Florida, who draws benefits based on Social Security credits he first began to earn by picking oranges at age 113.

There is some question about the nearly one million older people—the 5 percent—who are residents of some form of institution: Do all of them really belong there? Much has been written about the tragic fact that most of them are living under conditions certainly not worthy of an advanced society, relegated to live out their lives in depressing environments that invite decay and welcome and encourage apathy. Too often our system of care for the elderly is based on a tragic assumption that senility must be involved, even when none is present.

Many of those in nursing homes and other institutions may not belong there. Many who are there might be rescued and returned to more normal living if they were not so often treated as little more than children who require maternal supervision and, instead, received proper medical rehabilitation care. There have been investigations demonstrating that when rehabilitation involves goals to which the individual may aspire, remarkable physical and psychological benefits accrue.

It's not uncommon to find old people in a reasonably healthy condition who, when put away in custodial care facilities, totally lose interest in life, refuse to communicate and to eat, become bedridden, and waste away and die. On the death certificate, the reason for death should be "isolation," not "disease."

The treatment—or, rather, the lack of it—of patients in custodial care facilities compounds the erroneous notion that invalidism and quick decline are the norms for the aged and helps to sustain the ironical but vicious cycle in which little or nothing is done to help and so it is thought that little or nothing *can* be done.

The Neglect in Medical Training

The care of the elderly has been largely neglected in the physician's training. A study made for the Senate Special Committee on Aging found no mention whatever of the subject in the catalogues of fifty-one out of ninety-nine medical schools. Among more than twenty thousand faculty members, only fifteen were identified primarily with the field of aging.

With most schools having no programs designed either to emphasize or explain the special problems of the elderly patient, the negativistic feeling is reflected widely in attitudes of resident staff physicians, who frequently show no interest in patients over seventy or seventy-five although such patients may have medical problems fascinating from the standpoints of both diagnosis and treatment.

Ironically, although medical students will be dealing more and more with elderly patients throughout their professional careers, they get little training in care of the elderly, while getting much training in exotic diseases that most of them will never see throughout their careers.

The fact is, too, that most physicians are trained to look after acute illness and to gain satisfaction from it, and the satisfaction is often there in the form of dramatic responses to treatment. But the major problems in the elderly are chronic ones and by their very nature do not respond dramatically, and it appears that medical students too rarely are taught to gain satisfaction from less spectacular improvement.

Nor does the fault for failing to interest students in the care of the elderly lie only with medical schools. After four years of medical school, plus internship and residency, a physician may spend several impressionable years in the army. During internship and residency, there is no effort to make the study of old age interesting. In the army, of course, virtually all patients are young, perhaps 90 percent of them between the ages of eighteen and twenty-four.

In view of these factors, medical educators sympathetic to the problem worry over the difficulty of orienting the medical student in geriatrics for a whole lifetime. How in the world, they wonder, can they, in a four-year course, make a medical student highly oriented toward the care of older people when in his next six to eight years there is no plan in that direction!

There is at least some encouragement in the fact that medical educators and authorities are beginning to struggle with the problem and that some efforts are beginning to be made to give aging its due in curricula and to find ways of maintaining and building young physicians' interest in care of the elderly beyond medical school.

The Need to Cure and Nothing Less—and So, Nothing Less

From the standpoint of some physicians, the elderly are guilty of a sin: They remain alive but they don't yield to quick cures. Feeling threatened by patients who are so inconsiderate as to fail to be curable, such physicians hasten to apply the label "old crock" and to take refuge in the notion, "Well, he's old; what can you expect? There is nothing to be done."

Some physicians may be driven by a need to cure because, to some extent as the result of training and to some extent as the result of personality, they have come to expect that patients will view them as all-powerful—and they may even half-believe themselves that this is what they are. An incurable patient threatens them, muddies their image of omnipotence, and, not necessarily with deliberate, conscious intent, they may prefer to ignore the patient or categorize him as beyond any help.

But this is to deny the patient what help he can have—and that help often can be considerable. When, say, Mrs. Smith at eighty-two suffers from severe arthritis, failing vision, loss of hearing, and digestive troubles, is her case really hopeless? Not necessarily. It may well be possible to improve her vision and hearing, relieve and even possibly cure her digestive disorder, and relieve and control her arthritis, even though not to cure it.

Worthwhile medical accomplishment is hardly limited to the quick, dramatic, outright cure of disease. It extends to providing relief, to achieving a degree of control, to rehabilitating at whatever level is possible.

Condescension medicine, of course, is not strictly an American phenomenon. For some years in Canada concern has been expressed about the urgent need to end the defeatist, negativistic approach of some physicians there to the treatment of the elderly, about their proneness to regard the elderly as hopeless, incurable, and irremediable cases.

Noting that though most conditions of the elderly are presently not amenable to cure but are remediable to a certain extent, Canadian doctors have pointed out that older people often can be rehabilitated by the same techniques used in rehabilitating younger people, with some modifications to suit their physiological state. Where restoring a younger person to optimal function might be considered to mean a return to gainful employment, for most older people, independence, ability to get around, capacity to perform activities of daily living including washing, dressing, eating, and toilet functions could be considered optimal function, especially if accompanied by good psychosocial adjustment. To make an elderly person self-sustaining is certainly a desirable goal for medicine and an achievement that could mean much to the elderly person and his family.

The Balky Elderly Patient "Problem"

Some physicians complain that the elderly are difficult patients, balky, unable to understand explanations, unable or unwilling to follow directions.

Some may be. But so are many younger patients.

Medical educators have pointed out that there are, in fact, at least four types of balky patients at all ages.

There are people who insist upon denying illness and on not taking medications—more often men than women, because men are supposed to be strong and medicine-taking may be looked upon as a confession of weakness.

There are patients, classified psychiatrically as obsessive-compulsives, who have a need to be perfect, to have perfect control of their bodies. They may avoid doctors and, if they see one, may fail, completely or partially, to follow his directions.

There are hypochondriacs for whom illness is a life-style and who look upon any medication that may eliminate their illness as a threat. Such people may say they want help; they may go from doctor to doctor, collecting prescriptions but filling none and telling each successive doctor that nothing helps. Some do take prescribed medications—but in inadequate amounts on the one hand or to excess on the other hand so that they suffer undesirable reactions and the medications have to be stopped.

There are patients of all ages who are afraid of medications or who become easily confused about when to take them and how much to take.

Some patients—at any age and certainly at older ages—can, indeed, be difficult but not impossible to help with some effort and understanding on the part of the physician. It may be necessary to fit the treatment and approach to the patient's particular personality—and this is done frequently by experienced physicians.

Many physicians have learned, for example, that a hypochondriac patient, young or old, who may not want to get fully well, can be approached with the assurance that cure is impossible but that some improvement may be possible—and, knowing that he is not going to be robbed of his precious hypochondriac life style, he often will be glad to have some degree of relief and take his medicine.

Interested and knowledgeable physicians have learned to make their instructions for patients, young and old, very specific and, if there is the least likelihood of forgetfulness or confusion, to write the instructions down in simple, clear terms. They regard the time spent in this as essential, hardly any less important than other aspects of treatment.

No less than a younger patient, an elderly person with a physical ailment may also be suffering from anxiety or depression. In fact, the likelihood is greater for the elderly person. He may have been anxious or depressed before the ailment became pronounced and the anxiety or depression may be heightened by the physical problem and even by the circumstances of tests, diagnosis, and treatment. Unless the anxiety or depression is treated as actively as the physical problem, he may well become a "bad" patient, made so by his festering psychological state.

If, moreover, a sound doctor-patient relationship is critical for the effective treatment of younger people, it can be even more critical in the case of older people. The elderly person, often very conscious of the infringements on his dignity in everyday life, must feel that he is being treated with dignity by the physician, that the physician is genuinely interested in him as a person and not just as a fractured hip or a congestive heart, that the physician takes seriously his doubts, fears, and questions and gives him opportunity to express his concern.

Many physicians have learned that just a few minutes spent listening with interest and sympathy to a patient can heighten the patient's self-esteem and, in the process, do much, sometimes more even than medication, to reduce anxiety or depression and materially aid the treatment of a physical problem.

But this, of course, takes deep insight, concern, and dedication on the part of the physician, not readily attainable starting from a base of condescension.

3

MYTHS, MISCONCEPTIONS, AND REALITIES

From earliest times, the mystery of aging and a hopeful dream of perpetual youth have intrigued priests, poets, and philosophers. In 1909, the word "geriatrics"—from the Greek *geron,* old man, and *iatrikos,* medical treatment—was coined to focus medical attention on aging and to suggest that a special branch of medicine might be devoted to diagnosing and treating diseases of the aged. But not until the last ten to fifteen years did geriatrics, even as a word, come into fairly general use.

Another, more recently coined term, gerontology, is meant to stand for a science of aging in a very broad sense that brings into play all the sciences—biological, physical, and social—and is concerned with changes that may occur before old age, beginning even at maturity and perhaps even earlier.

But while, gradually, facts have been uncovered about aging—about what happens with the passage of time and what does not happen, about which changes in older people are really due to aging and which to disease or disuse—misconceptions still abound. To some extent, they may affect medical attitudes; to a larger extent, they affect social attitudes; and they may affect, harmfully, individual elderly people and their families. Some myths and misconceptions, although now clearly invalidated scientifically, continue to prevail and to distort elderly people's views of themselves and society's and their children's views of them.

The Myth of Old Age as Disease

The notion that old age itself is a disease is a pervasive one. But it is a basic myth.

To be sure, there is a link between old age and disease. Chronic disease is more common among the elderly. Old people are likely to have multiple diseases and diseases that may speed the aging process. But these generally are diseases that the aged have accumulated over a lifetime and bring with them rather than acquire afresh in and as a result of old age.

Until very recently, for example, it was supposed that coronary artery disease was an accompaniment of aging. This is the disease—the choking up of the coronary arteries feeding the heart muscle—that produces angina, the severe chest pain on exertion, and that leads to heart attacks. As an accompaniment of aging, a result of the passage of time, it was presumed to be unassailable.

But the age-association misconception was exploded during World War II, when physicians began to note heart attacks in relatively young men in the armed forces. They gathered data on 866 cases of heart attack in men aged 18 through 39. Most of the men had been in apparent good health until the very moment of heart attack and sudden death. Sixty-four of them were less than 24 years old; more than 200 were under 29. Autopsy studies showed changes in the coronary arteries much like those found in elderly victims of heart attack. They helped to provide convincing evidence that heart attacks were not matters of advancing age but of advancing disease.

During the Korean War, physicians took the matter a step farther. They performed postmortem studies on many soldiers killed in battle. They found evidence, when the coronary arteries of these young and apparently healthy men were examined, that disease was present at an average age of twenty-two—and in 10 percent of these very young men, the silent atherosclerotic process had already narrowed by 70 percent or more the channel in one or both coronary arteries.

The aged suffer from other problems—strokes, arthritis, high blood pressure, kidney disorders, kidney failure, vision and hearing difficulties, and many others. But so may the young; so, in fact, do many of the young. It is now recognized, for example, that high blood pressure affects at least 10 percent of the total population, young and old—and, indeed, high blood pressure recently has been discovered in as many as 10 percent of teenagers in some areas, and even in young children.

So diseases of the aged are not peculiar to the aged.

But there are changes that go with aging. There are realities of altered physiology with time.

Changes That Accompany Aging

Some, of course, are obvious: The eyes become less bright; height diminishes a bit; the nape of the neck becomes more round; on the skin appear brown so-called "liver" spots and wrinkles; hair becomes thinner, grayer.

But there are others.

Although some body functions do not change with age, there is generally a gradual decrease of functions beginning at age twenty-five to thirty and continuing thereafter.

The rate of decrease varies with different functions—in many cases, considerably. Thus, the maximum excretion ability of the kidneys generally falls by 50 percent between ages thirty and ninety, but the speed of conduction of nerve impulses diminishes by only 15 percent in that time.

With age, there is some alteration of the functioning of the nervous system in its role as coordinator of interactions of muscles, glands, and blood, and this could account for the fact that with aging there is likely to be a gradual decline in muscular strength. Muscular strength may reach its peak by or before age thirty and, commonly, baseball and football players, boxers, and track athletes seldom perform as well after thirty as before.

Because many acts of everyday living—walking, lifting,

getting up, bathing, cooking, for example—involve many nerve-to-gland, nerve-to-muscle, and nerve-to-nerve connections, such activities, too, may be affected to some extent by changes in nervous system functioning.

Some investigators have found that a decrease in heart output begins at about age twenty and, with advancing age, certain cells (epithelial) of the heart increase in volume, but the aged heart is not necessarily a diseased organ. However, as in the young, such conditions as high blood pressure and hardening of the coronary arteries feeding the heart may lead to a state of disease.

There are changes in the digestive system. A decreased flow of saliva which sometimes may lead to dryness of the mouth is a complaint of some older people. The amount of gastric juice secreted and the acid and pepsin content of the secretion tend to decline, and there may be some reduction in motility of the stomach and in contractions of the muscles of the intestinal tract, leading to constipation.

Only a few people beyond the age of seventy are entirely free of kidney changes. Blood flow through the kidneys may be reduced. There are conflicting reports about how common the enlargement of the prostate is among elderly men, with some studies indicating that 30 percent of the male population will have some enlargement at age sixty or beyond; others indicate some degree of enlargement in as many as 76 percent of those over age fifty-five.

With advancing age, lung capacity may be reduced, and obesity and weakening of muscles that lift the rib cage for breathing may be factors in such reduction.

There are bone changes. Between youth and age, about 15 percent of bone may be lost. The loss is usually somewhat greater for men than for women and for whites than for blacks.

Tooth loss and gum disease are often marked in the aged, and there may be stiffening of joints and difficulty in particular in bending the hip and knee joints.

The senses change. There is reduction of the sense of touch and pain, of taste, and of ability to perceive odor. Hearing may be affected. Many older people are able to "hear" but, as they say, not "understand" speech; the exact cause of the condition, called presbycusis, is unknown. With changes in the lenses of the eyes that may occur with aging, accommodation may be slowed, tolerance for glare diminished, and there may be some shrinkage of visual field and delayed adaptation to darkness.

One of the most striking effects seen with aging is the response to stress, whether physical, as in vigorous activity, or emotional, as in fear or excitement. Stress imposes demands which the body meets by hormonal and other changes. Afterward, body functioning shifts back to normal functioning for routine demands. With increasing age, the rate of recovery from stress—the shifting back to normal—is slower.

But There Are Some Compensating Changes, Too

There is a misconception that aging is all decline and there are no compensations. But the fact is that as some attributes decline, others may be strengthened.

Memory may decline, but judgment and the ability to appraise significance improve with age. While there may be some loss of visual acuity, the ability to comprehend what is seen improves with experience, and experience depends upon time and therefore grows with age.

It is of interest that investigators have found that the number of duodenal ulcer cases actually decreases with advancing age. They have also determined that while high blood pressure is abnormal at any age and is reflected in shortened life expectancy, elevated pressures of equivalent levels have far greater adverse significance at younger than at older ages.

The same is true of obesity, which is less ominous in older than in younger people; of abnormal glucose tolerance tests (for diabetes); and of electrocardiographic abnormalities.

Even cancer pursues a less fulminating course as a rule in older than in younger people. Heart attacks are fatal in a high percentage at all ages, but the likelihood of surviving the acute episode is much better the later the age at which it occurs. "If one has to be afflicted with cancer or a coronary attack, it is better to have it happen at the age of seventy than at forty," one medical editorial has pointed out, "and not simply because one has already lived a long life."

The Variability of Change

There are great individual differences in rates of aging and in the way people age. Moreover, different organ systems in the same person age at different rates. One seventy-year-old may have a heart output no better than that for an eighty-year-old, and another may have an output fully as good as that of a forty-year-old. But the seventy-year-old with the forty-year-old heart may have kidney function like that of an eighty-year-old.

Individual variability, of course, has significance for investigators; in it may be clues to causes and underlying mechanisms. It also has, or should have, great significance for physicians. "It means," a Public Health Service publication called *Working with Older People—A Guide to Practice* points out, "that the elderly patient must be carefully assessed and dealt with as an individual and not as a member of any age group, since groupings based on chronological age are much less homogeneous in the old than in the young."

The Alterability of Change

Are the changes—and losses—with age subject to control, to being held in check or at least slowed?

Actually, it is apparent not only to scientists but to many observant nonscientists that today's generation of older people is physiologically younger than the generation at the turn of the century. "Many of our 65-year-olds today," Professor Walter M. Beattie, Jr., of Syracuse University points out, "are more like their 50-year-old counterparts at the turn of the century due to improved nutrition, health care, and environmental sanitation. Whistler's mother, who epitomizes 'old age,' was 44 years of age when she sat for that famous painting."

Here is a sampling of recent scientific reports touching on the alterability of the changes seen in aging:

● Muscle tone and strength can be regained by sixty- to ninety-year-old men—and by older women as well—with an exercise program of six to eight weeks.

● Improvement in diet is able to reverse some of the fatigue, irritability, insomnia, and even confusion in elderly patients.

● Loss of bone density—osteoporosis—which is a common problem in the aged, particularly among women, may not be a change dictated by aging but the result of a lifetime of faulty diet and hormone imbalance; and the loss of calcium from bone, which is involved, might well be modified with attention to diet and general health throughout life.

- Tooth loss and gum disease are not inevitable; preventive techniques can effectively minimize the destructive processes.
- Provide an attractive eating situation to a person who is old and alone, and failing appetite improves, energy increases, and disease susceptibility decreases.
- Healthy sexual activity can continue into the eighth and ninth decades; all that is needed is an "interested and interesting partner" and some reeducation.

Consider these findings and you may well agree with Dr. Ruth B. Weg of the University of Southern California Department of Biology that, "It would seem, then, that an important percentage of the diminished function (of the aged) may be due to society's attitudes, disuse, misuse, lack of information, rather than solely a function of age."

Pockets of "Unusual" (or Normal?) Aging

For several years recently, scientists have gone to "exotic" areas of the world to study people who at age 100 and beyond lead active, productive lives.

In particular are studies in three areas: in Vilcabamba, a tiny village in the rugged Andean mountain terrain of Ecuador; in the district known as Abkhazia in the Caucasus Mountains of the U.S.S.R.; and in the province of Hunza in the Karakoram Mountains, a part of Pakistani-controlled Kashmir, on the borders of Afghanistan and China.

The 1971 census in Vilcabamba found nine people aged 100 or more in a total population of 819—a projected rate of 1,100 centenarians per 100,000 population, clearly an exceptional situation compared with the United States, where there are three centenarians per 100,000 population. In the Caucasus Mountains, the projected rate has been reported as 35 to 65 per 100,000 population. No figures are available for Hunza, but there is evidence that people there live to ages comparable to those in Vilcabamba and Abkhazia.

Investigators found a remarkable lack of disease among many of the aged who, although wrinkled, are vigorous. Striking photographs were obtained of people of advanced age: a 95-year-old man in Hunza, in the field, binding hay for animal fodder; a 95-year-old in Abkhazia chopping logs; a 98-year-old in the Caucasus spinning sheep wool as his daily responsibility; a 105-year-old woman near Vilcabamba sewing without need for eyeglasses.

In 1969, when a team of Ecuadorean physicians went into Vilcabamba, they studied some of the aged, making many diagnostic tests, checking hearts, lungs, blood pressures, carrying out laboratory and other procedures. They found a 100-year-old businessman, entirely without symptoms, with normal heart and lungs and with a remarkably low blood pressure of 125/70; a 120-year-old active farmer with a blood pressure of 135/60, and also classified as in normal health; another 120-year-old farmer, also normal, and a 100-year-old homemaker entirely normal except for cataracts.

The purpose of the studies was to try to identify, if possible, factors common to exceptional longevity—to old age without debility and senility.

Heredity is generally considered a significant factor in long life—and it does, when favorable, confer some advantage, yet many studies have shown that the advantage is a modest one. For example, a study of longevity based upon life insurance records found that offspring of long-lived parents had a life expectancy at age twenty that probably does not exceed three years more than the expectancy of a similar age group whose parents were short-lived. And while it was found that in Vilcabamba and Hunza the elderly seemed related to one another, that wasn't the case in the Caucasus, where the centenarians included Russians, Georgians, Armenians, Turks, and others.

Diet was checked. It varied, being almost exclusively vegetarian in Vilcabamba, largely so among Hunzakuts. But it was not so among people in the Caucasus, who consume animal products almost daily, although the animal fat intake there is half that in the United States. Overall, the dietary factors uniform to all three regions were a low intake of animal fats and a moderate caloric intake, under 2000 calories a day and often 1800 or less, some 600 calories less than current recommendations of the United States National Research Council.

Another factor checked was physical activity. The level was striking in all three areas. All are mountainous locations, and it was found that an incredible amount of physical exertion was essential just to attend to the daily business of living.

And, although it came as something of a surprise, psychologic factors are very significant in exceptional longevity.

In all three places, social status is largely age-dependent, and the older a person is, the greater the regard by both contemporaries and by the young. There is no retirement; old people continue to work and to participate in the economy and social life; their activity may become less vigorous, but activity remains; and a sense of usefulness and purpose in life pervades the atmosphere for the elderly in all three places. They drink; they smoke; and interest in the opposite sex persists into old age. Where only one of the partners of a marriage survives, remarriage even at ages up to 100 is common.

An overall myth that aged people are all alike and "all decrepit," as Dr. Ruth Weg has termed it, has been a drag on both cultural and medical attitudes. It needs to be cast aside; it is beginning to be—as are some of the sub-myths that go with it or otherwise impede real understanding of aging and valid efforts to help the aged.

The Myth of Mental Decline

There has long been a fallacious notion that human intellectual capacity reaches a peak early in life—in the late teens and early twenties—and thereafter begins gradually to diminish until by the sixties it has fallen very low.

Within recent years, however, many studies have produced evidence to upset the whole idea. They indicate that if the factor of speed is separated out, virtually no changes in intellectual capacity are identifiable until extremely late in life. Older people may not do well where rapid response is required but when the pace of a learning task is slowed, the elderly improve significantly in performance.

In 1955, the National Institute of Mental Health began a human aging study, following a group of men as they moved from an average age of seventy-one to eighty-one years. That study, too, has provided evidence to upset the myth of mental decline. It found a "remarkably high quality" of mental functioning despite fairly advanced age. Retests of the men at the end of the ten years revealed performances remaining to a considerable extent close to what they had been at the beginning of the study.

While there are some declines, "what stands out are the residual capabilities," the human aging study discovered. And this is no small matter although it has had relatively limited attention. The aged may be getting less credit than they deserve, the study indicates, for the extent of their intellectual, perceptual, and personality strengths and capabilities, including their capabilities for acquiring new knowledge, concepts, and skills.

On some intellectual tasks there may even be an increase in capability with age. Stored information is continually increasing with age. If, for example, as a college graduate, you knew 20,000 words, by age 65 you are likely to know 40,000. So intellectual function, in terms of stored information, increases with the years.

On the other hand, with age, the store of knowledge and experience is searched more slowly. While quick response is an attribute of youth, the more reasoned approach goes with age. The young do far better under time pressure than do the aged. Boxers, because they must respond quickly, are "old" at thirty. Golfers, however, because they need not hit the ball until ready, can take advantage of experience and do well in the late years.

Older people have a sense of competence when they have the opportunity to make maximum use of their experience on a self-paced basis, which is why, for example, writing is a skill that often flourishes in late life. Research in occupations has shown that, if given a choice, men and women, as they age, move from jobs subjecting them to the pressure of time into jobs that are self-paced.

An understanding that slowing is a normal part of aging and no indication of mental decline could help the aged themselves as well as their families and physicians. There is no need for the aged to be embarrassed about it.

"I don't feel particularly embarrassed if someone should tell me that I don't process as much information per unit time as I used to. This is no ego blow to me," says Dr. James E. Birren, Director of the Ethel and Percy Andrus Gerontology Center at the University of Southern California.

"There is a concept I use to help me over any residual ego concern that may be involved in the fact that I am no longer as good an information processor," he adds. "I explain the change using a conceptual approach. . . . If you have a secretary who puts letters in the file as they come in, you will have a complete chronological file, but one where it's difficult to have easy access to any one letter. So access time lengthens purely as a function of the amount stored. In our brains we take care of this filing problem by organizing information into a conceptual store. What were previously discrete bits of information now form a concept group. You reach through the concept to relevant experience.

"Let's take a practical example. We did interviewing at the University of Chicago of successful middle-aged men and women. One of the things they talked about is that they had come to deal with professional matters with less intensity in middle age. A high school principal said, 'When I started out, each disciplinary problem in the school was a special problem for me. I intervened; I went all out for it. Now I withdraw a little more and let the teacher handle it until I can see what is going on.' As another example, the firstborn child is a big crisis for the man and the woman. The first time the baby cries at home, the mother cries. There is much emotional involvement. This is not so with the second and third child. If only mothers could begin with their fourth child, then they could deal with the issues conceptually. With maturation comes a greater conceptual grasp so that we can size up the situation and then look to the relevant items in our store. This is what I call the race between the chunks and the bits. While younger people, say those between 18 and 22, can process more bits per second, and even though by age sixty that number may be halved, the older person may process bigger chunks. The race may go to the tortoise because he is chunking, and not to the hare because he is just bitting along."

The Myth of Unproductivity

Another myth that can have devastating effects on the aged themselves and on the attitudes of those who care for them is that somewhere along the line, at age sixty-five or sixty or even before that, a person changes purely because of aging and becomes unproductive, doesn't really have any interest or any wish to be productive or to work with and associate with younger people, but wishes for segregation.

Yet no one changes drastically because of the passage of some given number of years. Unless there is debilitating illness, people of advanced age can and often do maintain interest in the world around them, in making some contribution. If they have been creative, they remain so. If they have not been creative, they may even become so. In addition to painters, musicians, scientists, and executives who continue to perform with virtuosity in their seventies and eighties, there are many instances of late bloomers—a Grandma Moses becoming a creative painter for the first time in old age, for example.

The attitude that creativity and ability to acquire new skills diminish rapidly with age has become an American disease of epidemic proportions.

In industry, Jack W. Taylor, the director of executive development at Planning Dynamics, Inc., Pittsburgh, has been refuting the common reactionary view that a business organization can achieve creative impetus only through acquiring "new" young minds and sticking with the false hypothesis that the human brain tends to stultify at some time after age thirty-five.

In addition to pointing to repeated scientific studies showing the hypothesis to be false, Taylor has proved the falsity by actually setting up a number of creativity-development programs in major United States business organizations.

The programs demonstrate that, if anything, when it comes to creative accomplishments and productivity, the older person has the best of it. At later ages, there is less waste of and greater conservation and use of vital energy; activity has much greater directness and control and therefore efficiency; older people are inured to work; they have the experience to avoid fads and pitfalls that often trap the young; they have tenacity, willpower, and persistence needed for creative achievement, the stuff to decide, start, stick with, and finish; they bring better continuity of attention, interest, and motivation to their work.

"Contrast all of this," says Taylor, "with the all-too-observable tendency of so many youngsters toward short attention spans . . . preoccupation with status, personal advancement, politicosocial relations, etc., rather than self-fulfillment . . . proclivity for 'reinventing the wheel,' not knowing what has already been tried . . . grasshopperish pursuits (as of conquests rather than concepts, for example) . . . desire, as C. F. Kettering once expressed it, to 'revolutionize the world without having to bother with the necessity of first building a working model' . . . and the like. And the contrast becomes sharp indeed!"

In each of the creativity-development programs Taylor set up in industry, there were pretests of the creative ability of participants, comprehensive training in the principles, methods, and techniques of creative thinking, testing to measure the results of the training, and continuing follow-up to evaluate the participants' subsequent creative contributions.

Analyzing the results of these programs over a period of

nearly twenty years, it was found that the greatest positive response as shown by performing in post-training versus pretraining tests was made by the older men. Where average improvement for those under thirty was 62 percent, it was 146 percent for those over forty.

Moreover, the highest level of post-training test scores was achieved by those over forty. The under-forty men earned average scores at the 78th percentile; the average for those over forty was at the 92nd percentile.

And, most convincing of all, in the practical application phases, 80 percent of all the most workable and worthwhile new ideas later came from those over forty.

The "Set-in-Their-Ways" Myth

It is commonly believed that older people are set in their ways, extremely conservative, intolerant of and extremely resistant to change.

The myth is harmful on many counts. It may make it seem necessary to segregate the old, to get rid of them, to retire them as soon as possible in the interest of progress. It is also part of the stereotype of the elderly medical patient who is not worth full effort because the effort would be wasted, because he or she cannot be counted on to cooperate, to try a new treatment or procedure, to be hopeful of its success, or to make a change in a living habit that might help.

Yet the alleged "setness" and balkiness and resistance to change are exaggerated. And what there is of such seeming attributes of aging may not be due to aging at all but to social and economic pressures. When, for example, an older person opposes civic improvements, school bonds, tax increases, the opposition very often stems not from a wish not to change but from a painful awareness of further incursions into his fixed and low income. The aged, too, may very well oppose some schemes out of wisdom, aware of previous failures of exactly the same schemes—and they certainly are not without insight into questionable motives of others and of incompetence as well.

The Tranquillity Myth

One of the prime myths about the aged—at once ironic and with potential for grave harm—is that old age is a time of ease, of relative peace, of tranquillity, a time when people can "relax and enjoy the fruit of their labor after the storms of active life are over."

Rarely, if ever, is old age that.

Research psychiatrists who have thoroughly examined the stresses of the aged find that the elderly experience more stress and more severely than do younger people.

The ability of so many of the aged to endure such stresses is remarkable. Yet often it is these stresses, which include solitude and financial hardship, that are responsible, partly or wholly, for the depressed states, anxious states, and psychosomatic illnesses frequently found in the elderly.

Depression among the elderly is common—and why not! Depression can stem from grief, from despair, from loss of personal and social status and lowered self-esteem. It can stem from isolation. And it can stem from prolonged physical problems that do not yield to treatment and which, in fact, may not be receiving adequate treatment or any treatment.

Anxiety reactions are also common in older people and may be manifested in various forms, including rigid thinking and behavior often mistakenly blamed on aging.

The notion that age is a period of tranquillity when, in fact, so often it is a time of mental stress, can stand in the way of helpful treatment. It may suggest, on the one hand, that since the life of the elderly is tranquil there should be no mental or emotional component to physical illness, excluding that avenue of possible help—or, on the other hand, that if an elderly person is mentally or emotionally disturbed, the disturbance must be linked with aging and is therefore untreatable.

The reality is entirely different.

"Despite the therapeutic pessimism and at times nihilism concerning the psychiatric disorders of old age," says Dr. Robert N. Butler of George Washington University School of Medicine, "physicians who actually work with elderly patients report impressive therapeutic results. Unfortunately, many general physicians refer the aged to a psychiatrist only late in the course of their illness or never refer them at all. These practitioners feel that they cannot treat geriatric patients because their 'mental' conditions are 'irreversible.' Some psychiatrists on the other hand regard the mental disorders of old age as primarily physical—and thus beyond the scope of psychiatric treatment. Fortunately, these attitudes are changing—even if slowly."

4

NEW HOPE FOR THE SENILE (THE FALSELY SENILE AND THE TRULY SENILE)

During a visit to Canada late in his life when he was still president of France, Charles de Gaulle, never noted for tactfulness, made several remarks about internal Canadian politics that caused a furor in Canada and worldwide. A European diplomat, although he had no business doing so, was led to diagnose the problem: "You might as well talk to a wall," he announced. "De Gaulle is getting old—he is nearly 77." Whereupon, some Montreal wags hastened to suggest, "France's new rallying cry might be Liberté, Egalité, Senilité."

In covering the story, one American newsmagazine observed that senility is a vague term that stands for all the physical and mental infirmities accompanying aging but popularly is applied to failing mental processes. With age, muscles may weaken, bones grow brittle, and blood vessels harden, but none of this necessarily affects mental processes until, sooner or later, blood supply to the brain is impaired. Then, old people often become illogical, sloppy, pay no attention to details they once cared about, are insensitive to the feelings of others and oversensitive to their own; any earlier neuroses become more acute, and at times they become cut off from reality.

But, the magazine quickly added, ancient bodies often support vigorous minds: Konrad Adenauer remained in power in Germany until his death at ninety-one, Toscanini conducted from memory right up to retirement at eighty-seven, Mr. Justice Holmes stayed sharp to retirement at eighty-seven.

And, however upsetting de Gaulle's remarks in Canada might have been, the magazine also noted, they were no indication of any lack of mental soundness: all the evidence from those who knew him well, from physicians who attended him, and from many French physicians who had observed him closely though never as his doctor, indicated the absence of any signs of a senile mind: no mental lapses, memory as striking as ever, speeches meticulously prepared and delivered from memory without notes, firm grasp of detail, and impeccable bearing.

So de Gaulle, though aging, was not senile; nor are many of the noncelebrated aged. And while there are some aged who are senile, their senility may not be inevitably hopeless—though it has long been considered to be so not only by lay people but also by some otherwise knowledgeable members of the medical profession.

The Wastebasket Diagnosis

Senility is the extreme. It can happen to anyone—it is not a matter of sex or color or race or social class.

Perhaps you have a parent or someone else in the family who you suspect may be senile or who has been diagnosed as that. Perhaps you have been led to believe that nothing can be done.

That need not be the case at all.

Too often, senility has been a wastebasket diagnosis—in

reality, no diagnosis at all, but, rather, an easy disposal category.

The tendency to link senility with just one thing —hardening of brain arteries and chronic brain disease—has been pronounced. And since the elderly have aging brains and aging cannot be reversed, the argument has gone, nothing could be done for the senility; it could only get worse.

Yet senility is *not* invariably linked with hardening of brain arteries. Many symptoms of mental "deterioration" have nothing to do with brain disease. They can result from emotional reactions to aging, from physical diseases including previously unrecognized conditions, and from deprivations and insults a long way removed from the brain. And these are often treatable—controllable in many cases and sometimes even curable.

Moreover, even when the brain is involved, when the vessels there are diseased, the situation is far from hopeless. When diseased vessels impede circulation to and nourishment for the brain, there may be measures, often relatively simple ones, that can be used to improve the nourishment. The measures include, and are not limited to, overcoming heart failure, correcting anemia, actively combatting emphysema, and overcoming vitamin and other deficiency disorders.

Senility involves the whole person. It is not an isolated disease, confined to a single body compartment. Many alterations, often subtle ones, individually or collectively can conspire to create the appearance or actuality of senility, and they must be understood and taken into account. The list of possible factors is a lengthy one, with a range all the way from thyroid and other hormone disturbances to low blood sugar, and from infections and injuries to intoxications from self-administered drugs such as bromides and sometimes from physician-administered drugs. And when these disturbances are sought for and actively treated, the diagnosis of senility may be abandoned or the hopelessness about it may vanish very quickly.

With any mental illness—certainly with senility—there is need for total concern, for investigating the possibility of every type of contributing factor.

Unfortunately, some physicians still have an "either/or" orientation; they feel that a patient's ills are either physical or functional. Yet there is much overlap between the two. Many physicians now recognize very well that a patient who has suffered a heart attack, for example, may be responding to medical treatment but will not get well unless an associated mental depression is recognized and treated. As much as mental state can impinge on physical, so can physical on mental. More than half of a Temple University group of psychiatric patients had some physical problem, and, in many cases, when the physical problem was corrected the mental problem diminished.

How Many Are Committed to State Hospitals—and Needn't Be?

State mental institutions have been used, almost indiscriminately and almost routinely, for "warehousing" disturbed elderly patients. California's alone has had more than eleven thousand like Mrs. X.

At age ninety, Mrs. X was arrested on a Superior Court-approved petition for mental illness. She had had a fall a short time before, during a dizzy spell, and thereafter was unable to walk or talk. She was confused and there was some mental deterioration. She went through a routine five-day "period of observation" in the psychiatric wards of the San Francisco General Hospital and then, almost routinely, was committed to a state hospital, away from family and friends, on a diagnosis of chronic brain syndrome.

Yet that five-day observation period had only intensified her emotional disturbance and increased her agitation. This may have helped make up the court's mind to order commitment. But her commitment was inappropriate. She was a sensitive, suffering, living being—sick but not harmful, not dangerous. She was committed just three months before a special geriatric screening project got under way. There would have been a tremendous difference—for her and her family—if only the onset of her problem had been delayed those three months.

The screening project, supported by the state of California, was set up in San Francisco to determine whether elderly patients headed for commitment to state mental hospitals really belonged there, whether some less drastic means of care couldn't be found.

One reason for setting it up was a special study that had been conducted in one state mental hospital. It had revealed that the majority of the elderly there did not need and would not benefit from care in such a hospital. Their real needs were for changes in living situations, for some supervision, and for active treatment, both physical and psychiatric.

The screening project staff was very small—one half-time internist, one half-time psychiatrist, two psychiatric social workers, and a stenographer. But they diagnosed, evaluated, made recommendations, offered consultation, worked with private physicians, got the help where necessary of community resources such as homemaker services, Meals-on-Wheels, visiting nurse care, and public health nursing services.

In the four years just preceding the project, there had been an average of 486 elderly people a year committed to mental hospitals from San Francisco. In the first full year of the project, the number dropped to 40; in the second year, to 12; in the third, to 3. And the majority of those screened were able to live in their own homes; others went to nursing or boarding homes.

The project clearly demonstrated that vast reductions in commitments of the elderly can be achieved with enlightened screening and real effort by a dedicated staff to muster all available community resources to meet the needs of old people. Unfortunately, warehousing of the elderly in mental institutions remains a widespread problem, although here and there it is receiving attention. Recent legislation passed in Illinois specifies that elderly persons whose mental processes are impaired only by advanced age will not be committed to mental institutions. In 1969 a committee that looked into the problem of the elderly and their institutionalization in state mental hospitals in New York State declared, "To place aged patients in the State hospitals unless it is necessary and clearly indicated is a shocking and inhumane error for all concerned."

The experience of a dedicated admitting psychiatrist at Bronx State Hospital in New York is disconcerting. The hospital, affiliated with the Albert Einstein College of Medicine, making an effort to develop a more rational program for elderly patients, had set up strict standards for admission. No person would be admitted for purely social reasons such as lack of money or difficulty in obtaining suitable housing accommodations, nor when the prime cause of his psychiatric symptoms was a physical illness. Nor would any person be admitted because of such characteristics as forgetfulness, a tendency to wander, or an eccentricity that caused problems for others. Although such characteristics could be a burden to relatives or friends, other solutions to these difficulties, including care in nursing or old age homes, are preferable. Similarly, no person would be admitted because of a disability which made for difficulty in ordinary tasks such as cooking, shopping, cleaning; other community services could and should help in such a case. And, finally, no person would be admitted "in order to increase the profit of the operator of a private nursing home, or to spare the budget of a locally operated community facility."

Yet, in a two-year period, against his judgment and will, because of outside pressure over which he had no control, the admitting psychiatrist had to admit sixty-six patients who did not meet the criteria for admission, including twenty-nine who had been previously rejected one to three times.

Of the sixty-six, forty-nine were not psychotic at all and were not sufficiently disturbed to require admission to a mental hospital; the remaining seventeen had such mild degrees of disturbed behavior that with proper medication they could easily be kept in the community.

If that was heartbreaking to begin with, so were the results of hospitalization in these patients who were warehoused—essentially, abandoned and shunted off—and who didn't belong in a mental institution. They remained in the hospital at more than three times the rate for other patients who belonged there when admitted. They improved to convalescent status at only one-seventh the rate for those who had met admission criteria, and to complete discharge status at only one-third the rate. Moreover, those who were improperly placed in the mental hospital had a death rate three times that for those who met the criteria for admission.

The psychiatrist has since died. Although he obviously felt strongly about the whole matter, he kept his report scientifically factual and drew no inferences about why the misassigned patients did so poorly. It would not be unfair, however, to infer that they may have given up hope, realizing that they did not belong in a mental institution, that much could have been done for them outside if community services had been mustered, that they were abandoned.

"Water on the Brain"

The situation is all too familiar. The patient is elderly (sometimes even middle-aged). His bizarre behavior, forgetfulness, and growing slovenliness have brought his family to the point of despair.

Physical examination, routine laboratory tests, and even a neurologic examination if done have shed no light on the problem.

More often than not, the diagnosis will be senile dementia if the patient is old, presenile dementia if middle-aged, and quite probably the patient will be permanently institutionalized.

Yet, at least in some cases, if the patient is lucky, encounters a bit more diagnostic persistence, and gets the benefit of more sophisticated diagnostic techniques, occult hydrocephalus ("water on the brain") may be uncovered and, with surgery, symptoms may be reversed and the patient saved from a life of vegetation.

The report in 1965 by a Harvard team of a small series of elderly patients who responded, plus many other reports since, have opened up a whole new vista for many of the seemingly hopelessly senile.

For an understanding, we need just a brief look at the brain. It's a well-protected organ. The skull, a tough bony cage, surrounds it completely; it takes a strong blow to break the skull. The skull itself is protected by the scalp, which is made up of five layers—skin, cutaneous tissue under the skin, fibrous tissue under that, then loose tissue, and finally periosteum, another layer covering the bone of the skull—and the scalp can absorb some tough blows.

Still more protection is provided. Inside the brain are four reservoirs, the ventricles, which contain fluid; and, with fluid circulating around it, the brain in effect floats on and in fluid. It is an ideal shock-absorber system.

The brain, of course, is part of the central nervous system, which includes the spinal cord. The spinal cord is suspended in a protective cylinder formed by the bones of the spine and it, too, has fluid to cushion it from shock.

It has long been known that when the regular flow of the cerebrospinal fluid is impaired by a congenital malformation of the internal skull, the fluid accumulates in the brain and enlarges the ventricles. This is hydrocephalus (literally, "water brain"), which in children causes enlargement of the cranium.

When a child has hydrocephalus, it is soon obvious. Normally, the cerebrospinal fluid forms in the ventricles, flows out through openings in the brain and arrives in the fluid cushion surrounding the central nervous system. In addition to routine flow, there is routine absorption of fluid by large veins in membranes covering the brain to balance new fluid formation in the ventricles.

In a hydrocephalic child, the fluid can't get out of the ventricles. Pressure increases. The ventricles become distended. The distention makes the child's still-soft skull bones spread and the head balloons grotesquely. Most cases begin shortly after birth or during infancy, and, if unchecked by early childhood, the condition may lead to mental and physical deterioration as well as massive head enlargement.

Surgery for hydrocephalus in a child is designed to divert fluid around an obstruction and into the blood circulation. Through a small scalp incision and a burr hole in the skull, a fine, spaghetti-thin tube is inserted into a fluid-stretched ventricle. The tube is then threaded under the scalp and under the skin of the neck to the jugular vein, then down through that vein to an entrance chamber of the heart, an atrium. This is a ventriculoatrial shunt or bypass. By reestablishing fluid flow, it works wonders for a hydrocephalic child.

But hydrocephalus in an elderly patient does not give itself away by obvious signs. It does not produce the enlarged head common in children. It need not even be marked by increased pressure. The first report from Harvard told of hydrocephalus in three elderly people who had no head enlargement, no increase of pressure within the brain.

One was a sixty-three-year-old woman whose illness started with a peculiar episode of weakness, giddiness, and pallor, from which she recovered the following day. From then on, however, she became easily tired, uncertain of gait, forgetful, less able to concentrate and organize her daily affairs. Several times, she lost urinary control.

Six months after onset of her illness, she entered Massachusetts General Hospital, a Harvard teaching institution in Boston. There, among the studies performed, was one for cerebrospinal fluid pressure and another in which her skull was X-rayed. Both were normal. However, a pneumoencephalogram—an X-ray of the brain after injection of air—showed massive enlargement of the ventricle system. Quickly, after a shunt operation done much as for a child with hydrocephalus, she began to improve—and continued to improve. At age sixty-six, her intellectual performance in standard tests was "superior" and her general memory "very superior." Her recovery was complete and remains so.

The other two patients also made dramatic recoveries after surgical shunting. Within four weeks both were judged by their families to be their former, cheerful, alert selves again. One, a sixty-two-year-old pediatrician who had shown symptoms of early senility including forgetfulness, unsteady gait, and bedwetting, could return to his practice in perfect health.

What actually produced the senility symptoms? There is some belief that the cause was directly related to the cerebrospinal fluid pressure even though the pressure remained within normal limits. There is some possibility that at the beginning of illness, the intracranial pressure does increase—but only until the ventricles become enlarged. Then, with the enlarged ventricles providing a larger surface to absorb the pressure, the pressure is reduced. Yet the increased area over which the lower pressure is applied results in a considerable total force exerted on surrounding brain tissue.

Hydrocephalus without increased intracranial pressure may occur following injury, hemorrhage, meningitis, or brain tumor. But it may also occur for unknown reasons in patients who have had none of these.

The original Harvard work has been confirmed now at many major medical centers.

At Mount Sinai Hospital in New York, one patient was a sixty-six-year-old judge who first experienced an episode of confusion, disorientation, and severe headache lasting several hours. Over the next two years he gradually deteriorated, his personality changing markedly toward increased suspiciousness. Two months prior to admission he fell without losing consciousness but thereafter deteriorated rapidly. On admission, he was confused, disoriented, had memory deficits, anxiety, depression, marked paranoid suspiciousness, insisting that he had evidence of his doctor accusing him of all kinds of crimes. His gait was impaired, and he was incontinent of urine and feces. Within forty-eight hours after a shunt was inserted, he was alert, cheerful, oriented, and his incontinence and paranoid thinking disappeared.

Another patient, a man in his mid-sixties, had noted onset of difficulties ten years earlier. He had been successful in his profession, enjoyed family and social activities. But where he had always been mild-mannered, unassuming and slow to anger, he began to notice, as had family and others close to him, that his personality was undergoing change and he was becoming increasingly impatient, quick-tempered, argumentative, and belligerent. After several years, he developed gait disturbances and began to repeatedly lose his balance and fall. Finally, his deterioration became so pronounced that he had to be hospitalized; he suffered severe headaches, irritability, depression, memory deficits, and disorientation and could walk no more than a few steps without falling. Again, results of a shunt were dramatic. Within days, his symptoms were almost completely gone. Within weeks, he could return to his profession and he has worked full time since.

In both these cases, serious consideration had been given to permanent institutionalization and, based on Mount Sinai's experience with them and with other patients, many more may be going unrecognized and untreated. Patients over fifty who seem to have psychiatric problems very often receive limited or no diagnostic neurologic examination, and, as a result, some who might otherwise be treated are sent to nursing homes and state hospitals to await demise.

At the Veterans Administration Hospital in Cincinnati, seventeen of the first twenty-eight patients to receive a shunt showed improvement. In a report from Episcopal Hospital, Philadelphia, shunting for twenty-eight patients with senilitylike dementia produced a good response in eighteen.

Detection of occult, normal-pressure hydrocephalus now is being aided by refined diagnostic techniques. In addition to pneumoencephalography, cisternography is valuable. The latter is a technique in which a material (radioiodinated serum albumin) is injected and demonstrates whether cerebrospinal fluid is being adequately reabsorbed; if it is not, the indication is that the patient may benefit from a shunt.

Shunting is not a panacea. Nor is it a minor procedure. As with any surgery, there is some element of risk of infection and of other possible complications. But it is clearly a worthwhile procedure when appropriately used—when studies are made first to be reasonably certain that a patient has not suffered irreversible brain damage and has a good chance of benefiting from the operation.

"Attitude Therapy" and Senility

From the Veterans Administration Hospital in Tuscaloosa, Alabama, come reports of elderly men and women, once considered "hopelessly" senile, some of them almost vegetables, returning to active, meaningful life.

They have included patients who had little apparent capacity for rational thought and little or even no control over natural functions, who were unable to dress or feed themselves and were unable to give their own names.

Some of the recoveries sound like "old-time medicine-man advertisements." In one case, a man who had been confined for a year had been keeping two orderlies occupied much of the time just dressing him because his sole occupation was taking off his clothes. Currently, he is caring for himself and helping to care for his wife.

The treatment used at Tuscaloosa, known as "attitude therapy" and "reality orientation," rests on principles that go against much of the folklore about senility. One principle is that however senile a patient may be, there is still something left to work with; there may be brain damage, but capabilities remain. A second principle is: Demand more of a patient and often, surprisingly, he may rise to the demand.

Typically, for example, many of the senile have fantasies and their well-intentioned, concerned families humor them. Not at Tuscaloosa. If, for instance, a patient says that he is waiting for a loved one, perhaps his wife Mary, to come, when actually Mary died years before, a sympathetic family may change the subject, hoping he will not think about it. At Tuscaloosa, he is told not to expect Mary; she will not come; she is dead.

At that, he may experience great sadness and cry, and the treatment may seem cruel. But Tuscaloosa personnel find that the treatment is really kind rather than cruel; that evading the facts may lead a patient deeper and deeper into unreality; and crying is an essential part of returning to reality.

At the hospital, each senile patient is carefully studied and then a specific basic approach is prescribed.

For example, for an apathetic patient with little interest left in life, the approach is "active friendliness"—everything possible is done to show interest in his ideas and activities and to give him pleasure.

For a suspicious, paranoid patient, the approach is "passive friendliness"—much like the "active" type but the patient must make the first move.

On the other hand, for a depressed patient, "kind firmness" is the approach. He may be required to do repetitious, even useless chores under critical supervision—and the aim is to move him toward expressing negative, hostile feelings which, until now, he has been directing inward.

Once a patient has been analyzed and an approach prescribed, it's used consistently by everyone in the hospital who has any dealings of any kind with the patient, from psychiatrist to nurse's aide.

The methods used at Tuscaloosa are hardly a cure-all. They may work dramatically in some cases but certainly not in all or even a majority. Much depends upon the patient, his age, how long he has been senile, how motivated his family is. Out of one group of a hundred, perhaps only five may improve; out of another group of a hundred, fifty may. Some veterans reach the hospital with histories of thirty years of senility; if they are in their eighties, the hospital may count it a success if they are kept from going downhill.

What is noteworthy and heartening about the Tuscaloosa effort—and many other efforts now—is that they are positive, determined, rather than defeatist, achieving gains that sometimes are small and sometimes great, and engendering reasonable hope that more gains can be achieved.

Actually, striking evidence could be found even long ago that positive attitudes and efforts could help if only they were tried. Dr. Karl A. Menninger, chief of staff of the Menninger Clinic, recalls that one of the brightest spots in his life was working with Dr. Howard V. Williams of Topeka who, twenty-five years ago, took over a ward in the local hospital, a ward for the patients with "senile dementia." ("I apologize for this abominable term," writes Dr. Menninger. "It is what we called the state of utter despair and demoralization some of our old people reached as they lost their faculty for readaptation and coping. We know now that the condition is not properly called a 'dementia.' ")

Every state hospital had many such patients who had become isolated from their families, confused, restless, irritable, forgetful, unsocial, and often plain nuisances. So off to the asylum they went where they were allowed to lie in bed or sit idly in a chair. At Topeka State Hospital there were eighty-eight such patients, average age sixty-eight. Fifty-one were constantly bedfast and had been so for an average of ten years, and about a score had to be spoonfed at every meal.

"Picture this ward full of longtime bedridden, incontinent,

hopeless, vegetating patients waiting to die," says Dr. Menninger. "Then picture an eager young doctor (Howard Williams) coming in with his team of cheerful nurses, aides, social workers, and psychiatric residents. Things began to happen. Every patient became a focus of attention."

The ward was fitted out with music, television, cages of canaries, potted plants, new lighting fixtures, curtains, and draperies. Birthday parties were held and relatives invited to them and for weekend visits. Many social activities were instituted by patients, staff members, and volunteers. Patients painted a shuffleboard court on the floor of a previously sacred "sitting hall" and built a ramp over a difficult flight of steps so bedfast patients could be moved into the social center.

Results? "A change in the clinical status of the patients was perceptible immediately," says Dr. Menninger. "Three weeks after the program had begun, one patient was discharged to relatives delighted to have their old father rise, as it were, from the grave. . . . By the end of the year twelve of these eighty-eight patients had gone home to live with their families. Six had gone out to live by themselves, and four had found comfortable nursing-home provisions. Four were now gainfully employed and self-supporting. . . . What had become of the dementia?"

Thinning the Blood and Senility

The first patient with progressive senile dementia to receive the treatment was a sixty-six-year-old woman who had deteriorated steadily over a three-year period. She no longer could use the bathroom, dress herself, or light her own cigarette.

She was given a drug, Dicumarol, an anticoagulant, designed to thin the blood. The theory was that senility often is due to insufficient blood supply to the brain. As arteries feeding brain areas become narrowed, the amount of blood they can transport diminishes and the obstructive narrowing of the vessels may also lead to some thickening of the blood getting through them and reaching the brain. The thickened blood then cannot flow freely through the brain capillaries, the tiny vessels through which nutrients and oxygen from blood move to brain cells, with the result that some of the cells may be prevented from functioning normally. Hopefully, by thinning the "sludged" blood, it might be possible to get more of it to deprived brain cells to help restore normal functioning.

After two months of treatment, the patient did show noteworthy improvement. In addition to becoming able to take care of herself and carry out her own personal hygiene, she managed now to do meticulous needlework again. She was continued on the drug during the remaining eighteen months of her life, living by herself most of the time and even doing some of her own interior decorating, before she suffered a fatal heart attack.

Of the next thirteen patients who underwent Dicumarol treatment, none deteriorated while on the drug, three became able to feed themselves, and one became well enough to be discharged. The work was done by Dr. Arthur C. Walsh, clinical assistant professor of psychiatry at the University of Pittsburgh School of Medicine and director of the Day Hospital, Western Psychiatric Institute and Clinic, Pittsburgh. It was a promising start.

More recently, there was another trial, this time coupling brief but intensive psychotherapy with Dicumarol treatment. Twenty-two patients took part. They ranged in age up to eighty-nine; eight were under sixty-five, including a sixty-four-year-old physician and a fifty-two-year-old nurse. The most deteriorated was a woman who could not put together a normal sentence; the least deteriorated was a sixty-three-year-old man who still was able to work in his office but in a demoted position. Seventeen patients had been treated elsewhere without success and were considered hopeless and had continued to deteriorate. Most of the patients had symptoms of organic brain disease: disorientation, impaired memory, poor judgment, or other loss of intellectual ability. Eight suffered mainly from emotional reactions—anxiety, depression, bizarre hysterical behavior such as inappropriate exposure of the body, paranoid ideas, or combinations of symptoms.

Treatment began with a two-month trial of Dicumarol. During that time, psychotherapy also was used. The objective was to get patients to express feelings of fear, frustration, persecution, abandonment; once exposed, the feelings could be discussed in order to reduce stresses to a minimum. If improvement occurred during the two-month trial, patients then were referred to their own physicians for maintenance therapy.

All the twenty-two patients showed some degree of improvement by the end of the two months. In eight, the improvement was marked. In fourteen, results were classified as good: memory considerably improved, confusion greatly reduced or eliminated. Prior to the trial, most patients had been receiving antidepressant or tranquilizer drugs, or both; at the end of the two months, most could do without drugs or needed greatly reduced doses. "This," Dr. Walsh believes, "can be attributed to improved brain function from better circulation and to the resolution of many emotional conflicts."

The fifty-two-year-old nurse with presenile dementia—dementia occurring before age sixty as contrasted with senile dementia occurring after sixty—illustrates some of the values of psychotherapy added to Dicumarol. She had had a three-year history of symptoms which had led to loss of her job. Her mental picture of herself was that of a menopausal woman with hardening of the arteries and deterioration of the brain. She was anxious over that, anxious too over loss of her job and the eating up of all her savings, and had become depressed enough to consider suicide.

She began to improve intellectually during Dicumarol treatment but remained anxious and depressed. However, as psychotherapy began to elicit her concerns and as she talked about them, antidepressant and tranquilizing medication could be reduced. A social worker saw her family—basically, a supportive but poorly communicating family—and made them fully aware of her financial problems and the fact that she could not yet cope with them herself because of brain damage. Social security benefits (which the patient was not aware she was entitled to) were obtained and her brothers and sisters provided contributions she could depend upon. As her brain function began to improve, her emotional and social problems also were relieved.

"This total approach," says Dr. Walsh, "undoubtedly accounted for the marked improvement in contrast to the limited recovery that would be expected from attention to only one aspect of the problem."

Today, the patient is doing increasingly well. She drives her car and is bright, cheerful, optimistic. The outlook is that if continuing intellectual improvement occurs, she may be able to return to work in her profession. It will take at least a year, Dr. Walsh expects, for her to recover emotionally from her harrowing three-year experience.

Videotape interviews with a sixty-four-year-old retired executive before and after treatment provide permanent records of the improvement in orientation and intellectual ability. Before treatment, the man had to be assisted out of his chair but after seven weeks of therapy he easily rose from the chair himself and walked unescorted from the room. He was able to look about and recognize his wife, which he could not do earlier. In seven weeks, he became able to dress himself, go to the cafeteria for meals, and remember his physician's name, none of which had been possible before.

Dicumarol treatment is not without risk. The drug is not a new one. It has been used frequently for heart patients. Whenever it is used, it must be used carefully, under close medical supervision, for an excessive dose, by thinning blood too much, can lead to hemorrhaging. To begin with, a daily blood test may be needed to make certain that the proper dose of Dicumarol is being used. Later the tests can be spaced at much greater intervals, as long as every four weeks. In seven years of trials, Dr. Walsh has had only one case of serious hemorrhage and that one, he believes, could have been coincidental.

Anticoagulant treatment for senility must still be considered experimental. Before it is generally accepted, many physicians will have to test it. Such testing has begun. At Maimonides Hospital and Home for the Aged, Montreal, a recently reported study compared two groups of patients suffering from advanced senile dementia, half of whom received Dicumarol while the others, for comparison, received placebos, or inert capsules. In the placebo group, after a year the mean memory quotient had declined by two thirds; in those receiving Dicumarol, the decline was about 10 percent. Tests for other characteristics showed much greater deterioration among the placebo group.

In their report, the Montreal investigators noted, "Our study showed that anticoagulant therapy is a safe method in carefully selected aged patients, when proper precautions are used and regular hematological [blood] and medical control is exercised." They also observed that they have reason to believe the treatment would have been more effective if earlier cases had been chosen. They are beginning a follow-up study with a larger group of patients.

Dilating the Vessels and Senility

In Europe, and more recently in this country, physician-investigators are reporting worthwhile, though far from panacealike, effects in elderly people treated with a preparation called Hydergine, taken in tablet form.

Animal studies have indicated that one effect of the preparation is dilation of brain blood vessels. Another is believed to be reduced blood-vessel resistance to blood flow. And some experiments suggest that the preparation also may improve utilization of oxygen.

A group of volunteers in Europe, aged fifty-nine to ninety-five, received either 0.5 milligram of Hydergine or a placebo, administered under the tongue, six times daily for twelve weeks. The treated patients improved markedly by the end of the first month and continued to show improvement through the third month, with no untoward side effects. They experienced less dizziness, ate better, had improved coordination, and tended to be less agitated and to tremble less.

On the other hand, patients who received placebos generally tended to improve during the first month, but failed to maintain improvement during the second and third months of the study and, by the third month, had reverted almost to pretreatment levels.

In another study with eighty other persons, with a mean age of sixty-five, not only did some receive real medication while others received placebos, but neither patients nor physicians knew who was receiving what until the trial was over. This is called a double-blind study, and eliminates the effects of hopefulness and enthusiasm engendered not only by the mere fact of taking part in a trial but also by physicians' attitudes and enthusiasms. Patients on the real medication became more receptive to new experiences, and the narrowness and inflexibility that often characterize the elderly were lessened.

Another double-blind study, in a Massachusetts home for the aged, was pursued for twelve weeks, and covered forty geriatric patients with cerebrovascular disorders. These included patients with mental deterioration diagnosed as due to cerebral arteriosclerosis or senile cerebral degeneration. Hydergine relieved a number of manifestations of cerebrovascular insufficiency, including inability to perform basic self-care tasks, some physical complaints, some aspects of mood and attitude, and intellectual deterioration. In the following areas, patients receiving the real medication improved to a greater extent than those receiving placebos: appetite, headache complaints, emotional instability, anxiety and fears, impairment of recognition, and ability to follow instructions. There was also some diminution of memory defect and confusion.

In some respects, American trial results do not agree completely with those reported in Europe. Some European studies indicate that Hydergine produces greatest improvement in symptoms relating to attitude and mood, some improvement in daily living activities and physical manifestations, with little change in "mental status." Other European investigations indicate relief of physical complaints and improvement in ability to perform self-care tasks, but no change in physiological status. The American investigators found relatively small change in patients' daily living activities, some improvements in physical complaints, attitude, and mood, but a most promising change in mental or cognitive capacities.

Obviously, Hydergine is a long way from being a specific treatment for senility, but it may be helpful in at least some patients in ameliorating some of the problems associated with senility.

Fats in the Arteries and Senility

A ninety-six-year-old man with severe atherosclerosis had very marked vision impairment. When first examined by an ophthalmologist, he could, with uncorrected vision, just barely see well enough to count fingers at a distance of two feet with his right eye and six inches with his left. While on treatment with a special drug, he could see well enough to count fingers at eight feet with his right eye and at four feet with his left.

The drug is a recently developed compound, clofibrate, which has come into use as a means of reducing excessive levels of cholesterol and fatty materials in the blood—materials associated with development of our most significant blood vessel disease, atherosclerosis. In atherosclerosis, fatty deposits are laid down on the walls of vital arteries, narrowing them and impeding blood flow. For unknown reasons, the coronary arteries, which feed the heart muscle itself, are most prone to develop atherosclerosis, and coronary atherosclerosis is the reason for most heart attacks.

But arteries anywhere may be affected by atherosclerosis. Commonly, those of the extremities are. And also the brain.

High levels of cholesterol and other fats (triglycerides) in the blood that appear to be involved in atherosclerosis development often can be reduced and kept under control by dietary measures—reduced intake of foods rich in cholesterol (such as eggs), and reduced intake of fats in the diet. But in some cases such measures are not enough, and clofibrate has been found to be helpful in lowering otherwise recalcitrant high serum fat levels.

Now, in addition, it seems that clofibrate may help relieve many symptoms in patients with impaired circulation.

Clofibrate was administered to fifty-seven men and thirty-eight women. Twenty-seven had histories of one or more heart attacks and currently suffered, as did a number of others, from symptoms of impaired blood circulation to the heart muscle. Others had evidence of impaired circulation to the limbs and to the brain.

As expected, blood cholesterol levels fell in eighty-eight of the ninety-five patients. In those with impaired circulation to the heart, electrocardiograms showed improvement, the need for nitroglycerin and similar medication to relieve chest pain was halved, and ability to tolerate exercise increased by more than 100 percent. Exercise tolerance also doubled in patients with impaired leg circulation. It was notable, too, that twenty-two of twenty-three patients with vertigo or dizziness associated with poor brain circulation reported relief.

Like other measures, clofibrate is hardly a specific for senility. But, consistent with the growing conviction among authorities that, if senility itself is not presently directly attackable, control of any factors associated with it or tending to exacerbate its effect is very much worthwhile, clofibrate may be of some limited value in some patients with senility.

Heart Failure and Senility

It has an ominous sound, but heart failure does not mean that the heart stops beating. Rather, long overburdened for any of several reasons, the heart loses its ability to pump as effectively as it once did.

We shall be considering heart failure in greater detail in a later chapter because of its significance for many of the elderly who are not senile. But we mention it here because any factor that reduces blood flow to the brain may be involved in senility, and heart failure—really pumping-efficiency loss—can reduce blood flow markedly to all areas of the body including the brain.

Yet, properly evaluated and treated, as we shall see, heart failure very often can be brought under control: a plus on the side of improving mental as well as physical health in the elderly.

Hypertension and Senility

Hypertension, or elevated blood pressure, is extremely common at all ages. Some twenty-three million Americans today are estimated to have the problem, and at least half of them don't know it.

While hypertension sometimes may produce such symptoms as fatigue, nervousness, dizziness, palpitation, insomnia, weakness, and headaches, it can exist for years without giving itself away by symptoms. It can have widespread effects. It is now recognized to be an important factor in heart attacks, strokes, and kidney failure.

We shall have more to say about hypertension and its many effects on the elderly in a later chapter, but, for now, it is pertinent to note that, by its influence on both artery hardening and heart pumping failure, it can reduce blood and oxygen flow to the brain and in so doing may contribute to senility.

Moreover, evidence of the effects of hypertension on the intellect of aging people has been observed in 202 men and women in their sixties and seventies over a ten-year period. At the beginning and at intervals thereafter, each man and woman had blood pressure taken and was given a battery of intelligence tests.

Surprised investigators found that, among subjects in their early sixties when the study began, those who had normal pressures showed almost no intellectual decline at the end of the ten years, whereas those with high blood pressure had drops of almost ten points in test scores.

Dr. Carl Eisdorfer, who headed the research, remarked: "The purpose of our study is to demythologize the aging process, which is full of misconceptions. The more we accept intellectual deterioration as inevitable, the less likely we are to do anything about preventing it."

Hypertension today is a correctable problem—happily, in the overwhelming majority of cases, relatively simple to correct.

Anemia and Senility

Of all the problems of human health, perhaps none is at once more widespread, misunderstood, mistreated, and outrightly neglected than anemia.

There are many types of anemias, but the important fact is

that their diagnosis by a physician is not difficult, and, in the vast majority of cases, they can be corrected. Their correction can do much to reinvigorate any victim at any age, including many elderly people without senility but dragging along because of unrecognized and untreated debilitating anemias. And for the senile, anemia correction, when it exists, while hardly likely to eliminate manifestations of senility, may help minimize them.

Anemia is not a disease in itself; except for fever, it is probably the body's most common and important danger signal.

Nor is it just a matter of a pale face or tired look. When mild, anemia can produce weakness, easy fatigability, irritability, vague abdominal pains, and many other insidious symptoms. When severe, it can lead to palpitations, vertigo, pounding headaches, spots before the eyes, and even psychotic behavior. And although it is rarely if ever a cause of senility, anemia can be responsible for many disturbances in the elderly and can contribute to senility. Because of its effect on blood capabilities, including capability for carrying oxygen, it can make a bad situation much worse. And its correction may make considerable difference to a person who seems to be hopelessly senile.

The problem is far more common—and at all ages—than most people think. It has been discovered in at least 20 percent of all patients admitted to general hospitals, no matter for what reason. Although nobody knows the total incidence—since many who don't enter hospitals are affected—moderate or severe anemia is extremely common in young children, in pregnant women (affecting as many as 70 percent, according to some estimates), and in the elderly.

Anemia means an abnormal condition of the blood—and it is best understood if you have a clear understanding of the workings of that remarkable internal sea.

Constantly bathing all parts of the body—flowing through some sixty thousand miles of arteries, veins, and capillaries to do so—blood consists of a fluid called plasma, which contains red and white cells.

The white are protective. Prick your finger, for instance, and if bacteria enter and start to multiply, white cells are mobilized at the site to fend them off. But day in and day out, it's the red cells that maintain life. They're saucer-shaped particles so tiny it takes three thousand to cover the space of an inch, and there are enough in the blood—about thirty trillion—to encircle the earth four times if lined up in a beadlike chain.

Red cells owe their color to hemoglobin, a pigment with great affinity for, and ability to grab and hold, oxygen. And it is through hemoglobin that the red cells carry life-supporting oxygen from lungs to all body tissues. Created mainly in the marrow of short, flat bones, red cells can function for up to one hundred and twenty days and then, worn out, are removed from the circulation and destroyed by the spleen.

Protein and iron from foods go into the making of hemoglobin; other dietary substances, including vitamins and minerals, help build the red cells. And if all goes well, red cell and hemoglobin formation keeps up with body needs; every hour, some ten billion red cells are produced to replace those worn out.

Anemia develops when there are not enough red cells or when they contain inadequate amounts of hemoglobin. The most common reason for anemia is iron deficiency and the resulting fall in hemoglobin levels produces a general oxygen deficiency that can interfere with efficient functioning of brain cells, heart muscle, and other organs, and can lower the body's general resistance.

Iron-deficiency anemia is common in childhood because of too little iron in the diet, especially when large amounts of milk are consumed to the exclusion of other foods. It is common in pregnancy because the mother must supply the baby's needs for it; all through the menstrual years, when she is losing some iron in menstrual flow, a woman is often in precarious iron balance.

Iron-deficiency anemia is common in the elderly, often simply as the result of poor diet and inadequate iron intake. In some cases, too, there may be blood loss and siphoning out of iron stores because of internal bleeding—from an ulcer, for example. Yet, the onset of the anemia in the aged is so gradual that many do not recognize the symptoms until effects become apparent by inability to work.

The medical detection of iron-deficiency anemia—and of other types of anemia—is easy enough with simple blood tests. And all that may be needed to correct iron-deficiency anemia is the use of a suitable iron supplement. An alert physician, suspecting the possibility of internal bleeding, can use tests to check further and, if a source of such bleeding is found, it often can be corrected.

While iron-deficiency anemia is most common, there are other types. Hemolytic anemias are caused by excessive destruction of red cells, outpacing the bone marrow's capacity to provide replacements. The destruction may result from exposure to excessive amounts of some chemicals such as lead and arsenic and to poisonous substances produced by bacteria during the course of severe infections. The anemias respond when the chemicals are avoided or infection is overcome. Some people have a specific inherited defect of the red cells that makes them sensitive to certain medications—sulfa drugs, for example. They may go through life without developing hemolytic anemia unless they happen to take a sensitizing drug, which must then be stopped promptly.

There are many other anemias in which the problem is inadequate red cell formation. Pernicious anemia is an important one. It was once a mysterious and deadly problem, hence the now-outmoded term "pernicious" because today it need not be pernicious at all.

Usually insidious in onset, pernicious anemia may produce some soreness of the tongue as a first complaint. Then may come loss of appetite, nausea, attacks of abdominal pain, and such general symptoms as weakness, shortness of breath, and palpitations.

Pernicious anemia stems from failure to absorb vitamin B_{12} from the intestine. The vitamin is essential for bone-marrow activity. When it is lacking, red cells formed in the marrow are abnormally large, fail to divide, have an abbreviated life span. The fundamental defect is a deficiency of an "intrinsic" factor normally present in the gastric juice and required to promote B_{12} absorption. Today, pernicious anemia is readily treated with periodic injections of vitamin B_{12}, circumventing the intrinsic factor deficiency.

Blood cell formation also may suffer from lack of another vitamin, folic acid. Such anemia often develops as the result of disorders impairing absorption of the vitamin from the intestine. Administration of folic acid by injection or even by mouth usually produces prompt response of the anemia while the underlying condition is treated by diet or other means.

Bone marrow depression and reduction in new red cell formation sometimes is associated with chronic infection such as tuberculosis or sinusitis, or with inflammatory conditions such as rheumatoid arthritis. Though supportive measures, including adequate diet and vitamins, help, the basic treatment is to actively combat the infection, inflammation, or other underlying problem.

Nutrition and Senility

We shall have more to say about the vital importance of nutrition for the elderly in a later chapter. But we have already touched briefly on it in connection with anemia and, because it can influence other problems of senility as well, we should go into it a little more here.

Although this is considered to be an affluent nation, the amount of malnutrition is staggering—and not just among the poor. People of good incomes, even the wealthy, are often victims of poor eating habits. It is possible to be overfed yet undernourished. And malnourishment may contribute to many physical problems of the elderly and, to some extent, to senility.

Recently, many thoughtful physicians such as Dr. Harold H. Sandstead of Vanderbilt University School of Medicine have become aware that they have been "taught to place so much emphasis on the systemic and pathologic factors of disease that they sometimes overlook significant signs of nutritional disorder, even when such signs are frankly apparent."

It may seem incredible that even hospital patients, technically supposed to receive the greatest amount of medical care, can be neglected nutritionally. Yet many experience loss of appetite, and if there were any routine examination of food trays after meals it would show large amounts of food uneaten.

Poor eating habits can lead to weakness, fatigue, weight loss, and other disorders that may falsely seem to be results of the patient's illness. One now-wiser physician doesn't hesitate to tell about a patient who had chronic lung disease and, on top of that, a long bout of pneumonia. She ate poorly, but when she began to suffer mentally, becoming confused and disoriented, the blame seemed to lie with her physical disease. But then the physician noted that her tongue had become purple and had lost all of its covering. He realized she must not have been eating well and could have a vitamin (nicotinic acid) deficiency. The surest way to find out was to give her vitamin supplements along with her diet. Not only did the condition of her tongue improve; so did her mental status.

Nutrition has much to do with physical health and with the state of the mind as well. And, unfortunately, as many authorities point out, the problem of dietary deficiencies is especially widespread among elderly people, too many of whom are "tea and toast" types. Because of poor appetite or lack of money or desire to cook, they live, if not entirely, primarily on bread and hot water.

Of considerable interest is a recent discovery about taste-sense disturbances that may have something to do with at least some cases of malnutrition in the elderly as well as in younger people.

Taste-sense disturbances—actual loss of all taste or distortions of taste that make many good foods taste foul—have long been considered to be psychiatric disturbances. But the discovery is that, in reality, taste is lost or becomes disturbed as the result of a deficiency disorder which is much more common, especially in milder forms, than used to be thought. And, fortunately, there is a simple effective treatment for it—with zinc.

One hundred and three patients aged twenty-five to eighty-one were given a zinc supplement four times a day in doses of 25, 50, and 100 milligrams. In most, blood levels of zinc were found to be abnormally low before treatment. All showed increases in the blood levels with treatment; all showed improvement in taste; and two-thirds became completely normal.

Emphysema and Senility

Pulmonary emphysema, a chronic lung disease, was once thought to be a symptom of aging, an inevitable concomitant of growing old. It is no such thing, but, if uncontrolled, it is a problem that can make life difficult and miserable for the aging.

Emphysema has become one of our most rapidly increasing basic health problems. It is far more prevalent a problem than lung cancer and tuberculosis combined and, in fact, affects more than ten million Americans, most of them in middle and older age groups.

We shall be considering emphysema in more detail in a later chapter, but we must mention it here because it can be a factor that contributes to and exacerbates senility.

In emphysema—a Greek word meaning inflation—the lungs are puffed up with air the victim is unable to expel properly. As he expends more and more energy trying, he has less reserve to do anything else. With emphysema, the amount of oxygen flowing to body tissues, including the brain, may be markedly reduced. And with advanced emphysema there can be disturbances of heart function as well, contributing still further to reduce flow of blood and oxygen to body tissues, including the brain.

Yet emphysema is not a disease beyond treatment. Changes in the lungs are irreversible, but it is possible to give patients considerable relief from such symptoms as wheezing, cough, labored breathing, and to increase the functioning capacity of the lungs. That can mean more blood and oxygen circulation.

Infection and Senility

Physicians have been discovering that bacteriuria—a very low-grade urinary infection that may produce no symptoms at all—is a chronic problem in many people of all ages. There is growing evidence that, however silent, its presence for years may lead to chronic pyelonephritis, an inflammatory disease of the kidneys, and to disturbances in blood circulation to the kidneys. Moreover, with advanced chronic pyelonephritis, blood pressure may become elevated and may have serious consequences for health—including, some late evidence indicates, mental health.

When sought for, bacteriuria can be detected readily enough and, with persistent treatment, can be eradicated or brought under tight control. And this is no less true for other chronic infections, which can begin as acute infections—colds, sore throats, and the like—that seem to respond to treatment, to subside, but do not disappear entirely; instead, they smoulder and become chronic. And on occasion, without previous acute infection, a chronic infection may develop and, without apparent symptoms, silently produce its harmful effects.

Thyroid Gland Problems

A woman patient had long experienced dizziness and, more recently, for about eighteen months, had felt light-headed and had noticed increasing deafness in both ears. Careful study also showed mental slowing. Within two weeks after starting thyroid treatment, she could walk without feeling dizzy. At the end of six months, there was definite overall improvement and at eighteen months, with continued treatment, she was completely well.

Can abnormal thyroid gland functioning be a factor in mental disturbances and perhaps contribute to some of the manifestations of senility? Of course.

In 1949, a now-classical study drew attention to "Myxedematous Madness," reporting on fourteen patients with hypothyroidism, or underfunctioning of the thyroid gland, who had gross psychiatric disturbances. Twelve suffered from marked confusion and disorientation and nine were sufficiently psychotic to have been committed to a mental observation ward before the diagnosis of hypothyroidism was made and effective treatment for that begun.

Other investigations since have shown a relationship between mental disturbances and abnormal thyroid functioning—and not only thyroid underfunctioning. In some as many as 20 percent of patients with hyperthyroidism, overfunctioning of the gland, had psychotic symptoms. Research suggests that, as in hypothyroidism, the hyperthyroid individual experiences a disturbance of intellectual function. One study found a group of ten hyperthyroid patients to be "strongly similar," in their performance on a series of tests, to individuals with proven organic brain changes. Treatment of the hyperthyroidism led to improvement of performance.

Recently at the Mayo Clinic, Dr. G. M. Cremer and his colleagues found that hypothyroidism sometimes can produce poor equilibrium and incoordination of the limbs, muscle disturbances such as weakness, aching, and stiffness, plus hearing disturbances and nervous-system changes leading to burning, prickling, and other abnormal sensations. Thyroid treatment usually led to marked improvement.

Physicians are continuing to find that thyroid disorder—either excessive or insufficient gland activity—can produce mental and emotional disturbances that often are readily helped when the thyroid problem is corrected.

Seventeen patients were examined, ten with hyper- and seven with hypothyroidism, severe enough in seven of the hyper- and six of the hypothyroid to constitute psychiatric illness. Most obvious was impairment of recent memory and difficulty with psychological tests demanding attention, abstract reasoning, and memory. Hypothyroid patients were frequently depressed, whereas those with hyperthyroidism were frequently anxious and irritable. Both groups improved after treatment for the thyroid problem.

The Great Need for Sensory Stimulation

One of the most valuable contributions made by space research—a contribution for use here on earth—was the discovery that the same kind of mental deterioration and debilitation which, for a long time, has been thought to be part and parcel of aging, can be brought on not by age but by sensory deprivation. When denied the normal, complex sensory stimulation—the sounds, sights, tastes, feel of the outer world and interaction with it and with people—even a healthy young person begins to show disorganization of the ability to think.

Just as the need for good nutrition, a balanced diet, does not change with age, neither does the need for varied human experiences. But changing conditions—job, family, daily living, coupled with problems of physical health—often make such experiences and the varied and beneficial stimuli they supply less and less available.

In his book, *Games People Play,* Dr. Eric Berne considered the great need for stimuli and the probability that "emotional and sensory deprivation tends to bring about or encourage organic changes." He remarked that, without sufficient stimulation, degenerative changes in brain cells may occur, and that though "this may be a secondary effect due to poor nutrition . . . the poor nutrition itself may be a product of apathy. . . . In this sense, stimulus hunger has the same relationship to survival of the human organism as food hunger."

In growing recognition of this need, varied searching attempts to meet it have been made and the results, if not dramatic, are, indeed, hopeful.

A pilot program was devised and carried out by an educational consultant, a casework supervisor, and a recreational therapist for one of the senile wards at a home and hospital for the aged. The program's keynote was sensory input, and aimed at overcoming the lack of stimuli for the elderly. Because the medical staff was skeptical, the test was confined to just one ward of twenty female patients, aged eighty to eighty-nine, in various stages of physical and mental deterioration. Most of the women needed constant physical care; many were confused, disoriented, withdrawn, depressed, or apathetic.

The team visited the ward daily and engaged the patients in arts and crafts and handwork projects at their bedside; twice a week, there was a live musical program with piano and guitar, with patients singing along, dancing, or clapping, and later sipping wine; once a week short movies were shown or bingo games played; and a day was set aside for recorded music while giant balloons were bounced and tossed to the rhythm.

To avoid routinization, variety and change were constantly introduced, always keeping in mind the fullest possible involvement of the senses.

After six months the reactions and attitudes of patients showed a marked degree of improvement in recognition, in recall, in relating to staff, relatives, and one another, and in overall behavior. Subsequently, every discipline working in or near that ward requested similar programming for other wards.

The same success has been achieved in Australia, with "stimulation therapy" over a six-month period for twenty-five women patients with senile dementia, and in the Virgin Islands, where such therapy has produced an outlook of restored confidence and self-worth on the part of the patients.

A registered nurse who met one hour a week with a group of seven aged, disabled hospitalized patients became increasingly aware that what concerned them most was psychologic deprivation. They felt isolated, alienated, bored; life was monotonous. Her original reason for meeting with the group was her acute awareness of the isolation of patients in the nursing homes in which she had once worked and still often visited, and to which dear neighbors of hers had been admitted. When she began, she had only one main goal: "to increase communication among a group of bored, isolated, disabled, aged patients."

She was severely limited in what she could do because of the conditions of the patients. Only two could walk. The group included a man confined to a wheelchair; a tottering man with glaucoma; an obese, arthritic wheelchair-bound woman who never stood or walked; a woman with shaking palsy and stammering speech; a man who had had a stroke twenty-five years before and had residual paralysis and slurred speech; and two very withdrawn, wheelchair-bound women.

She could not play cards, chess, checkers, or dominoes with them; could not show movies or slides because so few could see them. But she finally arrived at doing some very simple things.

She made it a point to touch each patient, and before long they began to shake hands and to touch one another. She sought to be a "pseudo family" for them, responding to their questions and sharing some of her world with them, and soon they became actively interested, asking her about her job, commuting, and so on.

The reason these patients hadn't talked together before was that they were unable to understand one another because of shaking palsy, heavy accent, residual effects of stroke, and so on. So the nurse spoke loudly and slowly and often repeated herself when one of the group did not seem to understand; she was serving as a role model. And it worked. Attention spans became longer; long periods of silence vanished; the patients began to talk to one another as soon as they entered the room.

She found that many of the patients feared getting lost if they went outside their own rooms because the large hospital had a maze of corridors. So she wheeled them to and from their rooms often and later they began to navigate on their own. They even began to be anxious to get out of their rooms. One woman began spending her afternoons in the hospital foyer after two years in her room. One man began to walk long distances in the hallways.

They were unable to see their TV sets and had no idea of or interest in what was going on in the outside world. She encouraged them to listen to their radios and discussed current news with them; soon they became actively interested in the outside world. In one more way they were beginning to get out of themselves, to become curious and less bored, and life seemed less monotonous.

She then went to work on their bland, salt-free, and diabetic diets, often unpalatable or uncolorful. She talked with doctors and was allowed to give weekly snacks to all patients in the group. A small thing, but they appreciated it.

It was by just such small things that progress was made—and it effected a change in the staff who cared for these patients.

Such programs carried out in institutions suggest guidelines for how families, at least to some extent, may provide stimuli for older people at home. An occasional treat, a game, a touch or caress, a conversation—all these seem like very little things, perhaps unimportant things, but they add up to rewarding stimulation.

No Small Problem: Hearing

Shouting at an elderly deaf person does no good, only causing low-frequency sounds to boom without increasing audibility of higher-frequency consonants, which is why so many older people protest, "Don't shout; I can hear," when, in fact, they do not understand what they hear.

Many people in their seventies and eighties do not necessarily have a flat loss in all frequencies; in fact, the two lowest frequencies are often useful but the higher ones may be useless. As a result, hearing may be fair for the lower vowel sounds but poor for upper frequencies which include consonant sounds needed to differentiate words. For example, "fog" and "hog" may sound like "og."

Many elderly people thus become "tuned out" of their social environment, and it can have a strong emotional impact that increases tension, agitation, or depression.

Often, the aged with hearing difficulties can be helped by hearing aids. But patience may be required—by the hearing specialist as well as the patient. Too often patients with problems not amenable to medical or surgical treatment are referred by many of these otologists to commercial dealers for a hearing aid instead of evaluating all possible suitable hearing aids and selecting the best themselves. Such otologists feel that their time and expense are not justified because it is commonly believed that no significant differences in individual hearing-aid performance exist.

But there can be great differences. In their experience with more than six thousand hard-of-hearing patients, Baylor University specialists found that often the first five or more aids were all uniformly poor in performance; but then, finally, one aid was found that produced excellent results. In many cases, they had to test ten or more aids to find one satisfactory for a particular patient. With such differences in such a large proportion of patients, the time and effort needed to find the right aid, the most useful one, for a patient would hardly seem to be unjustified.

Nor is it always a matter of need for a hearing aid. A striking discovery—and follow-up—at Elgin State Hospital, an Illinois mental institution, could offer new hope for at least some institutionalized patients and for some who seem to be candidates for institutionalization. When screened for hearing, fully 42 percent of the hospital's population failed the test. The majority who failed had impacted wax in both ears; some had otosclerosis, a disease of middle-ear bones. While impacted wax does not handicap all individuals, removal of the wax—sometimes so impacted that general anesthesia was needed to remove it—often showed up other problems such as infections, cysts, and perforated ear drums. Elimination of even a little hearing loss or an infection may often bring significant changes in behavior and, in addition, facilitate mental therapy. After treatment, more than fifty patients from Elgin improved to the point that they have been placed with families outside the hospital.

But only about twenty-five institutions (eighteen in Illinois) for the mentally ill in the entire United States provide speech and hearing services by qualified speech pathologists.

Psychiatric Help

The diagnosis of senility too often has been a dead-end one.

The very word implies inevitable deterioration, hopelessness. And it is very often not so much a diagnosis as a substitute for one and for active therapeutic effort.

The elderly quite commonly suffer from depression. The depression may have various causes. In some cases, it may yield to companionship and hope; in other cases, good nourishment may work wonders; in still others, effective treatment for a nagging physical problem may lift the melancholia; and, finally, there are those who can benefit from antidepressant drugs.

But depression does not respond to therapeutic nihilism—the kind of therapeutic nihilism that accompanies the diagnosis of senility. Nor do other emotional problems respond to such nihilism.

Yet mental and emotional impairments of all kinds frequently affect the elderly, including many of the elderly with brain syndrome.

We shall have more to say later about the treatment of depression and other psychiatric problems in the nonsenile aged. But the point to be made here is that when depression or other psychiatric disorder exists on top of senility, its treatment may make considerable difference to the senile—just as may treatment for impoverished circulation, failing heart, and other physical problems.

Total Care

Rescuing the elderly from mental institutions is a significant part of the treatment provided in Oxford, England. Although the United States rate is eight long-stay beds for every thousand elderly people, the rate in Oxford is only one per thousand—not because of shortage but rather as the result of a radical departure in treating the elderly that is aimed at getting them out of bed.

The working principle in Oxford is that many cases of confusion or general disorientation among the elderly are the consequences of organic brain diseases that stem from physical anomalies—and if medical resources are brought to bear, the organic disorder can be kept from progressing to the point where the patient is left mentally and physically helpless.

In the Oxford plan, a patient's ability to function is constantly assessed and reassessed. He may need immediate intensive care but, as his condition improves, he is gradually moved out of such care and encouraged to learn to take care of himself. The first step back into the community is a halfway house where therapists and social workers prepare the patient for independent living. Although many patients still appear to be candidates for commitment when they arrive at the halfway house, they recover enough to return home and resume living with their families.

If an elderly person's family needs advice or instruction, a member of the family can stay overnight or for several nights with the patient in the halfway house, watching how the professional team there and in the day hospital cope with him.

Once the patient returns home, a schedule is worked out with his family that allows him to return periodically to the hospital. It has turned out that much of the stress on the family can be eliminated by having the patient return to the hospital, off their hands, every now and then. In many cases, the patient is scheduled for return for two-week periods every three months and is readmitted when his family goes on vacation.

In Oxford today, of the fifty-three thousand elderly people in the community, fewer than fifty—less than 0.1 percent—are committed to mental institutions, although about seven hundred of the two thousand admitted to the plan yearly could be certified for commitment at the time they enter. In contrast, in New York State, for example, 1.5 percent of all people over sixty-five—fifteen times as many—are committed to mental hospitals.

Obviously, the possibility of applying such a program and attitude here should have active consideration—and possibly it will have.

Even short of it, there is new and growing hope for the elderly, including the senile. If senility at this stage cannot be cured, there is much that often can be done to relieve its manifestations, to make its victims more comfortable, to restore their dignity, to give them new hope, and perhaps even to allow at least some of them to resume relatively normal lives.

5

THE GREAT MASQUERADER

For just a moment, let's forget about older people and briefly consider two young people—a man of thirty-five and a woman of twenty-eight.

The man, a professional, has experienced a variety of disturbing symptoms: chest pains that worry him that he may have heart disease; headaches that seemingly come from the blue and do not respond to usual remedies; loss of appetite, and difficulty sleeping.

He seeks medical advice. When a thorough examination reveals nothing physically wrong, the physician refuses to leave it at that and gently prods with questions. He determines that the symptoms have appeared before; that there have been several episodes, each a little more intensive and prolonged than the preceding one; and, always, they have occurred in the midst of periods of job pressure and have been accompanied by feelings of discouragement and despondency.

The physician prescribes no battery of drugs—no extrapowerful analgesics for the headaches, no "tonics" for appetite, no sleeping pills for insomnia, no medication for the chest pains. The prescription is simply for a medication to help combat the man's "blues," his mental depression, and there is an extended session in the physician's office to consider the depression, to explain the connection with the varied symptoms, to reassure, and to offer hope.

The young woman, an attractive housewife, complains of fatigue and constant abdominal distress. She has tried vitamins, minerals, iron compounds, without benefit. When she finally seeks medical help, the physician examines her and carries out tests but also notes that she seems passive, withdrawn, lethargic.

He questions her gently but persistently. She had lost her mother some months before; and, yes, she responds thoughtfully, her symptoms had begun not long after her mother's death. And, like the young man, her problem too is diagnosed as mental depression and she receives medication for the depression.

The happy outcome for both these people is relief of their symptoms, not by piecemeal treatment for the symptoms but by treatment for the depression that caused them.

And even among the young, they are two of the lucky people.

Mental depression, long known to be an important problem, is now recognized as a *prime* one, accounting for a tremendous amount of human suffering, perhaps more than from any other single disorder. Of late, it has come to be regarded as *the most* prevalent of all psychic maladies in this country, so widespread that it has been referred to as the "common cold" of mental disturbances. A National Institute of Mental Health survey indicates that as many as eight million people a year suffer depression severe enough to merit treatment.

But it is sneaky.

It has been labeled "the great masquerader"—aptly—in recognition of its great propensity for mimicking a host of physical problems, often without giving itself away by any obvious mental indications such as a sad or despairing mood.

Not that its victims are not aware of sadness and despondency. They may be much aware of them, but often they are far more aware of, and concerned about, the physical problems.

A study of depressed patients in 1950, reiterated in 1966, found that the elapsed time from onset of symptoms to accurate recognition of depression ranged from three to thirty-six months during which patients often, if they received any treatment at all, were treated for other illnesses "while family difficulties worsened, financial resources were depleted, and suicidal risk continued."

For old as well as young, the suffering caused by depression—both mental suffering and extremely diverse physical suffering—can be severe.

It can be stopped—often with dramatic rapidity.

But whereas depression is a diagnosis missed often in all age groups, it is even more frequently missed in the sixty-five-and-over group because it may often be confused with senility. For the depressed elderly patient often appears to have memory loss, confusion, and other symptoms that may easily be mistaken for senility associated with cerebral brain artery hardening.

The Mood

All of us have our ups and downs, days when we feel "low" as well as other days when we feel on top of the world. But depression is another matter, no fleeting "down" feeling but rather a sustained, chronic change of mood, an extended lowering of the spirits.

At any time of life, depression may be brought on by a loss—the death of a loved one, a job loss, a financial setback. Such a depression arising from an external event is called reactive or exogenous.

Another type, the endogenous, comes from within. Again at any age, an individual may suddenly come to feel that he or she has failed in life. Although there may be no grounds for this, nevertheless this is how the individual sees himself and becomes bereft of self-esteem and self-confidence. And now matters that he once could handle without difficulty—everyday affairs, family problems, social problems, financial problems—suddenly bulk up as monumental, too much to cope with.

Often, depression may be mixed, both endogenous and exogenous. And some investigators believe that since many people suffer, for example, grief from a death in the family or other loss but, after a period of mourning, bounce back, there must, in those who go into prolonged depression, be some internal or endogenous factor that is responsible.

With depression, there is a lowering not only of mental mood but of general vitality. One indication of this is the proneness of the depressed to common illnesses and to greater difficulty in recovering from them. This has been shown by many studies. In one, for example, the winter after employees of a large business organization were given psychological tests, flu struck and many were affected. But the study revealed that those who had been found mildly depressed in the psychological tests required three weeks or longer to recover from the flu while others were over it in three to fourteen days.

Physical Symptoms

One of the most common symptoms in the depressed is overwhelming fatigue. It is often fatigue so profound that it becomes difficult to carry out even the most ordinary, routine, daily activities.

Sleeping problems are frequent. Most commonly, there is no great difficulty in falling asleep but after a few hours the depressed wake up and toss about for hours. "In a real dark night of the soul," the novelist F. Scott Fitzgerald wrote, "it is always 3 o'clock in the morning." Victims of chronic depression appreciate that melancholy phrase.

Headaches are also common. Out of 423 depressed patients in one study, 84 percent had headache as a major complaint and in some cases the only complaint. Depressive headaches do not necessarily have a favorite location but they do tend to be worse in the morning than in the evening and often stubbornly resist the usual headache remedies.

Loss of appetite is a frequent symptom. When the depressed seek medical help, their recital often may follow the lines cited by one physician: "Doctor, please give me something for these pains in my head. I feel so bad—such a pressure—like a heavy load weighing me down. I can't get interested in anything. . . . At night, I'm wide awake thinking of all kinds of terrible things, and even though I feel empty and hungry, the minute I see food I lose my appetite."

Gastrointestinal symptoms are diverse. Depression often accounts for complaints of gas and for abdominal pains unexplained by physical findings. Some of the depressed who suffer severely from digestive upsets, nausea, vomiting, constipation, or diarrhea may be mistakenly thought to have ulcers or colitis.

Nor does all this begin to encompass the varied symptoms that may stem from depression. The depressed may develop urinary frequency or urgency, sometimes accompanied by burning and pressure sensations in the bladder area. Many experience heart palpitations, chest constriction, and pain in the area of the heart and may believe they have heart trouble. Others may experience visual disturbances, ear noises, mouth dryness, numbness or tingling sensations, and skin blotches. Some experience difficulty in breathing that may arouse fears of lung cancer or emphysema or other obstructive airway disease. Physicians refer to these physical disturbances as the "somatic mask of depression." They often can be relieved effectively with antidepressant medication.

Depression in the Aged

It is impossible to determine exactly how many elderly people are suffering from chronic physical illnesses brought on or exacerbated by depression, or who appear to be hopelessly senile when in fact depression is a contributing factor or even sole factor in their mental deterioration. There is every reason for believing that the number is great.

For one thing, as we've noted earlier, the aged in a youth-oriented culture have many reasons for becoming depressed: their loss of status, their feelings of being useless and unwanted. Old friends, too, are lost. They see a future in which their alienation from life, their infirmities, and their helplessness can only become more complete. Some of these attitudes may not be entirely realistic or in some cases realistic at all. Often they can be changed by reassurance and other means. But they commonly exist.

For another thing, even in the young, depression is not easy to diagnose and in the old can be even more difficult. It may often go undiagnosed in both young and old because physical complaints are commonly the overriding ones, those for which medical help is sought. Few people know very much about depression, even less about its somatic guises. If victims, young or old, are aware of mentally depressed states along with their physical ills, they may see no connection between the two and not even mention mood. If anything, many of the elderly may be less likely to see an association between physical hurt and emotional state because of a tendency to associate the physical hurt with aging. It takes a discerning physician to penetrate the somatic masquerade to find the underlying depression.

The task may be complicated in the elderly patient because depression in the aged often may give rise to irascibility and irritability—personality changes which may repel family, friends, and physician. And, on top of that, what has to be overcome too is a feeling common among many physicians as well as lay people that the aged are too senile and too little in contact with reality to be depressed.

When It Is Recognized

Physicians who take genuine interest in problems of the elderly consider the possibility that depression may be at work and treat it when found—with gratifying results.

Consider, for example, a seventy-eight-year-old woman who was hospitalized because of weight loss, lower abdominal pain, constipation, and flatulence. The symptoms might well have indicated a serious problem, possibly a malignancy. There were thorough tests; they revealed nothing to explain her condition. Nurses' notes, meanwhile, indicated that the patient not only ate poorly but displayed little interest in her surroundings and what was going on about her.

Her family was questioned and reported that the weight loss and other symptoms had come on top of a period of decline, of gradual loss of interest in everything. She had reached the point of no longer wishing to see people. She just sat, had to be told when to eat, when to go to bed. Often, when spoken to, she gave no sign that she heard but would finally respond after being addressed repeatedly. She was not mentally ill, her family insisted, just "getting old," suffering from progressive hardening of the arteries.

When a psychiatrist was called in consultation while she was in the hospital, she did not at first even acknowledge his presence but stared straight ahead. Finally, in answer to his questions, she began to speak slowly in a low voice. When she was asked the date of her birth, she gave the wrong one. But when the psychiatrist insisted that she concentrate, she recalled the right date. Clearly, she was not interested in the questions. Clearly, too, while her thinking was retarded, her memory was good.

There was much to indicate depression rather than senile deterioration. Usually, for example, if senile deterioration is the problem, there is no loss of interest but rather a one-track kind of interest or many different interests but inability to focus for any time on any one. A senile person usually talks freely and what he or she says is rambling or retrospective. That is not the case with depression. There are often other clues as well. Commonly, a depressed person may feel, act, and seem much improved in the latter part of the day. A senile person usually has no fixed pattern but often mixes up days and nights, may sleep by day and wander about by night.

Depression also was the underlying problem for a seventy-one-year-old widow who lived with her daughter and was hospitalized because of abdominal pain, rectal bleeding, and weight loss. She was frail, weak, undernourished, but a thorough check, including a gastrointestinal X-ray series, revealed nothing but external hemorrhoids and mild anemia.

Nurses once again noted that she seemed withdrawn, lay in bed most of the time, not reading or looking at television, eating little, and expressing no interest in anything. Although friendly when spoken to, she often would lie on her side with her face to the wall, apparently to avoid contact with nurses and others coming into her room.

In talking with a psychiatrist called in for consultation, she proved to be coherent, possessed of a good memory, without confusion or disturbance of thought processes. She did, however, insist that she had an incurable disease of some kind, probably cancer, and was going to die, and that dying, in fact, would be a relief because life was only a burden. During the psychiatric interview, she even became animated and cheerful when the subject of death was discussed, quite possibly because this was the first time anyone had discussed death with her openly.

When urged gently to talk about her loss of interest in life, she did so, saying that many of her friends had died or moved away and she was tired of seeing relatives and other people who did not understand her and repeatedly insisted, "You are now looking good," and "There's no reason for you to be sick."

Both women underwent electric shock treatments. For the first woman, six treatments over a two-week period produced mild memory impairment and a bit of confusion at first. But then she became markedly more alert, began to take interest in goings-on about her, displayed improved appetite. Two weeks after she went home from the hospital—following the last shock treatment—she was more improved, and cheerfully exclaimed that she felt better than she had in years.

The second woman had five electroshock treatments and quickly showed marked improvement. At home, she ate well and gained weight. She became interested in social and church activities.

In the latter example, that of the seventy-one-year-old widow, we saw how she had yearned to discuss death. Actually, many elderly people have some preoccupation with death. They are aging; they have lost some friends; they think about death and they want to talk about it. But if they raise the subject with their families, it is often pushed aside hastily. There are well-intentioned denials and protests. "You are not going to die—not for a long time. Those are morbid thoughts; forget them." And it is not uncommon for physicians to make the same well-intentioned error.

Just because the elderly are told to give up thinking about death does not mean that they do or can. And where a frank talk could be comforting, they are left, instead, to consider, in loneliness, the reality of death. When they can talk to someone who is not afraid to discuss death and who encourages them to face the realities of life, aging and death, they are often relieved.

Once depression is lifted by electroshock, then talking, or ventilation—which is at the heart of psychotherapy—is of great value. "Electric shock therapy relieves the depression, but psychotherapy often helps prevent relapses," observes Dr. David H. Smith of the Wheeling (West Virginia) Clinic Department of Psychiatry. Often, in fact, if depression is not too deep, psychotherapy may be enough to bring about a remission without the necessity of resorting to electric shock therapy.

And even when depression is too deep to yield to psychotherapy alone, electroshock is not the sine qua non. Very often drug therapy works and works well.

Treatments for Depression

There is no shortage of effective drug treatments now for depression, however mild or severe, at any age. But they are not being used often enough and often, when used, they are not used properly.

Depression ranks as the most undertreated of all major diseases despite the fact that in most cases it is relatively easy to handle. "The discrepancy between the *availability* of treatment for depression and the actual *providing* of treatment is so great as to constitute a scandal," charges Dr. Nathan S. Kline, director of the Research Center at Rockland State Hospital, Orangeburg, New York.

The outlook for victims of depression should be bright, indeed. Some years ago a poll among more than 150 of the nation's leading medical researchers and clinicians about what they considered to be the most significant new drug developments in modern medicine found them agreeing that high up on the list belonged one antidepressant medication that first came into use in 1959, and another that was introduced in 1965. Even since then, many more have been added.

Among them, for example, are such agents as imipramine (trade named Tofranil); desipramine (trade named Pertofrane and Norpramin); amitriptyline (trade named Elavil); protriptyline (trade named Vivactil); nortriptyline (trade named Aventyl); doxepin (trade named Sinequan); and amitriptyline plus perphenazine (trade named Triavil and Etraton).

They're available enough for the using. Yet government surveys have found that in any given year 15 percent of adults between eighteen and seventy-four years—twenty million people—may suffer serious depressive symptoms, but less than 5 percent of those in need of help seek it at psychiatric treatment facilities. And even though some may go to their family doctor first for help, most physicians have had relatively little training in treating depression and have not applied themselves to learning, and some even have what authorities call a "superstition" that psychiatric treatment must or should be given primarily in a psychiatrist's office.

Today, an effort is being made to get rid of the superstition and to inform all physicians how they can treat depressed patients, young and old, effectively. Medical journals aimed at nonpsychiatric physicians are now full of information on proper treatment, the urgent need for treatment by nonpsychiatrists, and guidance on avoiding common errors in treatment.

The most common mistake is not continuing treatment for a sufficient period of time to allow the medication to take effect.

It's essential for both physicians and patients to know that the average antidepressant drug takes twenty-one days to produce an initial response. Unless patients know this, they often complain or even discontinue medication on their own after two weeks.

Patients need to know, too, the normal, not immediately dramatic, pattern when a drug is effective. There is no sudden lifting of mental or physical symptoms. Instead, the first thing the patient notices is that he is becoming a little more aware of and interested in his surroundings, on what is going on around him. Next, his family and friends begin to see a change. Then, last of all, the patient feels better.

Another common difficulty is inadequate dosage. In a very mild case, a very small dose—for example, just 25 milligrams of imipramine or amitriptyline or doxepin or a similar drug given once at bedtime—is often sufficient. But for any but the mildest depressions, the minimum dose would be 25 milligrams three to four times a day, and in some patients a dose of 300 milligrams or more daily is needed.

When drug therapy is properly used, there is great likelihood that depression can be terminated and recurrences prevented for long periods, especially when psychotherapy is also used. And the psychotherapy can be brief, provided as well by a sensitive internist or family physician as by a psychiatrist, and may consist of a few short, informal meetings devoted to letting the patient talk out his feelings, and offering him support and encouragement.

Such treatment can help the great majority of depressed patients. When it does not, electroshock may be used. Electroshock also may be used from the beginning in some cases when depression is very severe and/or a patient may be potentially suicidal, because shock treatment produces more immediate results.

When it was first introduced in this country as a psychiatric treatment in 1939, electroshock was administered without anesthesia and without muscle relaxation. It produced a powerful convulsive seizure, and several attendants had to hold a patient down during treatment in order to prevent bone fractures.

Today, administration is markedly different. The patient is put quickly and gently to sleep with an intravenous anesthetic and this is followed by medication to relax the muscles of the body. Electrodes resembling headphones are then placed on the head, an electric current is applied for no more than a second, and a mild seizure is produced—minimal twitching of muscles, no "shock" of any kind.

The patient is asleep during the treatment and remains so for several minutes afterward. Then he gradually awakens and is usually up and about in fifteen to thirty minutes after treatment has ended.

Exactly how electroshock relieves depression is still not understood. One theory is that somehow the electric current changes brain chemistry. However it works, shock treatment is often effective. Usually a patient recovers after a series of six to eight treatments.

Electroshock is not without side effects. In some patients, it produces troublesome temporary loss of memory and confusion. In others, there are no such effects. When the effects occur, they usually clear within two or three weeks after the last treatment.

There is still considerable controversy over shock therapy. Some physicians are fearful that, conceivably, especially if it is used excessively, electroshock could have permanent effects on the brain, impairing memory and cognition. It is not nearly so popular currently as are the antidepressant drugs.

On the other hand, many psychiatrists favor electroshock, consider it the most effective treatment in many cases of depression, often a lifesaver.

Is it unsafe for older people? Not according to many authorities. "There are physicians who refuse to treat their depressed arteriosclerotic, osteoporotic patients with electroconvulsive therapy," says Dr. Sidney Cohen. "It is true that such patients have an increased risk of complications, but if a course of antidepressant therapy is unsuccessful, electroconvulsive treatments should be considered. As they are presently administered, fractures are rare. Often only a few treatments suffice; an entire course is generally unnecessary. For an old patient to remain severely depressed is more dangerous than ECT."

Dr. John Romano, founding chairman of the Department of Psychiatry at the University of Rochester School of Medicine and Dentistry and now Distinguished University Professor of Psychiatry, has used ECT in people with late-life depressions, including people in their mid eighties. "Sometimes only one, two, or three ECT treatments have helped old people get better," he says.

The Heart of the Problem

In theory, clearly, the outlook for the depression victim is bright. With accurate diagnosis and really effective care, there is a 95 percent chance of getting back to totally full functioning.

But a critical problem that bears repeated emphasis is recognition of depression, especially in the aged, when it leads to distressing physical troubles or bizarre behavior, or both, that may be too easily attributed to aging and senility.

It would be ideal if anyone who felt depressed and who also had physical complaints would mention the depression as well as the complaints when seeking medical help. If an elderly person fails to do this, it can be most helpful if the family, knowing or suspecting that depression may also be present, imparts the information to the physician.

There may be clues to be noted, some of them perhaps more readily discerned by an interested physician but some that can be meaningful to the family. They may be found in the reactions of the elderly person to his physical complaints, reactions that seem excessive in view of the nature of the physical complaints. They may be found in attitudes of "giving up," of pessimism, of self-deprecation. They may be found in a look of sadness, in slow speech or movement, frequent sighing, and lack of interest in anything.

Loss is often a precipitating factor in depression, but it can be important to realize that it *does not have to be* what you would consider a major loss, such as death of a near relative or spouse, for example. Often, some seemingly minor event may be looked upon by the depressed as a serious loss because it has triggered the recall of many disappointments from his past life. One woman who was very poor and had worked and saved for a long time to buy a dining-room set she had long wanted finally got together the money she needed. Then the set arrived and the table was scratched. This little detail, though relatively insignificant to others, triggered deep depression.

If you have an aging parent who you suspect may be depressed, the suspicion may be no idle one. Diagnosis of depression belongs in the hands of an expert, and you can't expect to make it. But the suspicion deserves expert investigation.

6

OTHER PROBLEMS FOR WHICH PSYCHIATRY—OFTEN QUICK PSYCHIATRY—CAN BE EFFECTIVE IN THE AGED

The study was labeled "Geriatric Rejects."

It took place at Metropolitan State Hospital, Waltham, Massachusetts, and the objective was to see what, if anything, could really be done for fifty patients, twenty-one men and twenty-nine women, aged sixty-four to ninety, who had been sent to the state institution as "unmanageable behavior problems" by families, hospitals, and nursing homes.

The agitated patients, considered to be suffering from psychoses or senility, displayed such symptoms as confusion, anxiety, apprehension, crying spells, insomnia, violent outbursts, destructive behavior, hostility, delusions, untidiness, and psychosomatic disorders.

The effort was to provide intensive treatment for each patient as a *whole* patient. Medical problems received treatment. Surgical problems were attended to. And psychoactive drug therapy was tried along with formal and informal therapeutic programs such as occupational, physical, individual, and recreational therapy.

At the end of six weeks, thirty-six patients were so improved that they were ready for discharge; at the end of fourteen weeks, nine more were ready.

Evidently, even among the institutionalized, 90 percent could, given aggressive, hopeful, coordinated care—psychiatric as well as medical and surgical—take up lives again in the community, very greatly improved, with a potential for reasonably happy and rewarding living.

And much more can be done to make life more comfortable, pleasant, and rewarding for the noninstitutionalized aged—given good, and not necessarily extended, psychiatric help along with medical care.

Psychiatric Shunning of the Aged

Geriatric psychiatry has been a grossly neglected area. Training in it has been rare. Many psychiatrists have been concerned with what is called the YAVIS type of patient—YAVIS being an acronym for young, attractive, verbal, intelligent, and successful. In modern psychiatry, as one psychiatrist has remarked, old age, like its outcome, death, has been "shunned, avoided, and even denied."

However, the picture has begun to change. At least some psychiatrists are giving attention to the needs of the elderly. Recognition has been growing that the aged not only may have many of the same psychiatric problems that the young do but that they may have them more intensely and in far greater proportion, and they may suffer physically as well as emotionally from them.

During the five-year operation of a geriatric outpatient psychiatric clinic in a general hospital, where patients sixty years and over were referred from various hospital departments and every patient was seen by a psychiatrist and psychologist, only 9 percent were without psychiatric problems. Ninety-one percent showed evidence of emotional disturbance.

Recognition is growing, too, that psychiatric techniques—especially newer ones that are brief and incisive—can help many of the elderly as much as they help younger patients.

Given the availability of only extended psychoanalysis—with its three, four, five years or more of intensive probing—it may not have seemed practical to provide psychiatric aid on any large scale to the aged. But when psychiatry often can work in a few sessions—a dozen, half dozen, sometimes even just one or two—it becomes practical, indeed, to try to help the aged who need help.

The Emotional Problems

Many of the elderly have what are called neuroses of later maturity. Their problems are primarily those of adjusting to the facts of aging—biological, psychological, and social. Earlier in life, as younger people often do, they may have had difficulties in adjusting during critical periods and in situations of conflict. Now, with age, the important factors are loneliness, loss of prestige among family and friends, loss of occupation, reduced earning capacity, and, concomitantly, often drastically reduced income.

Often, there may be feelings of weakness, tiredness, irritability, and sometimes even hostility against a family member. Some complain of sleeplessness and loss of appetite whereas others may overeat, especially at night. Frequently, as with depression, there are complaints of physical illness, not all of which can be traced to actual physical disease. Undue fears—hypochondriacal fears—about the heart, lungs, intestinal tract, and even of impending mental disease are not uncommon.

The main factor in these neurotic conditions is anxiety—about growing old, losing an accustomed role in society, and becoming rejected and isolated.

Anxiety in itself, when it becomes chronic, can be painful. Anxiety is a nameless dread. The victim feels sensations of apprehension and increased tension that he cannot pin down.

Chronic anxiety can be so painful that heroic efforts may be made to avoid it. One doctor sees in psychiatric disturbances only the abnormal methods some individuals take to avoid anxiety.

Efforts to avoid anxiety can lead to phobic reactions, for example. Someone who suffers an anxiety attack while riding in a plane, train, or other vehicle may associate the anxiety with the vehicle and thereafter avoid the vehicle. He has a phobia about the vehicle. He may similarly develop phobias in other situations and thereafter avoid those situations, limiting his activities, sometimes with great penalty.

Many chronic anxiety victims develop psychosomatic conditions. Their physical symptoms, however painful, serve as distractions and help to lessen conscious anxiety, which can be even more painful. Almost no system of the body is immune from anxiety-provoked effects. Anxiety in some cases may account for migraine, elevated blood pressure, asthma, ulcers, colitis, urinary disturbances, skin outbreaks, seeming heart disease.

It is not a one-way street. While anxiety may provoke physical illness, physical illness can give rise to anxiety, and if the anxiety becomes chronic it can exacerbate the physical illness.

If Only the Regular Doctor Would . . .

Whether young or old, patients with emotional problems can be helped, and often the patient's regular physician could provide the help if he would.

Good medicine should include a thorough medical history followed by a physical examination, diagnosis, and treatment.

There is more to it than that. Almost every patient visiting a physician does so because he is worried. Unless his anxiety is dealt with, the visit is a failure. Once the disease is named, the patient needs to know about it: its nature, seriousness, how long it will last, whether it will recur. If no specific treatment is indicated, the patient needs reassurance. Often, reassurance is what the patient came for in the first place. Often, what he most wants is to vent his problems, his inner feelings, his doubts and fears.

But some physicians unhappily have an attitude of "So what . . . you can't treat them anyway" when it comes to patients' emotional problems. It never enters their minds that very often patients will feel better if simply allowed to talk to an interested physician.

They are ignorant of studies indicating that when a physician, in the course of carrying out a medical examination, talks with a patient and allows the patient to talk to him, when all the concentration isn't on physical problems but some attention is paid even in the most informal fashion to psychologic problems, 45 percent of patients experience *very* significant improvement.

Physicians ought to be aware that they themselves are extremely powerful remedies, more powerful than any drug in the pharmacopoeia. This is something the old family doctor understood; often having little else to prescribe, he prescribed himself, in large doses, which is why most likely he is spoken of nostalgically today.

One example of the emotional power of a concerned physician is reflected in the experience of the late great internist, Dr. Walter Bauer of Harvard University.

One of the residents serving under Bauer came to him for advice and help because of a patient dying on the ward with terminal cancer. Although the resident had given her four times the usual prescribed dosage of sedatives and analgesics, she got no comfort from the medication, was pain-racked, excited, miserable. What could he do?

Asked by Dr. Bauer to tell him something of the patient, the resident described her as a little, dried-up old lady. He did not know if she had a family, where she lived, what she did. He really knew nothing about her life; all he knew was that she had terminal cancer.

"What do you know about her feeling about dying?" Bauer asked. "Is she afraid? Does she want to die? What does she believe in, if anything? Find out. I want to you to do this next week. Give your patient a great big dosage of yourself. I want you to learn about her ambitions, her life, her joys and sorrows, her dreams—fulfilled or unfulfilled."

A week later the resident reported back that he had spent hours with his patient, had really got to know her, was ashamed to admit that the previous week he hadn't even remembered her name. "She is," he said, "a wonderful little lady. She now is really my friend. You know," he went on, "it is unbelievable, but she seems perfectly comfortable on a quarter of her previous medication."

Psychotherapy

Psychotherapy can help many of the aged with emotional problems. Often it can be brief psychotherapy. It is not exclusively the province of the psychiatrist. Any physician can, if he will, practice it. In fact, in recent years, postgraduate courses on psychotherapy for nonpsychiatric physicians have sprung up all over the country.

Brief psychotherapy can be a matter of up to forty sessions or so stretched over a period of six months or more. Not infrequently, it is a matter of half a dozen or fewer.

The strategy of brief psychotherapy is not to try to alter or reconstruct a patient's basic personality, not to change him, but rather to accept him as he is and alleviate his distress so he can function more effectively and comfortably.

Any and all methods that can help the patient are used.

Usually, patient and physician sit down in a quiet room and the patient is encouraged to speak freely about himself and his feelings. Often, as he does so—even without any interpretations or suggestions from the physician—he begins to see himself and his problems more clearly. He may lose some of his inordinate fears as the problems become clearer; he may develop different feelings about the problems.

A process called ventilation, already mentioned, is often used in brief psychotherapy. It involves letting a troubled person blow off steam. Although seemingly too simple to be of much use, the results often are astonishing. Ventilation alone may permit a patient facing some crisis to dislodge his feelings of gloom or panic and his inability to do anything constructive and restore his usual self-control.

For more serious emotional problems for which ventilation is not enough, reassurance may be added. This is informed, authoritative reassurance. Some of the first, most striking evidence of its value came during the Korean War when soldiers who had to be taken out of the line because of acute combat nerves could return to action after just a few brief sessions with a therapist who encouraged them to talk frankly about their fears and guilt feelings and could reassure them that virtually every officer and soldier is secretly afraid.

Because a patient in psychotherapy is aware that the therapist has no personal bias and is specially informed about psychological problems as no friend or family member usually is, he can take advice and suggestions he would not accept from others.

That brief psychotherapy can help the young and the middle-aged is now virtually taken for granted. But many of the elderly can, if given the opportunity, benefit no less.

Even experienced psychiatrists are themselves surprised at how effective such therapy can be, how often in five to fifteen minutes once or twice a week a physician can work wonders with a disgruntled older person. "We're never really certain ourselves what happens in some of our treatments," one physician remarks, "but it seems to me that what is benefiting the patient is the doctor's attitude of noncritical understanding and willingness to listen to the patient recite his difficulties. This can lessen the patient's fear and rage. And talking to an understanding person can relieve him and increase his self-esteem as well."

Cases

Let's look at a few examples of brief psychotherapy at work to help elderly patients.

A sixty-seven-year-old professional man who had been happy with his work and wound up in it—perhaps too much so, since he was working fourteen hours a day but nonetheless finding it rewarding—fell one night while going to the bathroom and hit his head against the bathtub. His left eye was so badly injured that it had to be removed.

The accident disrupted his life. Although he didn't necessarily have to, he gave up his work and then had no idea of what to do with himself. He developed an almost endless list of symptoms, including crippling anxiety and claustrophobia.

In psychotherapy, he was encouraged to "uncork the bottle," to talk out his inner feelings. As he did so, his anxiety and, after a time, his phobia, began to diminish. He began to look freshly at his talents and resourcefulness and put them to constructive use. He decided he most wanted to broaden his activities, to take courses, write, engage in volunteer work, and travel. Psychotherapy lasted five months. It didn't make him over. But all his life he needed to be busy. The need continued and soon he was busier and happier than ever, content with a maximum of three hours sleep a night.

A woman of almost seventy became severely agitated. She had been a beautiful woman when younger, with many suitors, an adoring father, and eight equally adoring brothers. She was narcissistic and her first psychiatric disturbance had come with menopause. Another came when her only son failed his doctoral examinations. Her latest problem coincided with becoming a grandmother.

She, too, needed five months of therapy to recover.

But often psychotherapy can be far briefer.

A sixty-nine-year-old man broke down under what seemed to him a burden of terrible events that left no room for hope. His wife had suffered a heart attack and was in a hospital in an oxygen tent. His son was in a mental hospital and had been given a series of electroshock treatments but seemed confused. His family seemed to be lost and, grieving and despairing, he found himself crying bitterly and almost continuously.

When he sought help, he broke into tears which he could not control at first. He was still crying at the second session. But then in the calm, noncritical atmosphere of the physician's office, he could begin to pull himself together. As he talked out his feelings, his composure began to increase. And he could then begin to see his problems more realistically. His wife was in fact feeling better and would recover; he could register that now. He could understand now, too, where he couldn't before, that his son's confusion was only a temporary effect of the electroshock treatment, and in fact the confusion was diminishing.

He had to face the reality that his family would be there even though not in prime health—and he could face it as his strength returned. The duration of treatment was six sessions.

A sixty-seven-year-old man was referred by his physician for psychotherapy because of loss of sexual potency. He was greatly disturbed. The basic emotional needs of people, especially sexual needs, do not change with age, no matter how old the individual.

In therapy, several things became apparent. He was able to have erections but could not maintain them because of his wife's lack of interest and cooperation. His wife had never been much interested in sex, yet his moral standards had not allowed him to seek sex elsewhere. He was also greatly dependent on his wife and feared any disagreement with her.

His "shame" over his loss of potency could be dissipated as he talked about it in therapy and received some understanding of why it had occurred. He was helped, too, by suggestions for how he might set about influencing his wife to be more cooperative since his need for intercourse was not frequent. Even more helpful were additional suggestions aimed at aiding him to establish what he needed most of all: a closer, warmer, more accepting relationship with his wife. The treatment was fruitful. It took eleven sessions.

Psychotherapy is sometimes referred to as "the talking cure." It may not be a cure in the sense of providing complete solutions for all problems, but it can do much—for the aged as well as the young—to help over the crises and rough spots, to point the way out of a morass of anxiety and despair, to relieve psychological distress and physical symptoms stemming from such distress.

Physicians who use it for the aged believe that it is especially rewarding. What makes it so, as one physician puts it, "is that in most cases one deals with mature people who have lived a long time and have experienced a great deal. These are people who understand more, are able to cooperate better, and as a rule do not expect absolute results."

Group Therapy

That group therapy, which is widely used for younger people, can be effective for the aged is also being demonstrated.

Group sessions are a valuable form of psychotherapy because patients react to one another as well as to the physician, and because their self-confidence is increased by being with people whose problems are similar to their own.

Groups may be formed by psychiatrists. Even hospitals are forming them because of recognition that medical services as a whole are not well equipped to handle the human side of sickness.

At Montefiore Hospital and Medical Center in New York, patient groups were begun as an experiment to see what could be done with the most serious asthma patients. Asthma was chosen because it is well recognized that asthma attacks can be caused by emotional factors.

Twelve asthma patients were drawn from a Montefiore outpatient clinic. Among them, in the six months prior to becoming a group, the twelve had had twenty-eight hospitalizations. Weekly meetings were designed to learn exercises and basic information about their illness, and to interact with one another. This first experimental group met for only ten weeks. Yet in the six months afterward, there were ony two hospitalizations among the twelve patients, some of whom have since been able to manage without drugs.

A group currently meeting at Montefiore is the "Thick Chart Group." It is made up of elderly men and women, all of whom have had several major work-ups over the years with no conclusive findings to explain their varied symptoms of illness.

Once a week, the group meets at the hospital. The members lie on the floor and learn exercises to improve their circulation and strength. They discuss diet and the general effect of nutrition on health. They talk about their anxieties—about becoming infirm and burdensome, for example. They visit each others' homes between meetings and sometimes bring their children in to talk.

One result has been a marked uplift of spirits. Importantly, too, the number of physical complaints has declined considerably.

7

AN ERRANT GLAND AND ITS BEWILDERING FACES

She had long experienced dizziness. For eighteen months more recently she had felt light-headed, and there had been increasing loss of hearing, along with mental slowing. There was suspicion of a brain tumor, but it was not a brain tumor. Within two weeks after the real problem was found and treatment for it started, she could walk without feeling dizzy. After several months, she experienced overall improvement, including return of hearing. At the end of eighteen months, with continued treatment, she was completely well.

Another patient considered herself a burden to her family. She had frequent thoughts of suicide and had become preoccupied with memories of her son killed in an automobile accident some years before. She wished she had been the one killed. She dreamed of digging him from his grave with her bare hands and heard his voice calling her. She felt she was being punished now by her illness. She responded to the same treatment provided for the first woman.

A sixty-seven-year-old man was rushed to a hospital because of a sudden attack of pain in the left side of the chest. Treatment for heart attack was begun but he didn't respond to it as expected. Getting a more detailed history, physicians found that he had been losing weight for a period of six months, had suffered from muscle weakness, nervousness, and intolerance to heat. Now suspicious, they carried out a test which confirmed their suspicion. Within forty-eight hours after proper treatment was begun, the man's abnormal heart rhythm had been converted to normal and electrocardiograms showed no further evidence of heart disease. In less than a month, he had regained thirteen pounds; in less than three months, thirty pounds. And other symptoms were gone.

Despite the diversity of their troubles, all three patients were suffering from a malfunctioning in one way or another of the thyroid gland.

Thyroid disturbance is by far the most common gland disorder. Exactly how common it is is difficult if not impossible to find out because it wears so many faces. It may share the blame—and sometimes may be entirely to blame—for a seemingly limitless variety of troubles. In one case, it may give rise to mysterious headaches; in another, to undue fatigue. Chronic infection, irritability, anxiety, depression, paranoid symptoms, hallucinatory disturbances, failing memory, difficulties in concentration—these are just a few of its possible manifestations.

If recent investigations indicate anything at all, it is that at any time of life, and certainly among the elderly, the possibility that thyroid disturbance may be involved in physical disorder or a mental disturbance deserves consideration. It may not be involved—but the possibility should not be overlooked. Yet it is too often overlooked, out of the failure by many people, including physicians, to thoroughly understand and appreciate the major role of the thyroid in health and disease.

The Body Controller

The small, one-ounce thyroid in the neck, which resembles a little pink butterfly, with its "wings" on either side of the larynx or voice box, was one of the first endocrine glands discovered.

There is an old medical saying that just a few grams of thyroid hormone can make the difference between an idiot and an Einstein, which summarizes the thyroid's role as a quickener of the whole tempo of life.

All the endocrine glands play remarkable roles in the body economy. Unlike the millions of other glands—the sweat glands in the skin, the salivary in the mouth, tear glands in the eyes—which perform only local functions, the endocrines pour their complex hormone secretions into the bloodstream, which carries them to work in all parts of the body.

From the pituitary in the brain come hormones that influence growth, sexual development, uterine contraction in childbirth, milk release afterward. The adrenals atop the kidneys pour out more than a score of hormones, including hydrocortisone and adrenaline, needed for the body's response to stress and injury.

Also in the endocrine system are the sex glands—ovaries and testes; the pineal gland in the brain, whose hormones are believed to play a role in nerve and brain functioning; the thymus behind the breastbone, which appears to be involved in establishing the body's immunity system.

The thyroid controls body metabolism—the rate at which chemical processes go on and energy is used. Minute thyroid secretions, something less than a spoonful in a year, are responsible for much of the body's heat production. They help maintain the circulatory system and blood volume; without them, the heartbeat slows, many blood vessels close down, and fluid leaks out of the bloodstream. They're necessary for muscle health; in their absence, muscles become sluggish and infiltrated with fat. They also heighten sensitivity of nerves.

Just as tadpoles deprived of thyroid glands (in a famous experiment performed more than fifty years ago) never became full-fledged frogs, so children without any thyroid secretions would remain dwarfs and become idiots.

Total lack of thyroid hormone is extremely rare. But unbalanced functioning of the gland—so that its secretions are either too much or too little—is not rare at all.

Many of the manifestations of severe malfunctioning are well known and almost unmistakable.

The severely hyperthyroid person—whose thyroid produces grossly excessive amounts of hormone—is nervous and irritable, tires easily, may lose weight to the point of emaciation despite good appetite. Often the eyes protrude and the skin is warm and moist. In addition, the pulse may race, blood pressure may shoot up—and, in time, the burden may become exhausting for the heart, leading to what is termed thyrotoxic heart disease.

In the other direction, the severely hypothyroid individual—whose gland produces grossly inadequate amounts of secretions—experiences a slowing of the whole body economy. Weakness and listlessness develop; the skin becomes dry; there is great sensitivity to cold; the speech may become slow and thick.

Such effects are readily recognized for what they are by physicians and even by many patients. They are the classical symptoms, and patients who have them are quickly given one or more of the medical tests which can confirm the diagnosis and permit effective treatment to be started.

In one test, which determines what is known as the basal metabolism rate, the patient inhales oxygen and the amount left in the exhaled air shows how much the body has used and indicates how the thyroid gland is functioning. The test is little used today because of the problems involved: the patient must go without breakfast and must spend a considerable time lying motionless.

A variety of other thyroid tests are available. In one, the radioactive iodine uptake test, a capsule of radioactive iodine is swallowed and a counter device detects how much gets into the thyroid gland. In another, the PBI, the amount of protein-bound iodine in the blood, is measured and provides an indication of thyroid functioning. There are still others, including one that measures the output of a pituitary hormone that stimulates the thyroid gland.

Once thyroid disturbance is diagnosed, treatment can be gratifyingly effective.

For hyperthyroidism, an antithyroid drug may be used. Such drugs, which include propylthiouracil and methimazole, interfere with and suppress excessive secretion. Over a period of several months, thyroid functioning may return to normal and drug therapy can be stopped. This method may not be suitable for some patients, including about 9 percent who develop skin outbreaks, fever, and other drug reactions.

Alternatively, depending upon the individual patient and his thyroid condition, surgery or radioactive iodine treatment may be used. Surgery, called subtotal thyroidectomy, removes part of the thyroid gland, enough to eliminate excessive secretion. Injection of radioactive iodine, in amounts many times those used for testing thyroid function, also may bring thyroid function down to normal.

For hypothyroidism, simple replacement therapy works. The patient regularly takes thyroid hormone pills, either extracted from animal glands or made synthetically in the laboratory, in the right dosage to supplement his gland's production of hormone and provide him with a normal amount.

Missed Diagnoses

It has become apparent recently that thyroid disorders can go undetected for long periods and can even be missed entirely.

Delays in diagnosis may occur even when there are classical symptoms because the disorders may develop slowly, and if the first symptoms are limited to relatively vague ones such as weakness, fatigue, nervousness, or irritability, they may be attributed by patients, and sometimes by physicians, to other causes.

On top of this, investigations in recent years have led to a whole series of new findings on the many guises thyroid disturbance can assume, the many troublesome symptoms, not classical at all, that both under- and over-functioning of the gland can produce. There have been studies, too, underscoring the need for alertness on the part of physicians and for the use of their clinical detective abilities if thyroid disorder is to be recognized in some of the less common but important and long-known guises it may assume.

Consider, for example, a woman in her mid fifties who had for a year progressively lost weight and suffered from weakness and episodes of diarrhea. When she was admitted to a Los Angeles hospital, she weighed only sixty-five pounds. She was thought to have gastrointestinal cancer, but tests for that failed to disclose malignancy. She continued to lose weight in the hospital.

Finally, two weeks after admission, thyroid disease was considered—and confirmed by tests. The diagnosis had been missed at first because she had none of the usual symptoms of severe hyperthyroidism, such as increased sweating or gland enlargement. With drug treatment to curb her excessive thyroid secretions, she gained weight rapidly and regained her strength and health.

A fifty-seven-year-old man was admitted to the same hospital and, after evaluation, to the psychiatric ward with a diagnosis of psychosis—serious mental disturbance. For a year his family had found him becoming increasingly unmanageable, subject to bouts of agitation, restlessness, and overactivity. Occasionally he became combative; sometimes he had delusions.

In the ward, he couldn't sit still. He insisted upon helping mop floors, wash windows, and bus trays; he rarely slept; he was constantly asking for extra portions of food. After two weeks of this behavior, a doctor in the ward suspected thyroid disease. Tests showed marked overactivity of the thyroid gland. The patient was transferred to the medical division of the hospital and treated with an antithyroid drug. He quickly calmed down and could be discharged home in good mental health.

Although it is medically well known that hyperthyroid patients may display bizarre and erratic behavior, this disturbance may still be misinterpreted as a psychiatric rather than a physical illness.

Investigators who have studied hyperthyroid patients have found that in as many as 20 percent there is serious mental disturbance. But the type of disturbance is not uniform. Anxiety and depression are frequent. So is destructive impulsivity on the one hand and social withdrawal on the other.

At the University of North Carolina, physicians studied a group of patients with thyroid disorders, including ten with hyperthyroidism, who experienced mental disturbances. In seven of the ten the disturbances were severe enough to constitute psychiatric illness. Four patients had noticed increased difficulty in concentrating and impairment of recent memory. One had loss of both visual and auditory acuity. Many had difficulty with simple mental arithmetic. Fatigue, anxiety, and irritability were common complaints. Two patients complained of depression. Two suffered from delusions of being persecuted and one of the two had hallucinations in which she saw "swarms of bees" flying toward her. In all these cases, there was remarkable improvement following treatment for the thyroid disfunction.

Other bizarre forms that hyperthyroidism occasionally may

take have been reported: myasthenia or muscle weakness; periodic paralysis of muscles; severe chest pain; heart failure; ankle swelling; and comatose states.

Hardly any less than overfunctioning, underfunctioning of the thyroid can produce a host of deceptive mental and physical symptoms.

The Under-Functioners

The two women whose cases were cited at the beginning of this chapter suffered from some of the many diverse effects that hypothyroidism may produce.

Patients with untreated thyroid deficiency can easily be mistaken for neurotics.

In one carefully structured investigation, twenty-four hypothyroid patients were studied. In addition to medical observation, they were interviewed extensively and given a battery of psychologic tests, both before they received any treatment for their thyroid deficiency and again after a mean interval of five months, at a time when treatment had overcome the deficiency.

Before treatment, the patients experienced extreme fatigue, decreased mobility, increased irritability, and nervousness. They were emotionally explosive. They regretted their behavior but were unable to control it. Sexual function was decreased. Such physical symptoms as vision disturbances, speech difficulties, and diffuse muscular pain were also noted.

After treatment, most of the symptoms decreased or disappeared. The patients experienced a sense of well-being and a feeling of integration of personality.

To the investigators making the study, it seemed that people with hypothyroid problems differ from neurotics in that they assume responsibility for their emotional reactions. Neurotics usually blame those around them or circumstances for their difficulties.

Another conclusion was that hypothyroidism might be brought on by pressures or stresses that an individual is unable to cope with adequately.

At the University of North Carolina, where investigators studied the mental changes accompanying hyperthyroidism, they also examined those associated with hypothyroidism.

Among their hypothyroid patients was a sixty-four-year-old woman suffering from confusion and depression; another patient, a fifty-six-year-old woman, experienced confusion and great anxiety. There were other patients who were depressed, some of them confused as well, and one considered psychotic.

Most of the hypothyroid patients complained of poor recent memory and difficulty in concentration. They experienced difficulties with simple dollars-and-cents arithmetic during interviews. Several of the women complained that they could no longer remember recipes for cooking without constant reference to a book. One had come to rely on other members of the family to remember where she had placed things in the house.

The hypothyroid patients, in fact, usually showed greater emotional disturbance than the hyperthyroid. With thyroid treatment, they showed marked improvement.

Because they were impressed by the frequency of depression in the hypothyroid, the North Carolina investigators later went on to try thyroid hormone in depressed people even when they were considered to have normal thyroid functioning by all the usual test standards.

The results were striking. With a very small dose of a thyroid hormone, L-triiodothyronine, or T_3, added to usual antidepressant drug treatment, they found they could reduce by about half the time needed to bring patients out of depression. They also noted that some depressed patients, not responding to antidepressant drug treatment, did respond when thyroid hormone was added.

Underfunctioning of the thyroid gland sometimes can be responsible for many strange physical as well as mental disturbances: poor equilibrium and incoordination of the limbs (ataxia); muscle disturbances such as weakness, aching, and stiffness; plus hearing disturbances and nervous system changes leading to burning, prickling, and other abnormal sensations.

In one study at the Mayo Clinic, twenty-four patients with such disturbances—five men and nineteen women—responded to thyroid treatment. Among them was the first woman mentioned at the beginning of this chapter.

Thyroid Insufficiency in the Elderly, Chronically Ill

Heart disease, arthritis, obstructive lung disease such as emphysema, are among the chronic disorders that afflict many of the aged.

Can hypothyroidism be a contributing or aggravating factor?

When physicians at the Hôpital Notre-Dame de la Merci in Montreal studied elderly, chronically ill patients, they found that the majority had decreased thyroid function in contrast to the thyroid function of healthy elderly people.

Moreover, treatment with thyroid extract resulted in noticeable clinical improvement in 15 percent of the cases, with no undesirable effects.

A Radical Theory

A still-small minority of physicians today believe that a case is being built against hypothyroidism as an important factor in many chronic diseases of both young and old.

Evidence is being adduced to indicate that it may be a much more significant influence for heart attacks than cholesterol; that it may play a role in feared diabetes complications; that it could be of importance in the increasing incidence of lung cancer and emphysema; and that it may account for some chronic, unyielding infections and skin conditions.

Along with this, a radical theory has developed. It holds that hypothyroidism has been increasing, now affects as many as 40 percent of the population and before long will affect 50 percent. It also holds that much hypothyroidism is subtle—not necessarily detectable by conventional tests—but a very simple, unorthodox test can be used to get a clue to its presence.

It is a fact acknowledged by medical authorities that conventional thyroid tests, such as the protein-bound iodine and the radioactive iodine uptake, do not invariably reflect thyroid function correctly. The results of one or more of the tests may be upset, for example, by use of cough and asthma remedies, various medications employed for parasitic diseases, materials used in X-ray studies, many shampoo and skin-antiseptic compounds, aspirin, estrogens, or oral contraceptive drugs. Particularly when thyroid dysfunction is not extreme, it may escape detection.

An alternative test which has been used for many years by a few physicians is, indeed, remarkably simple. Called the basal temperature test, it is performed at home, takes ten minutes, and involves only use of a thermometer.

The thermometer is placed snugly in the armpit immediately upon awakening. Shaken down the night before and placed on the bedside table, it must be used first thing in the morning, before the patient gets out of bed and engages in any kind of activity.

The normal basal temperature, thus taken, is between 97.8 and 98.1 degrees Fahrenheit. A temperature below 97.8 degrees indicates the possibility of low thyroid activity.

One physician has reported using the test over the past thirty years in thousands of patients to discover hypothyroidism in many who had varied problems otherwise unexplainable and in whom conventional tests had failed to reveal hypothyroidism.

In such patients, he has reported, once the hypothyroidism was uncovered and inexpensive thyroid preparations were used to correct it, remarkable improvement has followed quickly.

The patients have included infants with previously recalcitrant eczema, women with menstrual disturbances, men and women with chronic headache and fatigue. About half of patients with psoriasis have responded. One, a retired dean at the University of Denver, had had psoriasis for fifty years which cleared entirely with thyroid therapy.

Among the patients, too, have been many with repeated infections throughout life. One man, seventy-nine years old when first seen, had had a left ear draining pus since childhood. For twenty years he had had a bone infection and had drained pus continually from his left thigh. His basal temperature was three degrees below normal. Three months after he was started on thyroid therapy, his leg infection cleared; after a year, his ear was clear.

Also among the patients were some who were diabetic. While thyroid treatment does not take the place of insulin or other antidiabetic medication, the correction of coexistent hypothyroidism appears to produce significant benefits. Wounds have healed promptly; infections are fewer; patients have more energy and a feeling of well-being. Over a period of years, the complications of diabetes have been conspicuously absent: no gangrene, kidney failure, stroke, blindness, or neuropathies.

Something else was noted: Among patients who had problems that could be solved by thyroid therapy, heart attacks had been conspicuously absent—and at a time when they were generally increasing rapidly.

Cholesterol was generally under suspicion as a culprit in the heart attack epidemic. The thyroid was believed to have something to do with regulation of blood cholesterol levels.

Beginning in 1950, each new adult patient, in addition to the usual screening for hypothyroidism, was questioned about heart disease history in the family and received a chest X ray for heart size, an electrocardiogram, and other heart studies. There was no reduction of fats or cholesterol-rich foods in the diet. The only change in daily routine was the taking of thyroid extract for hypothyroidism.

Some of the first patients could be followed for twenty years and longer; others, coming into the study later, for shorter periods.

Altogether there were 1,569 patients who could be followed at the very least for two years and could be compared, in terms of heart disease development, with expected incidence shown by national statistics.

There were 490 women aged 30 to 59; eight cases of heart disease were to be expected on the basis of national statistics; not one developed. There were 172 high-risk women (with high blood pressure or elevated cholesterol or both); at least seven cases were to be expected; none developed. There were 182 women aged 60 and over; eight cases were to be expected; none developed.

There were 382 men, age 30 to 59; at least 12 cases were to be expected; there was one. There were 186 high-risk men; 19 cases were to be expected; there were two. There were 157 men age 60 or over; 18 cases were to be expected; only one developed.

Thus, with seventy-two cases of heart disease to be expected based on national statistics and only four actually developing, treatment for hypothyroidism apparently produced 94 percent protection in these patients.

How Many Hypothyroids?

Is the rising epidemic of heart attacks—and possibly even of such other increasingly deadly diseases as lung cancer and emphysema—related to a rising incidence of hypothyroidism? And are both occurring because of a vast but not well-appreciated change that has taken place in mankind?

Up to this century, the argument goes, more than half of all children died before reaching adulthood. Beethoven, for example, was one of three survivors out of seven births. Premature deaths occurred because of infectious diseases, many of them rarely seen today. Epidemic diarrhea has been conquered; smallpox has all but disappeared, tuberculosis is no longer a top-ranking killer. Millions of deaths are prevented each year by antibiotics and other modern treatment.

Where in the past older people were largely those who were resistant to infectious diseases, now there are two groups of older people—those whose thyroids function well and aid resistance to infection, and those who, although susceptible because of hypothyroidism, have escaped death as the result of modern medicine.

And this second group, it is argued, now almost equal in size to the first, are prone not only to infectious diseases but also, because of that, to heart disease and even to such other degenerative diseases as lung cancer and emphysema.

Heart attacks were first associated with infectious disease during World War II, when there were 866 such attacks in American servicemen below age 40. Only two important correlations were found: A family history of the disease and a history of previous pneumonia in the men themselves. Pneumonia is an indication of low resistance to infectious diseases.

No country still with a high incidence of infectious diseases reports a high incidence of heart attacks, emphysema, and lung cancer because the infectious diseases kill off people at young ages before they can get these degenerative diseases. But, conversely, no country in which infectious diseases have been curtailed has failed to see a rapid rise in the deadly degenerative diseases.

If the theory is correct, given sensitive enough testing, quite possibly by use of the simple basal temperature test as a screening aid, two of every five people in this country might be found to be hypothyroid and could benefit from correction of the deficiency.

Can Thyroid Treatment Help the Already Severely Afflicted?

It is generally thought that nothing can be done to reverse atherosclerosis, the clogging artery disease that leads to heart attacks, strokes, and kidney deterioration and accounts for well over half of all deaths as well as many years of chronic illness.

But at least one recent study suggests that that may not be the case, that at least something can be done to modify the atherosclerosis, and that thyroid treatment may accomplish it, even when patients appear by conventional tests to have normal thyroid function.

Three hundred and forty-seven patients took part in the study. They fell into two groups—one with overt atherosclerosis, which was already producing symptoms, and the other without symptoms as yet but at high risk of developing them. They ranged in age up to eighty-six.

Among the men, twenty-three had already had twenty-seven known heart attacks, nineteen suffered from angina pectoris (the severe chest pain associated with heart disease), and there had been seventeen strokes. Among the women, nine had had heart attacks, nine had had strokes, and twenty-two had angina. Other patients without such obvious indications of atherosclerosis were known to be at high risk of developing it because of one or more such factors as high blood pressure, diabetes, high blood cholesterol levels, and electrocardiographic abnormalities.

Of all 347 patients, only 31 proved to be hypothyroid as determined by standard tests; the remainder, according to these tests, had normal thyroid function.

Yet, to determine the possible effects of thyroid therapy on atherosclerosis, all 347 were treated with thyroid.

Substantial improvement was measurable in a significant number of patients in both groups—with and without overt atherosclerosis manifestations. The mean blood cholesterol level was reduced by 22.2 percent, and a more favorable electrocardiogram pattern was achieved in 14 percent.

Moreover, during the course of the five-year study, there were only eleven deaths (at mean age seventy-five), a death rate less than half—only 44 percent in fact—of the expected rate as indicated by United States Life Tables.

Most patients in the symptomatic group reported increased sense of well-being, increased ability to exercise and be active, greater motivation and alertness. Even twenty-nine of the forty-one with angina at the start of the study reported they could be more active, had fewer and less severe attacks of chest pain, and had less need for nitroglycerin.

The study was undertaken with the purpose of determining

(1) whether there is anything a physician can do, possibly with thyroid, in his daily practice to prevent or alter the unrelenting downhill course of patients with symptomatic atherosclerosis, and (2) whether symptomatic atherosclerosis might be prevented or delayed by small, carefully regulated doses of thyroid.

Evidently the answer to both questions could be yes, and though thyroid therapy certainly cannot be considered a panacea, it deserves more extensive trial.

8

A COMMON, OVERLOOKED—AND EASILY REMEDIABLE—DISEASE OF THE ELDERLY

When physicians at the Virginia Mason Clinic in Seattle looked back at the record, they found that in an eighteen-month period they had seen eighteen elderly people, all of whom had arrived after a fruitless round of doctors. Hundreds of dollars had been spent for laboratory studies seeking evidence that arthritis or cancer might be the cause of their problems.

All had the same set of symptoms: crippling muscular pain, weakness, and low-grade fever. Some had simply awakened one morning to feel severe muscular pain of a kind that might follow unaccustomed hard physical labor, but there had been no such labor. Some traced the start of their pain to influenza several months before.

At the clinic, physicians found that the pain usually was in the neck, shoulders, and upper arms and that mild anemia was present, but there was no evidence of rheumatoid arthritis.

Everyone of the eighteen did, however, share one abnormality. A routine blood test, called the sedimentation rate, checks the rapidity with which red blood cells settle out of blood in an hour. It's based on the fact that inflammatory processes, if present, produce changes that make the cells cluster, which makes them heavier and more likely to fall rapidly. All eighteen had a high sedimentation rate.

With this finding, the physicians had a clue. They began to suspect that they could be dealing with something that had come in for some attention in Europe but had received relatively little in this country: polymyalgia rheumatica.

Muscular pain, weakness, and low fever are the earmarks of polymyalgia rheumatica. Investigators abroad had suggested that the somewhat mysterious condition might be linked with early temporal arteritis. It was well known that temporal arteritis stemmed from an inflamed condition of the temporal artery in the head and produced, as its chief symptoms, headache and pain and tenderness at the inflamed sites in the temporal artery.

But when the Mason Clinic physicians took small sample bits of tissue from the temporal artery in a dozen patients, they found typical arteritis in only three.

Still, they decided to try the treatment often used for temporal arteritis and began to administer a cortisonelike drug, prednisone, to their patients.

The results were remarkable. Within forty-eight hours, one elderly woman reported that she felt "perfectly well." Within three days, another patient was out of a wheelchair. On the average, the patients were feeling normal and were back to regular activities within two months and often within a month. When checked a year later, all remained fine.

Polymyalgia rheumatica, it seemed, was linked to arteritis—even when the temporal arteries revealed nothing. All eighteen of the patients had arteritis not localized in the temporal arteries.

So it appeared that temporal arteritis was really a misnomer for a far more widespread involvement of arteries. And in a report to the medical profession, the Mason Clinic physicians urged all physicians faced with elderly patients with muscle pains and high sedimentation rate to consider arteritis as a diagnosis and prednisone or a similar corticosteroid treatment, which might dramatically turn a bedridden, debilitated elderly patient into a self-sustaining individual.

A Common Problem

The exact incidence of arteritis—referred to medically as giant-cell arteritis because of the presence, with inflammation, of abnormally large cells—is not known. But it is estimated as about as common as gout and half as common as rheumatoid arthritis in older people, possibly affecting more than half a million of the elderly.

Mason Clinic physicians have been seeing two to three new patients each month with giant-cell arteritis. Studies there, at the Mayo Clinic, and at other centers in this country and abroad have been adding to knowledge about it: the many forms it can take, even leading to liver damage, stroke, heart attack, and personality changes; the ease with which it may be overlooked; and the often dramatic effects of proper treatment.

Among patients seen at Mayo Clinic was a sixty-seven-year-old woman who for six months had experienced increasing fatigue, loss of appetite, and aching about the shoulders and hips. She also suffered from morning stiffness and from pounding headaches over the right side of her head. Circulation in a number of arteries, including the temporal, was impaired, and no pulse at all could be felt in one arm. Laboratory tests also showed changes in the functioning of her liver.

Within one week after treatment was started with prednisone she was free of all symptoms, and within eight weeks her liver function had returned to normal. The prednisone was gradually decreased and then discontinued. Other patients too at Mayo and elsewhere had abnormalities of liver function associated with giant-cell arteritis, which could be reversed when prednisone was used to combat the artery inflammation.

The Many Forms

From what is now known, patients with giant-cell arteritis are always over fifty years of age, and usually over sixty-five. Women have the problem ten times more often than do men.

When the temporal artery in the head is affected, the major symptoms and signs are swelling of the artery, tenderness, and severe headache. But, commonly, too, there is intermittent pain in the jaws. A very serious complication that may develop if treatment is not insituted is blocking of blood circulation to the eyes, leading to loss of vision.

When other arteries, alone or in addition to the temporal, are affected, muscular pain is a frequent symptom. Severe aching may occur in neck, back, shoulder, upper arm, hip, and thigh muscles. Morning stiffness may occur. Pain and stiffness are in the muscles, not the joints. There may be no discomfort at rest, but any use of muscles causes pain. Often, too, the patient looks very ill and may suffer from mental depression. Yet the muscles and joints look and feel normal and there are no rashes or nodules or bumps. The clue to diagnosis lies in the rapid sedimentation rate.

Giant-cell arteritis is easy to confuse with other problems.

Because patients may complain of lassitude and appetite loss, because their muscular aches seem diffuse rather than localized, and because the usual physical examination shows nothing specific to explain the symptoms, it is all too easy to assign the blame to senile depression or to label it all as a matter of psychogenic aches and pains, although measurement of the sedimentation rate could quickly suggest the correct diagnosis.

Also, if fever, anemia, or weight loss is marked, as sometimes happens, the problem of diagnosis may be a little more complicated. Such symptoms can come from either infection or malignancy, and the sedimentation rate may be up in either of those as well as in arteritis. So appropriate tests for infection and X-ray studies of lungs, gastrointestinal tract, and kidneys may be needed to rule out infection or cancer before arteritis can be safely diagnosed.

Rheumatoid arthritis, too, can be confused with arteritis because both disorders may be associated with low-grade fever, weight loss, fatigue, mild anemia, and elevated sedimentation rate. But patients with rheumatoid arthritis have joint swelling and tenderness, and weak grips; in contrast, those with arteritis have normal joints.

What causes giant-cell arteritis is still a mystery. Nor is it clear why some patients with temporal arteritis get headaches while others suffer diffuse muscle pain and still others, with the same artery affected, have no localized symptoms, only anemia.

When anemia is the primary manifestation, the patient complains of fatigue and malaise; headaches and muscular pains are minimal or entirely absent. The anemia may be profound.

Somehow, the patient cannot produce enough red blood cells even though he has plenty of iron stores needed to manufacture the red blood cells in the bone marrow, where they are customarily produced. No one knows how arteritis leads to anemia—but still the anemia disappears when the artery inflammation is controlled.

Fortunately, all the symptoms of giant-cell arteritis can be eliminated with treatment of the inflammation. On a daily dose of forty to sixty milligrams of prednisone, or equivalent dosage with another similar corticosteroid drug, pain disappears, usually within twenty-four to forty-eight hours, and fever, apathy, and other symptoms also vanish.

The response, in fact, is so dramatic and invariable that it is considered a significant part of the diagnosis. If the patient does not show such a response, the diagnosis probably was mistaken. Even patients with anemia as the primary manifestation show prompt improvement, with the blood picture usually returned to normal within two weeks.

Corticosteroid treatment is the only effective therapy. The physician, noting not only the relief of symptoms but also the change in the sedimentation rate toward normal, may begin to reduce the dosage to a much lower level over a period of four weeks. In some patients, the drug can be discontinued entirely. In others, treatment must be continued indefinitely at a low level of about five to ten milligrams of prednisone a day, which is considered to be safe, well tolerated, and adequate to control the inflammation.

There could be additional benefits in combatting arteritis. For just as arteritis in an artery of the head may sometimes lead to blindness if not controlled—doing so by choking off adequate blood flow to the eyes—so arteritis elsewhere may sometimes contribute to heart attacks by reducing blood flow to the heart muscle and to strokes by reducing flow to brain tissues.

Obviously, physicians should be—and more are becoming—alert to giant-cell arteritis in elderly patients. But medical authorities still report that patients with the problem are coming to their physicians with a variety of nonspecific symptoms and are submitted to routine and unremarkable physical examinations, and then are often patted on the back and told to go home and "Get a grip on yourself."

When elderly people begin to fail, giant-cell arteritis should be not one of the last, but one of the first, diseases to be considered.

9

OTHER SIGNIFICANT DISEASES IN THE ELDERLY— COMBATING THEM, NOT AUTOMATICALLY GIVING UP TO THEM

The arthritic diseases, heart diseases, lung diseases the elderly suffer with, their hypertension and their sensory losses—none of these must invariably, inevitably, be invincible, any more than they must be in younger people.

Such chronic diseases may not often be curable, but they are often controllable at whatever age they develop. However, until now relatively little vigorous effort has gone into controlling them. The process of interesting many physicians in chronic illness has been long and slow, but vigorous treatment to control chronic diseases and to rehabilitate is available—and rewarding.

Active Treatment for Arthritis

She was seventy-six. Her suffering had begun with painful swelling in her left knee. Then followed painful swelling and morning stiffness in both her hands. Her personal physician had made some effort to help her but there was no improvement. He might well have considered that no help was likely. But at least he referred her for evaluation by an expert rheumatology group at a major medical center.

The diagnosis was rheumatoid arthritis. And at the medical center, active treatment for her was started without delay. At first blush, it didn't seem active. She was put at bed rest and given aspirin, but sizeable—and adequate—doses of the aspirin, twenty grains or four tablets every four hours. And that was all for a week. But by the end of the week, her acute arthritis had subsided.

Then began progressive exercises. Weights for resistance were applied to her legs and she worked at strengthening the muscles around the arthritic knee joint. Whirlpool therapy was used to maintain a full range of motion of the knee. Hot paraffin was applied to her hands daily followed by exercises, and splints were applied to rest the hands in between paraffin applications and exercises.

After a month, she could be discharged home, greatly improved, able to care for herself and to move about without difficulty. And at home, she took and still takes small doses of aspirin and carries out exercises as directed, making weekly trips to the medical center's rehabilitation clinic for help and support and to further aid her rehabilitation.

No cure; no miracles; but a seventy-six-year-old woman has hope, now suffers minimal discomfort, and can be independent and active.

She was seventy-three and a rheumatoid arthritis sufferer for nineteen years. There had been an abortive attempt at treatment—with gold. But she proved to be sensitive to the gold; it produced a rash. Treatment stopped. She went on suffering until an acute attack angrily inflamed her left wrist, and her right knee became swollen and agonizingly painful.

Then, fortunately, she found her way to the rheumatology clinic at the same medical center. For her, too, active treatment began with bed rest and plenty of aspirin and then went on to progressive exercises with weights. But she improved only slightly. It wasn't left at that. She received prednisone, forty milligrams a day. The acute arthritis subsided rapidly. More exercises followed. Soon the prednisone dosage could be cut to just five milligrams a day. Not long afterward, she could be discharged home, able to walk and to do her daily household chores. And she continues and is doing well under the supervision of the rehabilitation department as an outpatient.

Again, no cure—but rescue.

He was eighty-two. Both his hands were swollen, stiff, and painful. He couldn't move his neck without agonizing pain. He was thought to have rheumatoid arthritis and his personal physician couldn't help but did send him for expert evaluation.

He didn't have rheumatoid arthritis. That was a mistake. He had osteoarthritis. And it was cervical osteoarthritis—not in his hands but in his neck. The osteoarthritis compressed nerve roots in the neck region and, in addition to the pain there, caused the pain, stiffness, and swelling of his hands.

Hot packs were applied to his neck. He was fitted with a special cervical collar. And he was shown how to carry out cervical traction at home—stretching the neck area with light weights on a pulley system and then gradually increasing the weights he used for the stretching.

In one month, he was free of pain and all symptoms.

There is an important group of elderly patients who are believed to have rheumatoid arthritis but have osteoarthritis instead. The group is fairly large and includes a number with cervical osteoarthritis.

Arthritis still is too widely looked upon as virtually a hopeless disease and its diagnosis tantamount to a life sentence to progressing pain and disability. But though there is no known cure, available medical measures—if only they are used and used properly—can be of great value.

Rheumatoid Arthritis

Forty million Americans of all ages suffer from one or another form of arthritis, twenty million of them severely, twenty million others to a milder degree. The rheumatoid form is the most serious, painful, and crippling.

Rheumatoid arthritis is really a systemic illness that manifests itself primarily by joint pain and inflammation which may lead to deformities.

At first, many people with RA have only nonspecific symptoms such as fever, chills, poor appetite, and a general run-down feeling. Finally, the joints become stiff, sore, and painful. Most frequently the joints of fingers, wrists, knees, ankles, and toes, alone or in combination, are affected, although sometimes all joints may be involved.

In one type of RA, there is severe joint inflammation, with pain and swelling, often accompanied by fever and prostration. If the disease is not treated, deformities develop rapidly and may quickly become crippling. In the more common type of RA, the arthritic pains and swelling are not severe and disabling at first, and there may be intervals during which few if any symptoms are experienced. Gradually, however, over a period of years and often after several attacks of acute joint pain, the joints may become deformed.

Because the cause still has not been definitely established, there are no basic means of preventing RA.

Aspirin has been and even now is the mainstay of treatment. But it must be used in adequate amounts—at least twelve tablets a day in divided doses after each meal and before bedtime. Aspirin not only relieves pain; it also combats inflammation. Experts agree that, with active disease, aspirin should be taken on a regular daily basis rather than at will—and that there is no such thing as a standard dose. There is considerable variation from one person to another in the amount of aspirin in the blood produced by a constant quantity of aspirin. If need be, each patient should be given increasing amounts up to the point where noises in the ears develop as a side effect; then doses should be reduced a little below such amounts so the noises disappear.

While periods of rest during the day are helpful, complete inactivity must be avoided unless there is severe disease with markedly painful and swollen joints. Lightweight splints are often useful, insure correct position, and relieve the painful muscle spasms, or involuntary contractions, that otherwise develop.

Most patients improve if these conservative measures are

carried out for at least two months. To carry them out, the patient must be motivated, understanding; the physician should explain and encourage. Otherwise, two months is a long time to wait—in the dark—for improvement.

If a patient continues to have persistent symptoms, one tablet a day of chloroquine or hydroxychloroquine may be prescribed. Again, the patient must understand that no immediate effects can be expected, but after four to six weeks some patients show gratifying improvement.

When such measures aren't enough, gold salts may be used. Usually, there is a test injection of 10 milligrams of gold and if there are no undesirable reactions, this is followed in a week by 25 milligrams and thereafter by weekly injections containing 50 milligrams each. Improvement seldom occurs until 200 to 400 milligrams have been given. If there is no change after 1,000 milligrams, the injections are stopped. But if, as often happens, there is significant improvement on gold salt therapy, the patient continues to receive maintenance injections of 50 milligrams at about monthly intervals.

At all stages of the disease, and particularly when early deformity is present, physical measures can be valuable. There is an unjustified tendency even by many physicians, according to an expert committee of the American Rheumatism Association, to minimize the importance of physical measures. Local heat application through moist compresses or infrared irradiation, followed by exercises, often helps relieve joint pain and muscle spasm. The exercises help preserve joint motion and strengthen muscles.

If joint inflammation still persists, hospitalization may be advisable so even more intensive therapy can be used. Cortisonelike drugs in small amounts added to aspirin can have a dramatic effect in relieving pain and stiffness and can allow active exercise and other physical therapy.

There is no one best treatment for rheumatoid arthritis. What is needed is active individualized treatment; general treatment can be very destructive.

When a woman approaching sixty who complained of recurrent "bursitis" in both shoulders was, without thorough diagnosis, simply given aspirin, codeine, and local heat, she got enough relief to continue to be active. A year later, when her hands and wrists became swollen, stiff, and painful, she got some relief by soaking her hands in warm water for fifteen minutes each morning, by taking long hot baths, and by taking short courses of the drug phenylbutazone to combat the inflammation.

Four years later, the pain in her hands became more severe and prolonged, and pain and swelling developed in her left foot. Again, less than thorough, intensive medical care gave her some degree of relief, but not for long.

Finally, two years later, she got expert care. However, it was necessary now to start her on gold treatment and to fit her with an ankle brace for her right foot. The brace helped her get about with less pain. After 475 milligrams of gold, her foot swelling began to subside. After 650 milligrams, she was free of all symptoms and the gold was discontinued. Now, two years later, with a maximum of just two aspirins in the morning followed by a hot bath and use of the brace on her right foot, she is functional and pain-free throughout the day.

Osteoarthritis

Osteoarthritis, also called degenerative joint disease, is arthritis associated with "wear and tear" in joints. It does not usually manifest itself before middle age except when a joint has been injured or subjected to continued excessive stress, as in the fingers of some pianists, for example.

It is very common. By the time they reach sixty-five, two-thirds of all people experience at least some discomfort because of it. It is not considered to be a very severe disease in the sense that it does not involve inflammation and produces no constitutional symptoms such as fever—as rheumatoid arthritis does—but it may cause pain and in some cases joint disability. The joints most commonly affected are the weight-bearing ones such as hips, knees, and ankles. Affected joints may "creak" and grate on movement, and pain is increased by activity and relieved by rest.

What happens is that joint cartilage degenerates, becoming soft and wearing unevenly or sometimes even completely, so that bone becomes exposed or may thicken.

Osteoarthritis may well be one of the most undertreated of

all disorders—sometimes because a doctor is unaware of what can be done and fails to refer the patient to an expert or a clinic where proper care is available, sometimes because a doctor fails to encourage and support a patient, sometimes because a patient is diverted from even good medical care by well-meaning friends or relatives who insist that doctors don't know anything to do for arthritis and recommend some pet nostrum.

There is no panacea for osteoarthritis. The purposes of effective treatment should be to relieve pain, restore as much of joint function as possible, and prevent avoidable disability or disease progression.

Daily rest periods may be prescribed. The wearing of proper shoes, restoration of arch, or building up of one side of a shoe to shift the line of weight-bearing often can be helpful. So, too, the correction of any abnormal posture and reduction of excess weight. In some cases, to ease the load on affected weight-bearing joints, local support, including use of a cane, crutch, or other mechanical device, can be of great value.

Useful local measures include application of heat along with exercises designed to avoid or correct muscle wasting away, since muscle weakness intensifies joint instability and contributes to disability. Traction is useful when muscle spasm is present. A cervical or neck collar often helps patients with osteoarthritis affecting the neck vertebrae.

The mainstay of drug treatment for osteoarthritis, as for rheumatoid, is aspirin, with moderate doses—two tablets three to five times a day—often sufficient for osteoarthritis. If necessary, a cortisonelike drug may be used, but not systemically; rather, it may be injected into a joint to provide relief of symptoms for several weeks so that graded exercises can be begun with less discomfort.

Such measures are certainly not dramatic, yet they very often can contribute greatly to the comfort—and also mobility and independence—of an elderly patient with osteoarthritis. Provided they are used and used regularly. But because there are no quick changes, many patients understandably become discouraged and use them only sporadically or not at all. Family encouragement can be helpful, but there is no substitute for the support and reassurance of a concerned physician.

Even when there has been some neglect and osteoarthritis has become well advanced and has led to disability, active treatment may provide very worthwhile rehabilitation.

That is illustrated in the case of a seventy-five-year-old woman who, after many years of increasing pain and disability, particularly in her right hip and knee but also in both hands, finally sought help from experts at a rheumatology clinic. Her condition was such that it was thought best to hospitalize her in order to institute therapy.

For sixteen days, along with drug treatment for pain, she received physical therapy for both knees and hips, including first passive range-of-motion exercises in which her joints were moved for her, then active exercises in which she did the moving. Her hands were treated with paraffin and with increasingly active exercises.

At the time of her discharge, she could walk without pain with the help of a crutch and the range of motion in her severely affected right hip had been significantly increased. She had been taught how to use paraffin most effectively for her hands and was given a range of motion exercises for her hips, and, using both at home regularly, she is doing well. She isn't capable of dancing or anything like that, but she is happy to be able to get around without pain and to maintain her independence.

The Growing Role of Surgery for Arthritis

The number of surgical operations for the treatment of arthritis has increased tenfold over the past ten years and the curve is still rising. Surgery now offers hope for many of the most severely crippled, those unable to walk or move freely, to do housework or engage in any routine daily activities.

The increasing usefulness of surgery has been achieved through notable advances in the development of materials compatible with the human body, greatly improved methods of adhering them, and the growth of the field of bioengineering, in which engineers and other specialists work alongside physicians to design increasingly sophisticated prosthetic devices that can replace whole useless joints.

The Hip

One of the most dramatic developments has been total hip replacement.

The hip joint, a ball and socket arrangement, is a frequent target for both rheumatoid arthritis and osteoarthritis. With disease, the ball of bone at the head of the thigh bone (femur) can rub against the roughened surface of the socket in the hip and produce severe pain.

There had been many efforts to devise an artificial hip. But the material had to be strong enough to withstand the many millions of loading pounds placed on the joint over a period of years; it had to be compatible with, and remain uncorroded by, body fluids and tissues; and it had to be self-lubricating. Surgeons had tried using a stainless steel ball to replace the diseased femur head, screwing the ball into the thigh bone, but it sometimes came loose. They had made a socket of steel in which the ball could rotate, but a steel-to-steel joint had to be lubricated by body fluids and often these were inadequate.

Then, a little more than a dozen years ago, Dr. John Charnley, a surgeon at Wrightington Hospital, Wigan, England, decided to try the suggestion of a dentist friend that methyl methacrylate, a cement commonly used in dentistry, might hold both ball and socket in place securely—and, for the socket, Charnley tried a plastic, high-density polyethylene instead of steel.

The results in many hundreds of patients were gratifying. Some of the patients put on dramatic demonstrations at American medical meetings. A woman, previously totally incapacitated, walked without pain or limp after both hips had been replaced. A man handicapped for more than twenty years did a "go-go" dance.

At Massachusetts General Hospital, Boston, where one surgical team has performed more than 800 hip replacements, 96 percent of patients have gained better motion and freedom from discomfort. At Mayo Clinic, the results in the first 333 hip replacements who have been followed for at least one to two years suggest these prospects for arthritics undergoing the operation: 96 percent will have no pain or only slight pain; 97 percent will have no limp or only slight limp; 93 percent will be able to climb stairs with bannisters; 91 percent will need no support, or only occasional support, from a cane; 98 percent will be able to sit normally; 97 percent will be able to use public transport; and 98 percent will have no deformity.

Typically, in the operating room, while the surgeon removes a diseased hip joint, nurses mix a liquid and a powder to form a paste. The surgeon then pours the paste into place, molds it to shape, and it becomes cemented into the bones and provides a surface with much the same consistency as human bone. The artificial hip is implanted in the drying cement and by the time the patient is off the operating table the new joint is held securely.

Total hip replacement is a major surgical procedure, yet it does not leave the patient with the breathing restriction and discomfort that may follow temporarily after large-scale abdominal surgery. Patients, as a result, are able and nearly always eager to move around as soon as possible. But for the first four or five days the operated hip is rested. Walking is attempted between the fifth and tenth day, at first with a walker and then with crutches. Usually the hospital stay is three weeks.

Is the operation for the elderly? As a matter of fact, until recently, it has been largely reserved for them. Surgeons wanted more experience to determine how long the replacement functions well before trying it in young people with long life expectancies. Now, encouraged by the experience of Dr. Charnley's earliest patients, who are doing well after a dozen years, there is a trend to making the operation available for younger people who are severely afflicted.

The Knee

Total knee-joint replacement is now becoming feasible. The knee, which bears virtually all the body weight, is very susceptible to arthritis. Medical treatment is usually helpful when properly and actively used, but it does not suffice in about 10 percent of patients.

Surgery has been tried before. As a last resort, knees have been fused, made motionless, to stop pain. Some use has been made of partial prostheses, including metal discs, to separate the heads of thigh bone and shin bone (tibia). For years, surgeons have sought a total knee replacement, but the problem has been complex because the knee is inherently less stable than the hip joint. But recently several designs for replacement knees have been developed and two have been used successfully in several hundred patients.

One, the polycentric knee, consists of two crescent-shaped Vitallium metal half circles that are implanted in the thigh bone so only their rounded edges protrude. The shinbone is fitted with two matching polyethylene tracks or grooves in which the upper part can rock back and forth each time the knee is bent and extended. Both parts are cemented in place with methyl methacrylate, the same material used for hip replacement.

The second replacement knee, called the geometric, is basically a technical variant of the polycentric.

In 1971, clinical trials in this country began at five medical centers—Mayo Clinic, Johns Hopkins Hospital, Massachusetts General Hospital, Doctors' Hospital in Corpus Christi, and the University of California at Los Angeles Medical Center. Two hundred patients received the polycentric and one hundred the geometric knee. Results have been excellent in both. Length of rehabilitation varies among patients; some use crutches for three months; some use a walker until they feel comfortable with a cane and are walking with a cane in three and a half weeks.

A follow-up study, after a year, of sixty patients who had seventy-three knee replacements has found that the operation relieved pain in 84 percent and has provided normal stability in 93 percent. Seventy-eight percent of patients need no help in walking and six of nine patients previously unable to walk without aids have been able to throw away the aids, the other three use canes full or part time.

The Hand

Arthritis can twist and gnarl hands, producing, in some cases, both disabling pain and grotesque deformities.

When the wrist is affected, arthrodesis—a fusion operation that fixes the wrist in a neutral, undeformed position—often produces gratifying results. In 96 percent of a series of patients treated by surgeons of the Columbia University College of Physicians and Surgeons, New York, fusion led to increased grasping power and made the wrist pain-free and more useful.

Surgeons at Robert Bent Brigham Hospital, Boston, have reported on the use of arthrodesis in more than fifty patients. In one third, it was for pain alone; afterward, none had wrist pain. In another third, the major problem was wrist deformity or instability; the operation was successful in overcoming this in all. The remaining patients before the operation had no deformity and did not complain of pain; however, all had greatly decreased hand strength resulting from their having avoided strong gripping as a means of preventing pain. They, too, benefited.

Patients make excellent adjustments to wrist fusion. They develop new patterns of handwriting. They learn to make greater use of the elbow for such activities as combing the hair and dealing cards. No patient has felt that functional impairment from fusion was significant, and, in fact, all indicate that the increased function resulting from pain relief and increased strength more than compensates for loss of ability to bend the wrist.

Recently, too, synthetic finger joints made of silicone rubber, first developed by Dr. Alfred B. Swanson of Blodgett Memorial Hospital, Grand Rapids, Michigan, have proved their value.

A typical finger-joint implant resembles a piece of taffy which has been pulled out at both ends. After removing a deformed joint, the surgeon makes a channel in each bone entering the joint. The ends of the implant go into the channels and the device is positioned so its thickest part lies between the bones and keeps them properly aligned. For about three weeks the patient wears a movable brace to make certain that healing takes place in the right position.

The finger joints provide as much as 75 percent of the efficiency of natural healthy joints. In testing, they have been flexed 90 million times without breaking. In trials at 211 clinics throughout the world, they have been implanted in more than 4,000 hands and in 99 percent of cases have produced no adverse effects on surrounding tissues and no complications of any kind.

The Elbow

There is no accepted artificial replacement as yet for the elbow, but the need for one is less than for other joints. Despite arthritic changes, the elbow often remains useful and pain-free. When changes are severe, medication and exercises often suffice. When, however, such measures are inadequate, an operation, synovectomy, in which inflamed, overgrown tissues are removed from the joint, often can be valuable.

At the Hospital for Special Surgery in New York, for example, 89 percent of a group of patients so treated and followed for an average of three and a half years have had both relief from pain and extended range of motion.

The Most Common Operation

Synovectomy is the most frequently used operation for arthritic patients. It may be used for virtually any joint. While it has been used in the past largely to relieve pain and deformity, there are now some indications that its use at earlier stages may help to halt or prevent destructive processes.

To understand synovectomy is to understand how arthritic deformity develops. The synovium, lining every joint, is a membrane that produces fluid to lubricate joint surfaces. In rheumatoid arthritis, the synovium becomes inflamed and swollen. In severe cases, the swelling may be enough to distend the joint. Then ligaments, which connect bone ends in the joint, may become stretched and damaged; and tendons, which attach muscle to bone, may drift out of normal position and shorten, and the shortening produces deformity. In the hand, for example, the tendon shortening may pull the fingers into useless positions.

After World War II, during which surgeons made considerable advances in the treatment of battlefield-crippled hands, they turned attention to similar problems in the civilian population. They learned to remove swollen synovium, repair stretched ligaments, and put displaced tendons back where they belonged.

After a time, synovectomy was tried for other joints, including knees, shoulders, and elbows. There began to be observations that knee synovectomy, for example, not only often produced immediate benefits; it seemed to help arrest the rheumatoid process in the joint and halt further joint destruction. Studies revealed that the joint lining gradually reforms after operation and has the appearance of healthy lining.

Recently, excellent results of synovectomy have been reported from Duke University Medical Center, the Hospital for Special Surgery in New York, and other major medical centers, and include striking pain relief, chronic inflammation of knee joints controlled for extended periods, deformed hands made to look normal, and painful and unstable wrists made pain-free and stable.

Also recently, more and more surgeons have been performing synovectomies in early stages of disease with the hope of retarding, halting, or preventing destruction. There seems to be some justification for the hope. At the Cleveland Clinic, for example, 88 percent of patients who had early synovectomies of 121 finger joints have no pain or greatly reduced pain. And, for periods of up to five years and nine months thus far, deformity has developed in only one patient. Significantly, five patients already had deformities in one hand, and, thus, a demonstrated tendency to develop deformities. With synovectomies of their better hand, they have had no new deformities.

Currently, the Arthritis Foundation is carrying out a large-scale and long-term study to evaluate the preventive value of synovectomy, comparing the state of health of synovectomized joints with joints not operated on. Early results are reported to be promising.

Arthritics need all the help they can get. Today if medical therapy—active, determined, not abortive—is not enough, surgery has much to offer.

But surgery will never be the final answer to arthritis. That will come when the origins of the arthritic diseases are known and prevention becomes possible. And the search for origins is intensive.

No surgery can be considered minor. Always, there is at least a slight element of risk, some immediate discomfort. It isn't to be entered into lightly. It isn't indicated in many patients. It isn't needed in many, provided suitable medical care is used. Also, there is the expense; for a hip or knee replacement operation, for example, the bill may come to $4,000 or $5,000, though, in many cases, much or all of the cost may be met by medical insurance, Medicare, or Medicaid.

But when the best of medical care is insufficient to help, surgery may relieve pain, restore a good measure of joint function, and enable an elderly patient to lead a more active life.

COLD—Chronic Obstructive Lung Disease

Ten to twelve million Americans, mostly middle-aged and elderly, are struggling for breath today. They are victims of chronic bronchitis and emphysema—and many may be victimized by less than optimum care.

Because the distinction between chronic bronchitis and emphysema is hazy and because the two problems often coexist, they are often described together under the name of "chronic obstructive lung disease," or "COLD." Once considered rare and unimportant, COLD now kills more people, 70,000 yearly, than lung cancer. It makes invalids or near-invalids of many hundreds of thousands—and is the fastest rising of afflictions.

COLD takes a long time to become destructive and disabling. The lungs have great reserve and there often has to be 50 to 75 percent deterioration of lung function before it is noticed.

Thus, COLD is an insidious disease, a fact that complicates its early detection. But there *are* early clues. One is a history of chronic cigarette cough, usually worse in the morning on arising and often productive of sputum. Another is a history of frequent respiratory infections which are severe and take long to resolve. There may be other indications: an increase in chest diameter (called barrel chest) and some wheezing that occurs during a medical examination when a patient is asked to exhale forcefully.

Too often, however, it is severe shortness of breath or very severe respiratory infection which brings the COLD patient to medical attention for the first time, when much damage may already have occurred.

Several factors predispose one to emphysema and bronchitis. Chief among them is cigarette smoking, and it is rare, though not impossible, for COLD to occur among those who have never smoked. Air pollution and exposure to industrial fumes of some types may be involved. Recently, an inherited defect in the production of a certain body enzyme has been detected in some patients; it seems to be particularly common among those who are seriously affected at younger ages. Much more remains to be learned before there might possibly be practical results from the discovery.

The Disease

In chronic obstructive lung disease, changes occur in the passages—the bronchi and bronchioles—which carry air to the lung areas.

In addition to carrying air, the bronchi and bronchioles play a role in defense against infection. They contain special cells capable of destroying invading organisms. They also contain cells that produce mucus to trap foreign material. The mucus normally is washed up in the throat and swallowed or eliminated through mouth and nose. Smoking is known to impair these protective mechanisms, particularly hampering elimination of mucus. As a result, chronic infection may set in and may cause some destruction, weakening, or narrowing of the bronchioles. When mucus is retained instead of being eliminated normally, it tends to narrow the air passages, make coughing less efficient, and to lead to still more retention and narrowing.

With such obstruction and distortion of lung structures, greater effort is needed to expel air. This puts excessive strain on the walls of alveoli, the thin-walled lung chambers that are surrounded by networks of tiny blood vessels through which the exchange of oxygen and carbon dioxide takes place.

If you inflate a balloon just briefly to moderate size, it returns to original size and shape. But if you keep it distended for a prolonged period, it develops wrinkles. Similarly, with abnormally high and prolonged pressure, the alveoli become overdistended and disrupted. In addition, the abnormally high pressure may compress blood vessels, further impairing oxygen–carbon dioxide exchange.

Chronic bronchitis can be looked upon as the stage of the disease when mucus collects and chronic inflammation is present. Emphysema occurs when the alveoli are disrupted. During chronic bronchitis, the patient may have persistent cough and sputum production. When the alveoli become compromised, shortness of breath develops. Though chronic bronchitis may not progress to emphysema, this is the exception rather than the rule. Similarly, in some cases, emphysema may be present with little or none of the changes of chronic bronchitis.

Usually, in the beginning, there is persistent cough along

with repeated respiratory infections, sometimes complicated by pneumonia. Gradually, the infections become more severe and last longer. It may take ten years or longer before cough and sputum production become particularly troublesome. It may take as few as five or as many as twenty-five or thirty years before shortness of breath and wheezing develop. Later in the disease, heart failure—not a stoppage of the heart but a loss of pumping efficiency—may develop because of the long strain on the heart muscle, which has to pump blood through the vessels of the diseased lungs.

Conventional Treatment

Several measures are commonly used to treat chronic obstructive lung disease.

The patient is usually advised to give up cigarette smoking as a means of diminishing the quantity and tenacity of sputum. He may be asked to drink two to three quarts of water a day to help liquefy the sputum that is produced and so make it easier to eliminate.

He may also be taught to carry out a regular program of coughing to help clear his lungs of sputum and, as an aid to this, humidification, either in a steamy bathroom or through use of a heated nebulizer, may be advised.

Any chest infection will, if possible, be treated early with suitable antibiotics. Drugs also may be used to dilate the air passages when necessary. If congestive heart failure occurs, it is treated with diuretics.

This is symptomatic treatment, largely concerned with manifestations rather than underlying disease. As far as it goes, it is helpful. But is it enough? Is it all that can be done?

More Positive Treatment

Symptomatic treatment is what many medical centers as well as many individual physicians content themselves with. Virtually nothing is done to arrest progression of the disease, and little attempt is made at real rehabilitation.

Dr. Albert Haas, director of pulmonary services at New York University School of Medicine and New York University

Institute of Rehabilitation, has been involved for more than twenty years with a program he feels proves that COLD patients can be rehabilitated as successfully as patients who have neuromuscular and skeletal disabilities. The key to success lies not simply in treatment measures but in a conviction that such patients are not hopeless.

At the Institute of Rehabilitation, where sixteen thousand respiratory cripples have been treated, the approach is dictated by the philosophy that COLD patients deserve, and can have, more than a prospect of sedentary vegetation and can be given maximum use of their heart-lung reserve capacity

Each patient is studied for work tolerance, home situation, psychological status. A program is then tailored for the patient aimed at preparing him to take care of himself and often to return to work—either his original job or other work more in line with his capacity.

The program begins with a two-week hospital stay. The patient is given relaxation exercises, breathing exercises, and postural drainage. A family member is asked to join in so he can help supervise the patient at home.

Because COLD patients are usually tense and apprehensive, relaxation exercises are considered essential. In addition to easing tension and removing some of the apprehension, they help make patients more cooperative, more willing to try to work at breathing exercises and postural drainage.

Breathing exercises begin with the patient lying on his back and breathing deeply. He works through various positions and exercises until he reaches the point of being able to blow water in graduated amounts from one bottle to another through tubing. Oxygen may be administered as an aid to the exercise reconditioning.

Such rehabilitative measures can't erase damage already present but they bring significant gains, which are probably due to more economic use of heart-lung reserves and also, through the development of more efficient breathing patterns, a reduced labor cost of just breathing.

The fact is that in healthy people the diaphragm does about 65 percent of the work of breathing, and respiratory and other muscles do the remaining 35 percent. But this ratio is reversed in the pulmonary cripple.

The reason is that normally the diaphragm contracts during inhalation and relaxes during exhalation. And the recoiling action of the lungs helps the diaphragm do this. But in advanced obstructive pulmonary disease, the lung has lost elasticity and has become distended, depressing the diaphragm, interfering with its activity, and loading an increased portion of the work onto the muscles.

A more economical use of the breathing muscles is achieved by reestablishing the mobiity of the diaphragm. This is accomplished by teaching the patient to use his abdominal muscles. By contracting the abdominal muscles, he reduces the size of the abdominal cavity, thus causing the organs in the abdominal cavity to move upward. In doing so they push up the diaphragm.

The Institute of Rehabilitation gets patients with disease so advanced that in some cases it is possible only to teach them to take baths, shave, comb their hair, and carry out other self-care activities. But that represents a major accomplishment.

In some cases, much more can be achieved. Five years after treatment at the institute, one-fourth of 252 men have been able to resume full-time work, compared with only 3 percent of a group receiving no rehabilitation treatment. And, significantly, too, the death rate among the treated was one-half that among the untreated.

Who is responsible for neglect of the COLD patient? The fault lies equally with the patient's doctor who puts off referral until the last possible moment and the physiatrist, a specialist in physical medicine and rehabilitation, who is not interested, and the chest physician who is stepping into areas where he is not trained. There is an almost total lack of rehabilitation experience in the training of both the chest physician and the physiatrist.

The chest physician has to take over a rehabilitation program for which he has neither time nor adequate training. To satisfy the patient's demand, he uses just a few physical measures, such as breathing exercises and postural drainage, calls them rehabilitation, and generally turns to untrained nurses and inhalation therapists to do the work.

"The therapy itself," says Dr. Haas, of the Institute, "is usually poorly implemented; in most of the places that I have visited, even though the patients were taught breathing exercises, very few were given to understand that the purpose of these exercises extends beyond the recommended exercise period in order to change the actual breathing pattern."

There is no reason for the institute's program to remain unique. Almost every hospital has a rehabilitation service. What is needed is to make both patient and physician aware that the situation is not hopeless.

Other physicians who have taken an interest in rehabilitation of COLD patients agree. No such patient should be told his case is hopeless. The physician should adopt a cautiously hopeful and encouraging attitude. He should encourage work, hobbies, and mild exercises such as walking. He should urge the patient to participate in activities up to his level of symptom tolerance and to rest when tired. If exercise tolerance is very limited, oxygen therapy can help to increase it. Breathing exercises are important.

In a program in which 206 men and 51 women took part at Toronto General Hospital, activities included walking on a motor-driven treadmill, riding a stationary bicycle, going up and down stairs, and turning a wheel by hand. Before starting on it, 158 patients were limited by their breathing difficulty to slow walking on the level for less than two city blocks, and 75 were short of breath on any slight exertion. A definite goal for the patients was to be able to walk on the treadmill at the rate of one mile per hour for thirty minutes breathing room air. It was to be arrived at gradually. At first, 81 of the patients tested couldn't even begin to do the treadmill walking for just a few minutes without breathing oxygen-enriched air. Yet 42 percent of them were able to complete the program and achieve the goal, finally walking the treadmill for the full half-hour period without need for oxygen. Of the 176 patients who breathed room air from the beginning, 88 percent successfully completed the program. And 92 percent of patients who completed the program and could be followed up at intervals for a year afterward continued to be able to walk on the treadmill for thirty minutes. Their improvement was not fleeting; they had developed an increased exercise tolerance which, they reported, was making life more enjoyable.

Elsewhere, too, aggressive efforts to rehabilitate COLD patients have been found to pay off. At the Regional Chest Center of the University of Nebraska Medical Center, 140 COLD patients ranging up to 70 years of age who took part in an active rehabilitation program came out of it with improved psychological outlook and mobility and were able to perform more activities of daily life; many could return to work.

Given the will to try to help them, to be optimistic about helping them, chronic obstructive lung disease patients can be taught how to live with their disease rather than to cope with a living death.

The Older Person with Heart Disease

Within the next hour, 125 men and women in the United States will have a heart attack, and many others will experience their first attack of chest pain—angina pectoris. Some will be young, some middle-aged, some elderly. They will join the ranks of millions who have coronary heart disease, the clogging artery disease that produces heart attacks and angina.

What do they have to look forward to? Until recently the outlook was bleak. There was a pervading pessimism about atherosclerosis, the disease process underlying coronary heart disease. It was considered to be an accompaniment of aging. Little, therefore, could be done to prevent it or combat it when present.

But that picture has been changing. Atherosclerosis is present in many of the aged—but also in many of the young. It is not a result of aging. There are clues to its causes, to factors that start it up and may hurry it along. There is increasing optimism that the prevention of atherosclerosis is not impossible and that even when the disease is present and well advanced, when it has already manifested itself in angina and even led to one or more heart attacks, its victims need not invariably become invalids, withdrawn from life and waiting passively for death. No matter how old.

Real Heart Disease—and False

For many years, coronary atherosclerosis is silent. It may start early in life. As mentioned earlier, it has existed in advanced states, still silent, even in eighteen-year-olds.

At some point, the atherosclerosis stops being silent and may manifest itself in the first agonizing attack of angina. Almost two hundred years ago, an English physician, William Heberden, provided the first, and still unsurpassed, description of that experience: "Those who are afflicted with it [angina] are seized while they are walking (more especially if it be uphill and soon after eating) with a painful and most disagreeable sensation in the breast, which seems as if it would extinguish life if it were to increase or continue; but the moment they stand still all this uneasiness vanishes."

Angina pectoris—angina meaning suffocative pain, and pectoris meaning breast—may appear not only as the result of exertion but of strong emotion, and the pain may radiate beyond the chest to fingertips, pit of stomach, teeth, jaws.

Angina is really the cry of the heart muscle that it is not getting enough oxygen through the blood to meet demands placed on it. An attack is brief; if chest pain extends beyond fifteen to twenty minutes, it is not likely to be from angina. Usually, the pain—and anxiety accompanying it—are so intense that the victim must stop activity immediately and, with the reduced demand on the heart, the pain disappears.

But not all chest pain is angina. Many conditions that have nothing to do with the heart can produce chest pain that may be mistakenly thought to indicate heart trouble. Gallbladder disease, a mild rib inflammation, arthritis in the joints between rib and spine, bursitis (especially of the left shoulder), neuralgia, pleurisy—any of these can cause chest pain. Swallowing air, which becomes trapped in and balloons in the intestinal tract, is a common cause. Depression can trigger chest pain, and so can sleeping with arms or shoulders in a strained position.

Real heart disease is a vast enough problem, but an estimated twenty million Americans are carrying a needless burden of anxiety and many lead the lives of invalids because they think they have heart disease but do not have it. And many of them are elderly because they expect that inevitably with age any chest pain *must* come from heart disease.

Any older person who *seems* to have heart disease should have a thorough check. If it's real heart disease, it can be diagnosed as such. If it is not, the cause of it very often can be treated.

And if it is real, it need not be a hopeless matter at all.

A remarkable drug, nitroglycerin, is a common remedy and has been available for nearly one hundred years to provide relief for angina. It acts very quickly when dissolved under the tongue. It improves blood flow by, it is believed, dilating the coronary arteries and also by reducing the resistance to flow of other blood vessels in the body, thus easing the work of the heart. It is remarkable because it is quickly effective, inexpensive, harmless.

Many physicians advise angina patients not only to take nitroglycerin when an attack comes on but to use it to prevent attacks when they know they will be facing a trying emotional experience or doing something such as going out into the cold or engaging in the sex act which previous experience has shown to be likely to bring on an attack.

Yet, despite its proven value, many people still hesitate to use nitroglycerin. They have groundless fears that somehow it can do some harm or that they may become "addicted" to it. Or, if depressed, they may neglect taking it because of the apathy produced by the depression (see chapter 5).

When, as it so often can, nitroglycerin not only brings relief from angina attacks but minimizes their occurrence—and, additionally, by doing so may make possible progressive activity which, as we shall see shortly, may help—its use should be encouraged. For this, especially when the patient is elderly, a close rapport with the physician is important along with kindly, persistent efforts to educate the patient so he understands what his problem is all about, how nitroglycerin can help, and how other measures also may help what is not necessarily a hopeless condition.

What other measures may help?

Among the factors linked to the development and progression of atherosclerosis and heart disease are excessive weight, smoking, inactivity, excessive intake of fats in the diet, hypertension, diabetes, and gout. And it is not hopeless at any age, including advanced age, to try to combat these factors.

With gradual reduction of excess weight, the heart is helped because it does not have to work so hard if it need not carry the burden of pumping a considerable amount of blood simply to feed excess fat. Moreover, the less weight that muscles and weight-bearing structures must support, the less blood supply they need, further reducing the work of the heart. Additionally, weight reduction also often helps to counter diabetic tendencies and reduce elevated blood pressure—and when reduction is not sufficient, medication may be used.

No crash diets are needed; instead, they are to be avoided. Slow, steady loss of weight up to the desired point through a well-rounded diet—which avoids excessive fats—is what is needed.

And increased activity may be called for. However paradoxical it may seem at first, exercise may be good treatment for the heart patient. The heart, after all, is a muscle. Like any muscle, it becomes flabby with disuse. With exercise, muscle tissue may become able to contract more effectively so that with each beat of the heart more blood is pumped out. When that happens, the heart needs to beat fewer times to pump out the blood required for body needs. Investigators also are checking evidence that exercise may lead to the formation of new branch coronary vessels and connections—known as collateral circulation—to help feed the heart muscle, increasing blood supply even though main coronary arteries remain narrowed.

Physicians have noted that some patients who develop angina have such a great love for golf or some other activity that they refuse to give it up and insist upon trying to keep playing. At first, they may be able to play only a single hole before experiencing an angina attack. But as they persist, they gradually build up to the point of being able to play eighteen holes without an attack.

Exercise in a patient with angina, if carried to excess, can be dangerous. But if the exercise is carefully planned, starting easily and progressing very gradually, exercise tolerance may increase. And the patient who can become increasingly active not only is happier and has a psychological plus; he may well be healthier, too.

Some physicians now use this procedure with an angina patient: In the physician's office, the patient carries out very mild exercises while an electrocardiographic record of heart activity is made. When the patient exercises just up to the point where he feels that an angina attack may be about to develop and stops activity immediately, the angina attack does not come on and, significantly, the electrocardiogram shows no abnormal changes. That means that to that point of activity, the heart has experienced no shortage of oxygen.

The physician then may tell the patient to follow the same procedure in daily life without the electrocardiographic record: simply to carry out activities up to the point that there is the slightest indication that with any further activity an angina attack may develop. Most patients become extremely discerning—able to sense the point beyond which even just another few steps would bring on chest pain.

Even patients who have had heart attacks may benefit from the same measures. Many heart attacks are not fatal. In an attack, blood flow through a narrowed coronary artery may be shut off suddenly by a blood clot or by debris torn loose from the artery wall. The part of the heart muscle supplied by that vessel suffers acute deprivation of oxygen. More often than not, only a small portion of the heart muscle is affected. That muscle area dies, but the rest of the heart lives on and quite often is sufficient since the heart, like many other body organs, has reserve capacity.

After a heart attack, the same factors that led to it may still be present. But it is not inevitably too late to do something about them and to avoid invalidism and reduce the risk of another attack.

Many physicians now encourage patients who have recovered from a heart attack to engage in physical activity—very carefully graded and very carefully supervised. And the patients do well.

In patients with a healed heart after an attack, exercise may decrease or relieve angina, increase work tolerance, and improve chances of surviving future attacks if they occur; and patients without serious complications are capable of resuming former or new activity.

For the past eighteen years in Israel, rehabilitation programs for heart patients have included carefully graded and ultimately strenuous sports activities. For several months, patients go through mild warm-up and strength-building exercises. Within about nine months, they go on to systematic training in hiking, swimming, cycling, rowing, running, and volleyball. The program culminates in competitive team games. One study of 1,103 patients so treated and followed for five years found that the death rate was cut by more than two-thirds in comparison with a comparable group of physically inactive heart patients.

Recently, the American Heart Association has taken a major step through its Committee on Exercise. It has issued a guide booklet for physicians. In it a committee of heart specialists advises that regular, vigorous exercise is "an important therapeutic tool" in rehabilitating patients who have angina or are recovering from heart attack.

This instructive handbook gives physicians information on how to go about doing what few physicians had the tools to do before, even for younger people: give relatively simple tests to establish the immediate capacity of an individual, and, from the results of the tests, draw up a specific, individualized program of exercise likely to be most helpful and to have maximum safety.

There has thus been a tremendous change in medical attitudes and knowledge about heart patients from the days only a few decades ago when the patients were urged, in effect, to sit still and become invalids, with little to look forward to except eventual death. Unfortunately, there may be many heart patients, especially elderly ones, who have not yet had the benefit of the changed outlook and approach.

For an elderly patient with coronary heart disease who has not so benefited, a whole new look at his or her problem by the present physician or by another is in order.

Additionally, in some severe cases, new surgical techniques may offer new hope, as we shall see in the next chapter.

Congestive Heart Failure

Once, congestive heart failure had to be regarded as ominous. Today, many patients respond to vigorous treatment.

Congestive heart failure is no disease in itself. Rather, it is a constellation of symptoms produced by heart problems that include hypertensive heart disease (the result of untreated, uncontrolled high blood pressure), heart attack, congenital heart disease, and which sometimes may be produced by other conditions such as excessive thyroid gland activity, chronic lung disease, infection, anemia, emotional crises, and heart rhythm abnormalities.

Heart failure is not necessarily a final stage of disease. As pointed out before, it means that the heart's pumping performance has been impaired: the heart muscle has been so weakened that it cannot provide sufficient circulation for body tissues.

How does that happen? Actually, the normal heart has great reserve power. At rest, it uses only about 25 percent of its capacity. With strenuous exercise, it can quadruple its effort if necessary. It's normal for heart muscle fibers to grow in size to meet needs of people who do heavy work.

And the demands on the heart of even a very heavy worker or athlete are far from excessive. If, for example, you are sedentary, there are times during the day when you are more active than at other times, and during the active times, the work load on the heart may average about 150 percent of the resting work load. A laborer doing heavy physical work may impose an average 200 percent work load on his heart over a twenty-four-hour period.

But when an abnormal condition affects the heart, the work load can be much greater. If, for example, blood pressure is twice normal, the basic work load of the heart is doubled, and not just for a brief period but for twenty-four hours a day.

When extra demands are imposed on the heart because of

high blood pressure or other disease, the heart responds for a time. It accommodates by increasing in size and weight and carrying the load well. It may do so for months or years. But at some point it begins to falter. The muscle fibers become overextended; they lose strength, somewhat like an overstretched spring. Pumping efficiency is lost and less blood is pumped to the body; the heart may not completely empty. Pressure then builds up within the heart.

The pressure is transmitted back to the lungs, and shortness of breath develops. The kidneys, no longer supplied adequately with blood, no longer produce normal urine output. With urine output diminished and not enough water removed from the blood by the kidneys, the volume of water in the blood increases and adds to congestion in the lungs. Pressure may also extend backward from the heart to the body's vein system. Less blood then returns to the heart and fluid accumulates in body tissues, swelling the ankles and abdomen. When heart failure is far advanced, the patient is almost drowning in his own fluid.

Vigorous treatment for congestive heart failure aims at three things: to improve the heart's pumping efficiency; to eliminate excess fluids; and to reduce the overload on the heart, immediately, if necessary, by bedrest, and where possible by treatment of the condition that led to the failure.

To improve pumping efficiency, the drug digitalis is often used. For two hundred years, it has been a mainstay of treatment, a kind of tonic for the heart that strengthens heart muscle fibers and increases force of contraction so pumping efficiency improves. Digitalis may improve performance enough so that the heart can function efficiently even if the condition that caused the failure cannot be corrected. Even in advanced failure, it is not unusual for a patient to respond to proper digitalis dosage with a loss of twenty pounds of fluids from lungs, abdomen, and elsewhere.

The dosage of digitalis must be tailored carefully to the needs of the individual patient. Inadequate doses do little if any good. Excessive doses can produce unwanted effects that may include heart rhythm disturbances, nausea, vomiting, diarrhea, appetite loss, vision blurring, headache, lethargy, numbness.

To eliminate excess fluids, other measures also may be used. Reduction of salt in the diet can help because salt tends to hold water in the body. Diuretic drugs, which act to rid the body of excess fluids, also are valuable and may help, as a kind of extra dividend, to reduce elevated blood pressure if that is present.

In some cases when these measures are not enough and when retained fluid in chest and abdominal cavities makes breathing difficult, the fluid can be removed by needle. Its removal helps not only to make the patient more comfortable immediately, but also may allow diuretic treatment thereafter to become more effective.

Once heart failure has been overcome, proper care can help to prevent its recurrence. The care needed will vary from one person to another. It may include continued use of digitalis and diuretic, and limitation of salt intake. And it may include efforts to reduce the overload on the heart. This may, for example, call for the correction of anemia or overweight if either, or both, contribute to the overload. Often it should include control of high blood pressure, which commonly contributes to congestive heart failure, heart disease, heart attacks, and kidney failure.

Hypertension: Silent, Deadly, Overlooked

Hypertension—high blood pressure—is now known to be our greatest single cause of death—a long, silent, and largely overlooked and neglected disease.

It affects twenty-four million Americans of both sexes, all ages. Yet more than three-fourths of its victims don't know they have it or are not being treated adequately or at all for it, though effective, often simple, treatment is available.

While hypertension can occur at any age, it has its highest incidence in older people. To age twenty-four, 10.9 percent of men and 1.4 percent of women have elevated pressure. By age fifty-four, it affects 15.3 percent of women and 17.7 percent of men. By age sixty-four, 24.3 percent of women and 27.5 percent of men have it. And after age seventy-five, it affects 28.3 percent of women and 26.7 percent of men.

In people with high blood pressure, heart attacks are three to five times more common than in those with normal blood pressure; stroke is four times more common; congestive heart failure is five times more common. And the risk of kidney failure is greatly increased.

Contrary to what many people think, hypertension can be present for years without giving itself away. There may be no symptoms at all. When it does produce symptoms such as headaches, lightheadedness, dizziness, heart palpitations, insomnia, shortness of breath, or vision disturbances, the disease is already well advanced and the symptoms come from the complications produced by hypertension. Even then, they may be thought to be due to other causes.

When it is present silently, it is at work doing damage. It forces the heart to work harder to pump against high pressure in the arteries, and after a time the heart may weaken and congestive heart failure may develop.

Along with hypertension goes atherosclerosis, the building up of fat deposits in the arteries, leading to coronary heart disease, heart attack, and stroke. Hypertension may contribute to atherosclerosis in several ways. The excessive blood pounding on the artery walls may produce damaged sites where fatty deposits can settle. The pounding may even drive the deposits in. And recent studies indicate that, whatever the cholesterol intake in the diet, hypertension increases cholesterol production by the liver, thus increasing the cholesterol in the blood stream and in the artery walls.

What causes most cases of hypertension is still not entirely clear. In only about 10 percent or even less of the total is there a definite physical abnormality. This may be a faulty kidney artery, a benign tumor of an adrenal gland atop a kidney, a constriction or narrowing of the aorta, which is the body's main trunkline artery. In such cases it is often possible to achieve a cure, once and for all, by correcting the physical abnormality through surgery.

In the 90 percent or more of all cases in which such abnormalities do not exist, any one factor or several factors may contribute to the development of elevated pressure. Excessive intake of salt in the diet is one. Overweight is another. Often, mild hypertension may respond to limitation of salt and reduction of weight. Excessive emotional stress also may be involved.

Even though the cause is still not clearly established in the vast majority of patients with hypertension, in virtually every case, from mildest to most severe, the disease can be brought under effective control. Many drugs, from mild to very potent, are available for the purpose. And effective treatment does more than reduce elevated pressures; it sharply reduces the toll of premature death and invalidism from heart and blood-vessel disease.

Several problems have stood in the way of effective treatment for all who need it. For one thing, the only way hypertension can be discovered is by a simple check made by a physician. It takes only a minute or so but many people haven't had the check—some because they haven't seen a physician for long periods. For others it's because not all physicians have made the check a routine matter. Every physician now is being urged to do so no matter what the patient comes to see him about.

Additionally, some physicians, even after finding that a patient has hypertension, have done little or nothing about treating it. Except in the most severe cases of pressure elevation, they haven't been impressed with the need for treatment.

Moreover, the best treatment requires custom-tailoring. The right medication in the right amount has to be found. Sometimes it's found immediately; sometimes, after trial. Some patients have unpleasant reactions to some drugs, not to others. The right drug can be found but it may require effort. And some physicians, not overly impressed with the need for treatment, have shirked getting involved with it because it takes time and requires education and motivation of the patient, especially the patient who has none of the symptoms he mistakenly believes must be manifested if hypertension is present.

But there is now overwhelming evidence that even mild hypertension is important and deserves attention. And there is clear evidence now that with effective treatment, lives can be saved and much discomfort avoided.

Moreover, there is evidence now that even when a patient already has heart disease, treatment for previously uncontrolled hypertension can make a great difference. Even inadequately treated patients have much lower death rates than the untreated, and for the properly treated the death rates are still lower.

With all the new developments in hypertension—in the recognition of its great importance even when mild or moderate, the need for treating it, the preventive value of treating it, and also the therapeutic value even when heart disease already exists—every elderly person as well as every young one deserves a check for hypertension, and, if it is found, aggressive treatment for it should be pursued. And if its presence has been known, has been detected long before, and it has not been treated, a whole new look at it is very much in order.

The Eyes in the Aged

Three diseases—macular, cataracts, and glaucoma—or a combination of them account for as many as 83 percent of the eye problems in older people. Yet much can be done now to preserve and restore useful vision.

Cataracts

Cataracts are opaque spots that form on the lens of the eye and interfere with the passage of light rays. Often the first indications are blurring and dimming of vision. Gradually, the patient feels a need for a brighter reading light or for holding objects closer to the eyes. Continued clouding of the lens may sometimes cause double vision.

If an elderly person suffers from loss of vision, it can be better for him if the loss is due to cataracts than if it is due to almost any other eye disease. For if the retina is essentially normal, as it often is, the removal of the clouded lens can lead to restoration of a gratifying amount of vision.

But many elderly patients are frightened of cataracts—and of surgery for them—out of failure to understand the nature of their problem and its correction.

Technical advances in cataract removal have made the procedure a comparatively easy one for the aged and infirm. No longer is there the period of immobilization that was erroneously required years ago.

Cataract removal can be achieved under local anesthesia. Through an incision where the clear cornea and white of the eye meet, the lens is reached. It is then loosened by an injection of an enzyme, chymotrypsin, that dissolves the ligaments holding the lens without affecting other eye structures.

The lens then can be lifted out readily with forceps, a freezing rod that grips it, or an instrument with a suction cup. Once the lens is removed, the incision is closed with fine sutures which may be of a type that is absorbed and do not have to be removed later. Many surgeons now allow patients out of bed the day after cataract removal.

No longer is it considered necessary to wait for a cataract to "ripen." It can be removed anytime.

Since a lens is needed for focusing, glasses are required after its removal. They have thick lenses to make objects appear larger, but most patients adapt to them well. Instead of glasses, contact lenses may be used, but it is sometimes difficult to get older people to go to the trouble of learning to wear them. With glasses or contact lenses, the absence of the natural lens is not noticeable to others.

Even when a patient has a cataract so advanced that the ophthalmologist is unable to evaluate the condition of the retina because of the lens clouding, the lens may be removed beneficially.

Macular Disease

The macular area of the retina permits perception of fine detail such as print. In some elderly people, the area may degenerate, leading to loss of central vision and of ability to read and make out detail.

When macular disease is the result of inflammation, it may respond to administration of cortisonelike drugs that have anti-inflammatory effects. And even some noninflammatory cases of macular disease may respond to the same drugs, perhaps because they also remove excess fluid from the retina.

Macular disease is usually progressive. Yet, even when it has progressed to a considerable degree, the ophthalmologist can help many older patients with poor sight by prescribing special low-vision aids—magnifying devices now available in variety, both hand-held and incorporated into eyeglass lenses.

Glaucoma

By age sixty-five, about 10 percent of the population is affected by glaucoma, which is a major cause of blindness. Yet the disease can be arrested when detected early enough, often by eyedrops that control the production of aqueous humor or facilitate its drainage so pressure is reduced toward normal.

Glaucoma is often referred to, rightly, as "the sneak thief of sight." The chronic type, which is most common, causes no symptoms until damage has been done. It develops slowly and painlessly, although it can be detected readily by a medical eye specialist using an instrument to measure the degree of pressure in the eye. A less common acute form strikes suddenly, producing cloudy vision, severe eye pain, eye redness, and nausea. Though there are many varieties of glaucoma, all have in common increased pressure within the eyeball because fluid is unable to drain properly.

Inside the front of the eye, a circulating fluid, the aqueous humor, is continuously formed and normally drains off so the same pressure level is maintained. In glaucoma, as drainage of the fluid is impeded and pressure begins to build up, the pressure inhibits blood supply and gradually damages nerve cells.

The damage begins at the edges, slowly moving toward the center. The victim then loses side sight and develops "tunnel vision" so that he seems to be viewing objects through a telescope. He may also have blurring of vision and may see halos or rainbow-colored rings around lights.

If eyedrops prove insufficient surgery may be used. In one common procedure, a small segment of the iris—the colored part of the eye around the pupil—is cut off, leaving a small, almost invisible opening that allows increased drainage. The procedure can be carried out under local or general anesthesia, and the patient is out of bed within a day or two.

An alternative procedure is sclerectomy. A tiny hole is made in the outer coat of the eye, into the space under the sclera, which is the outer white eyeball sheath. This provides a new fluid drainage channel. No scar is visible.

While surgery for glaucoma is delicate, it is not life-threatening.

Other Eye Problems

With increasing age, the skin of the eyelids becomes thinner, wrinkled, and more pigmented and may develop various growths, or keratoses. Many growths respond to application of corticosteroid creams. When there are warts or other growths that stand out conspicuously, and if the patient desires, they often can be snipped off easily under local anesthesia in the physician's office.

Eyelids can become lax and not hug the globe, and excessive tearing of the eyes may follow. A fairly minor surgical procedure can correct the laxness and provide greater comfort.

A more serious problem involves the transparent cornea, or window, at the front of the eye. It may be affected by physical injury or disease, or sometimes with aging it may become less translucent so that vision is impaired. Although relatively few elderly people require corneal transplantation for corneal blindness, today this operation, in which a donor cornea is used to replace a damaged cornea, is much more easily performed by an expert than it was just a few years ago.

The transplant can be accomplished under local anesthesia. With present methods, the eye can be unpatched and the patient can be up and about within twenty-four to forty-eight hours, and the average period of hospitalization is less than ten days.

Yet the sad fact is that thousands of people who are blind because of corneal disease have long since abandoned hope of having their vision restored. Neither they nor their physicians have considered the possibility of a new eligibility for corneal transplant surgery as it is carried out today.

The Ear

According to current estimates, the number of the totally deaf who cannot hear the spoken voice at all is about 250,000, but the total number of people with some degree of impaired hearing is at least seventeen million and possibly twenty million.

As many as half of these cases of impaired hearing are due to defective conduction, a type of impairment for which modern surgical procedures are most effective. And age need not be a bar to them.

It is not difficult to understand the broad outlines of ear anatomy and the hearing mechanism, and what can go wrong.

The ear has three parts: outer, middle, and inner. The outer ear collects sound waves which then strike the eardrum, a membrane separating the outer ear from the middle ear.

In the middle ear are three small bones, or ossicles, called the malleus, or hammer, the incus, or anvil, and the stapes, or stirrup, because they do in fact resemble those objects. The three bones form a chain across the middle ear from the eardrum to an oval window in a membrane that separates the middle ear in turn from the inner ear.

In the inner ear is the cochlea, a spiral cavity containing a structure called the organ of Corti which translates sound vibrations into nerve impulses that go to the brain.

When a sound strikes the ear, the eardrum vibrates. In response, the bones in the middle ear, performing like levers, amplify the eardrum movement and pass the vibrations on to the cochlea. There, the vibrations are translated into nerve impulses that are transmitted via the eighth cranial nerve, the nerve of hearing, to the auditory center in the brain.

Conductive impairment—the result of mechanical interruption or resistance to the transmission of sound waves to the inner ear—is a major cause of hearing loss.

Sometimes it is only a matter of a foreign body or impacted wax in the outer ear canal that prevents sound vibrations from reaching the middle ear. Sometimes, it is a matter of a middle ear infection that needs treatment. In children, a common cause is overgrowth of adenoidal tissue, which blocks proper ventilation of the middle ear and interferes with its functioning.

But a most common cause in adults is otosclerosis of the stapes bone in the middle ear. In otosclerosis, the stapes bone hardens and becomes overgrown, and a barnaclelike crusting cements the normally springy bone to the tiny oval window of the inner ear against which it should beat like a piston. Now stuck fast, and unable to beat, the stapes cannot transmit sound vibrations. The victim loses hearing and may also experience ringing noises in the ear.

Although there were many efforts in the past, even dating back a century, to solve the problem of otosclerosis with surgery, it was not until the 1950s and the introduction of the operating microscope, which allowed very delicate work within the middle ear, that an operation called stapedectomy became feasible—successful in more than 90 percent of cases.

Stapedectomy is not a distressing operation. It is performed under local anesthesia supplemented with light general anesthesia to keep the patient drowsy. The stapes bone is removed along with the now abnormally hardened oval window membrane on which the bone rests. Either a small bit of vein or a plastic material is grafted over the window in place of the membrane and a miniature section of wire or plastic is positioned to bridge the gap between the window and the bone next to the stapes. With the new strut replacing the stapes, the conducting mechanism across the middle ear—from eardrum through conducting bones to inner ear window—is reestablished. The eardrum, which has been lifted out of the way for the operation, is replaced and not even sutures are needed; it stays in place. For twenty-four hours the patient is kept in bed, and hospitalization is a matter of only several days.

Hearing may return early in the postoperative period or as late as three weeks after surgery. Usually improvement is noted about a week postoperatively.

For patients who have normal nerve function—and this can be determined prior to operation—stapedectomy usually produces complete restoration of hearing. If a hearing aid was used before, it may be discarded now.

For patients with some degeneration of the auditory nerve, stapedectomy will restore hearing that is normal in most situations, somewhat limited in other situations—but, on the whole, patients will hear satisfactorily without use of a hearing aid.

For patients with marked nerve degeneration, the restoration of hearing will be limited. After stapedectomy, they will usually be able to hear close conversations and telephone conversations, and this gain may be enough to justify operation. For most social purposes, they will still need a hearing aid.

When nerve degeneration is advanced, the goal of stapedectomy is different. Often, with advanced degeneration, a hearing aid is of little or no value. Following stapedectomy, however, an aid may become useful for the first time.

Is age a bar to stapedectomy? It shouldn't be. It should have nothing to do with determining suitability for operation. A person of seventy-seven can be just as much a candidate for successful stapedectomy as a person of twenty-seven or thirty-seven. Some older people may have too much irreversible nerve degeneration to warrant operation. But this can be determined by testing and shouldn't be assumed.

Older patients as a group react well to the operation. And the lift they get from their new hearing is often remarkable. For them, to hear well again is something totally unexpected, and life, which may well have seemed drab, brightens again.

Perceptive Deafness

This is caused by disorders of the inner ear and the nerve of hearing. These can stem from many causes, which include infectious diseases such as meningitis and strep infections; injury by such substances as quinine, alcohol, salicylates (aspirinlike compounds), and some antibiotics; and even emotional disturbances, anemia, and marked underfunctioning of the thyroid gland.

Sometimes it is possible, with thorough investigation, to uncover a cause that will respond to vigorous treatment, and hearing improvement follows. In other cases, hearing aids often can help greatly.

The Jaw Joint

The temporomandibular joint, which is formed by the lower jaw bone or mandible and the temporal bone of the head, can give rise to a wide variety of harassing symptoms. And frequently they are not correctly diagnosed in the elderly patient who is told to "learn to live with" the pains.

According to a recent survey of both physicians and dentists, many in both professions still are either uninformed about temporomandibular joint dysfunction and the problems it can cause or are following outdated concepts of diagnosis and treatment.

Not only can it produce pain in the joint during chewing, and clicking sounds and limited jaw movement. It may give rise to headache, pain at the base of the skull, sinuslike pain, pain in the teeth, gums, tongue, or palate, burning sensations in the throat, or neck pain radiating down to the shoulders and back. It may also produce pain in or about the ears, vertigo, ringing of the ears, ear stuffiness, pain in or about the eye, and burning sensations in the eye.

The dysfunction may be due to "bad bite" or malocclusion, which is either hereditary or the result of loss of teeth. More commonly, however, it is due to fatigue and spasm in the chewing muscles, often caused by clenching or grinding of the teeth, usually unconsciously, as the result of emotional stress.

Only one of every three physicians checked in the survey tried to treat temporomandibular problems at all, and most of these simply prescribed or injected medication to decrease pain, without going beyond. The others often just sent patients to dentists for the purpose of "getting the bite checked" as if this was the only possible cause. And there is a suggestion from the survey that bite-altering dental treatments may sometimes be used indiscriminately.

What should be done?

It's important that a patient's symptoms be studied thoroughly by a physician to make certain that they are not caused by disease. He may want to use dental consultation before making a final diagnosis of temporomandibular joint dysfunction.

It has been the experience at the New Jersey College of Medicine and Dentistry that when no disease processes are involved and symptoms stem from temporomandibular joint dysfunction, treatment is curative for 85 percent of patients.

Treatment to bring quick relief for the symptoms caused by an inflamed temporomandibular joint and spastic, abnormally contracting muscles may include hot moist applications, pain-relieving medication, and sometimes local anesthetic injection or ultrasonic treatment. One or more treatments may be needed.

When the patient habitually clenches or grinds his teeth, a dentist can construct an appliance, a splint or night-guard, to reduce or eliminate the resulting muscle spasm. Muscle relaxants for a short time are helpful.

A planned program of muscle-conditioning exercises also is valuable. The patient may be shown how to place his elbow on a table and his fist under his jaw and to open the jaw against the resistance of the fist, and then to relax his jaw. He may do this five times in the morning and five times in the evening, increasing gradually, over a period of a month, to twenty-five times a day.

It may be necessary to replace missing teeth with a fixed or removable partial denture. If the patient has inadequate complete dentures, they must be remade.

10

TOO OLD FOR SURGERY? NONSENSE!

Mr. B was ninety-one years old when he was admitted to a New York City hospital, a very sick man, emaciated, weighing 110 pounds though six feet tall. He had a large mass in the upper right part of his abdomen. He complained of weakness, difficulty in breathing, severe constipation.

Examination showed that he had abnormal heart sounds, congestion of the lungs, a gallbladder stone, a hernia of the large intestine through the inguinal canal and a large scrotal swelling with fluid accumulation (hydrocele).

For ten days in the hospital, he was rested, treated for his heart condition, given daily enemas, nourished. When he showed marked general improvement, he was asked if he would consent to surgery, multiple surgery. He consented.

They opened his abdomen and removed a large, thickened gallbladder with stone. They covered that incision temporarily with a sterile towel and made another incision over the left inguinal region low in the abdominal wall. After drawing the protruding bowel back into the abdominal cavity and removing the left testicle with hydrocele, the hernia was repaired and the incisions closed. From start to finish, the procedure took seventy-five minutes.

Mr. B's postoperative course was uneventful. He could go home from the hospital seventeen days after surgery, free of all complaints.

Miracle? No.

In Mr. B's case, either one of his two major surgical problems could have led to an emergency situation. His gallbladder, large and mobile, could have become twisted at any time. His large intestine, protruding through the abdominal wall, caught in the hernia, could have become completely obstructed at any time. Either event could have been fatal without emergency surgery. And when surgery must be performed on an emergency basis because of a life-threatening situation in a patient made very sick and weak by the situation, the risk of surgery is substantially increased, whether the patient is young or old and even more so when the patient is quite old.

But when surgery can be performed with adequate preparation of the patient, the chances of success are greatly increased at any age and especially at older ages.

The ability of the aged to tolerate surgical procedures is becoming well established.

A distinguished American surgeon, Dr. Alton Ochsner, recalls that, in 1927, as a young professor of surgery at Tulane Medical School, he taught that an elective operation for inguinal hernia in anyone over fifty was not justified. Today such instruction would shock surgeons who know that repair of hernias can improve the quality of the lives of the aged and, in the presence of strangulation obstruction seen frequently in women with femoral hernias, can prolong their lives as well.

At Henry Ford Hospital in Detroit, in hernia operations on two hundred patients, men and women seventy years or older, including one who was ninety-two and one ninety-three, successful repair was achieved in 98 percent.

In a Louisiana community, of 131 elderly patients undergoing surgery for gallbladder disease and in some cases requiring multiple procedures, 98 percent experienced marked improvement or complete recovery from their disease. A seventy-two-year-old woman, in addition to gallbladder removal, required an operation for an abdominal aortic aneurysm (a dangerous weakening and ballooning out of the body's main trunkline artery). She also required another procedure to remove a clot from a leg artery. One elderly man required gallbladder removal, removal of a duodenal ulcer, and severing of the vagus nerve (vagotomy) to reduce stomach acid secretions. In addition, a perforation of the small intestine had to be closed.

In Milan, Italy, in a clinic where 3,000 patients underwent vascular (blood vessel) surgery, one in three was over sixty and many were over seventy. Fifty-eight percent survived for at least five years and 30 percent for at least ten years—contrasted with a 70 percent death rate in the first year of other patients with the same problems not operated on.

One of the first studies of surgery in the elderly came in 1935 and covered 293 patients over seventy years of age. Overall, the operative death rate was 19 percent, but for major abdominal operations the death rate exceeded 33 percent. By 1940, another study of abdominal operations in patients over seventy showed a halving of that rate to 16.6 percent. Eight years later, the rate was down to 11.1 percent. By 1957, it was down to 7 percent.

Surgery for Diverticulitis

Diverticulitis is a common problem in the elderly. A diverticulum is an outpouching, a kind of sac, that protrudes from the intestinal inner lining into the intestinal wall. There may be scores, even hundreds, of such outpouchings, especially in the colon or large bowel.

The pouches may act as traps for feces but in some people they seem to fill and empty efficiently and there are no symptoms. In many cases, however, inflammation develops and when the inflammation is severe, the result is acute diverticulitis.

Along with pain in the lower left abdomen, there may be nausea, vomiting, and abdominal distention. Bowel habits may change drastically; usually there is severe constipation but occasionally diarrhea may develop; sometimes diarrhea and constipation may alternate. Chills and fever may occur.

Medical treatment for acute diverticulitis may include bed rest, antibiotics to control infection, drugs to relieve pain, and liquid feedings, and these measures may succeed in some cases. But surgery is often needed, especially when the disease produces intestinal obstruction or becomes so severe that a swollen, inflamed diverticulum may burst, spilling intestinal contents into the abdominal cavity and producing peritonitis.

Is surgery for diverticulitis—which entails removal of the diseased section of bowel—dangerous for the elderly?

At a New York hospital, where 377 operations were performed for diverticulitis, the operative death rate in patients under 70 years of age was 2.5 percent; it was 4.4 percent in patients over 70. But when surgery had to be performed on an emergency basis, the death rate in patients under 70 almost doubled; in patients over 70, it almost tripled. There were no deaths at all in patients over 70 who underwent elective three-stage operations.

Three-stage operations are not always needed. When the patient's condition permits, the diseased bowel section can be removed and the healthy portions joined in a single procedure. There is no doubt anymore that when an elderly person has diverticulitis that cannot be managed adequately by medical measures, the odds are now greatly in favor of safe and successful surgical cure.

Preoperative Preparation

Of course, unless there is an emergency, surgical procedures for the elderly need not and should not be undertaken on a rush basis. Chronic diseases have to be considered and where possible given optimum treatment prior to surgery.

Older people's tissues may heal as well as those of younger people provided nutrition is normal. But while older people may rarely show obvious signs of malnutrition, many have diets deficient in proteins and vitamins. As a result, their wounds may be slow to heal and may not be as resistant to infection. Time spent before surgery in improving nutrition is not wasted.

Much can be done to minimize the likelihood of development of bronchopneumonia, the main cause of death after surgery. Bronchopneumonia may develop because of preexisting lung disease, lung changes during anesthesia, or failure to clear secretions from the respiratory passages because of discomfort. The lungs should ideally be at their best prior to operation; time spent in making them so—through cessation of smoking, use of breathing exercises, antibiotics, physiotherapy, and other measures—is well rewarded even though it may mean many more days in the hospital prior to surgery.

Each day of preoperative preparation may in fact take a week off the postoperative recovery time.

Successful Surgery Despite Chronic Afflictions

Despite the presence of chronic medical problems, with optimum postoperative as well as preoperative care, elderly patients who can benefit from surgery for a surgical problem can often come through the operation successfully.

At one hospital, for example, 608 surgical patients all over the age of 70 included many with diabetes and some with toxemia or peritonitis on admission. Almost two-thirds of them had high blood pressure, more than half had chronic respiratory disease, either bronchitis or emphysema. Two hundred twenty-five had heart failure, and 160 had had a previous heart attack, 29 of them less than six months before.

Three-hundred seventy-two of the operations were for gastrointestinal disease, including ulcers, gallbladder problems, cancers of colon and rectum, and diverticulitis. There were operations for many other types of problems, including many other types of cancer.

All were seriously ill patients with serious chronic ailments on top of the problems for which they underwent surgery. Yet the overall mortality rate was 13.3 percent, and, in the last year, thanks to the lessons learned in carrying out surgery for such patients, the mortality rate was reduced to 7.6 percent.

One of the lessons learned was that it can be vital to get an elderly patient moving as soon as reasonably possible after operation—not just sitting in a chair beside the bed, but up and walking. With enough encouragement and with sufficient support for an abdominal wound through use of a binder, most patients can be out of bed by the second or third operative day.

Surgeons at the hospital discovered that a major reason patients were kept in bed for longer periods was the belief that the elderly need more rest than younger patients and that it is cruel to force an older patient out of bed as early as a younger one. This concept, it appears, needs rethinking, and it can even be argued that the elderly should be out of bed earlier in the postoperative period than the younger, more fit patient. Not only does early ambulation help to improve breathing function; it also has an additional—and profound—psychologic effect. To the elderly, a hospital bed can seem as restraining as prison bars.

Heart Pacemaker? Why Not?

When is a heart patient too old to have a pacemaker, if that is what might be helpful?

Doctors today are extending the lives of tens of thousands of middle-aged and now, increasingly, the lives of many older people suffering from complications of heart disease that affect the cardiac electrical system, the vital natural circuit that makes the heart beat regularly at a rate suited to the body's needs. When that system is affected, the heart may stop beating or beat erratically, ineffectively, and extremely slowly, leading to fainting attacks.

A pacemaker is an electronic device designed to bypass the defective electrical system and thus keep an otherwise functional heart beating and pumping blood to meet a patient's needs. The first such device was placed in the abdomen of a Swedish engineer in 1949. He was then thirty-eight and a former hockey player, but, because the cardiac electrical system had become defective, he was at that point able to walk only a few steps. His heartbeat sometimes dropped to twenty-eight times a minute instead of seventy, and he often fainted from attacks that came unpredictably. With each attack, his wife or a friend—he needed someone constantly with him—had to thump on his chest to keep him alive.

A cardiac pacemaker has triggered his last four hundred million heartbeats and allowed him to fly around the world supervising the repair of electrical systems aboard ships. He prefers to walk rather than drive around Stockholm, and now is president of a group of electrical companies.

Since that first pacemaker, there have been many improvements in the device itself. The first to be available was a fixed-rate type that worked by producing constant electrical impulses. More recently, "demand" pacemakers have become available. They contain a special circuit that senses the heart's natural electrical activity. The circuit starts the pacemaker when it is needed to supplement that activity and to keep the heartbeat steady; it shuts off the pacemaker when support is not needed.

With little fuss now, doctors practicing not only in major metropolitan medical centers but in many community hospitals are inserting pacemakers that range in cost from $500 to $1,000 in young adults, middle-aged people, and even some children who need them, and more and more in the elderly.

At the William Beaumont Hospital, Royal Oak, Michigan, for example, gratifying results have been reported for pacemakers used in more than eighty patients, nearly two-thirds of them over seventy-one. The patients were given pacemakers in a technique which so simplifies and eases the surgery involved that, as cardiologists at the hospital note, the usual argument over whether a patient is too old or infirm has no significance.

The technique, called transvenous endocardial pacing, developed in the mid sixties, does not require surgical cutting through the chest wall and can be performed under local anesthesia. Electrodes are maneuvered up into the heart through a catheter or tube inserted into a superficial vein in the arm. The catheter is secured by tying it to the vein at the incision site, and the length of electrode remaining outside the vein is threaded beneath the skin and fat to a site on the chest or the abdomen where the pacemaker is sewn in place under the skin. Presently, an artificial pacemaker may last as long as five years, but usually is replaced in two or three years in a minor operation. However, now in sight are pacemakers, including nuclear-powered ones, that may not ever have to be replaced.

Open-Heart Surgery, Too

Even open-heart surgery—surgery within the heart—can be used successfully for elderly patients.

Until the advent of the heart-lung machine, the heart had remained the last frontier for surgery. To operate on a beating heart without disrupting circulation was extremely difficult. Complex heart problems could not be tackled until it became possible to use some system to take over temporarily the function of the heart.

The heart-lung machine takes over the work of the heart *and* lungs, giving surgeons time to make intricate repairs. While there are variations in the way the machine can be used, essentially blood returning to the heart after circulating through the body is diverted through tubing into the machine. In the machine's lung section, oxygen is added and carbon dioxide is removed. Like the heart, the machine then pumps the freshened blood out through more tubing into the arterial system of the body which carries it to all body tissues. And while the heart-lung machine is functioning, the heart can be stopped and opened, and repairs can be made.

Each year in the United States 30,000 to 40,000 infants—"blue babies" and others—are born with heart defects that now have become correctable with open-heart surgery. The defects include abnormal holes in the wall separating chambers of the heart, defects in heart valves, and pinching of the great artery (the aorta) emerging from the heart. Some children acquire heart defects as the result of rheumatic fever complications and other causes, and these too are often correctable now.

The same reparative treatment is now used for many adults with acquired heart defects and even with congenital ones. (Some defects produce no symptoms early in life but may do so later.)

Is there evidence that many of the elderly with such defects can benefit from reparative surgery? At the Texas Heart Institute, Houston, in a ten-year period, Dr. Denton A. Cooley and a team of surgeons used open-heart surgery for 292 patients, 192 men and 100 women, aged 60 to 84. Seven had congenital defects, 285 had acquired lesions.

One hundred forty-four of the patients had an aortic valve defect. The aortic valve regulates flow of fresh blood from the heart into the aorta. When the valve becomes stenosed, or narrowed, the heart has difficulty pumping the blood, and there may be chest pain with effort and easy fatigability to the point of invalidism. Sometimes the valve can be surgically opened up; that was the case for three patients. In the others, the valve was removed and replaced with an artificial valve.

Thirty-seven patients had mitral valve insufficiency. The mitral is the valve that controls movement of blood from a chamber into which it comes fresh from the lungs to the chamber where it is pumped out into the aorta to be distributed to body tissues. In mitral valve insufficiency, the valve cannot close properly after letting blood through and so blood leaks back and not all of it can go to the body. Weakness and fatigue may develop, also to the point of invalidism.

Twenty-nine patients had another type of mitral valve defect. The valve could not open properly, reducing blood flow to body tissues. Additionally, pressure builds up in the heart and is transmitted back to the lungs. At first there may be labored breathing only on exertion; then may come spitting of blood as small blood vessels in the lungs rupture because they are engorged with blood from the back pressure.

Twenty-three patients had double valve disease. Twenty others had an aneurysm of the aorta, a ballooning out of the great artery, which can press on nearby structures and produce coughing, chest pain, breathing difficulty. And there is danger it may burst and cause sudden death.

Thirty-two patients had had heart attacks that had left a dead portion of heart muscle that ballooned out to form a heart aneurysm. Unable to contract, it interfered with the heart's pumping work. If the aneurysm could be cut away, the heart could then work more efficiently.

At any age, heart repair operations carry risks. They are not entered into lightly. They are used when the patient suffers severely, nothing else helps, and the condition may be fatal.

Of the 292 patients, 44 died within the first month after surgery. Sixty-five patients had nonfatal postoperative complications such as wound infections and drug reactions. But 183, or 63 percent, had no problems and left the hospital without complications. The 65 who had nonfatal complications recovered and left the hospital greatly improved.

The fact that 248 of these 292 patients benefited from open-heart surgery is all the more remarkable in view of another fact: the usually advanced nature of defects in the elderly.

If elderly patients received earlier surgical care, before their defects have become extreme and they have been greatly weakened by them, the success rate could be increased. Even so, however, it would seem that the benefits of open-heart surgery should not be denied to a patient simply because of advanced age when he or she has, on the average, an 85 percent or better chance of benefiting.

And Surgery to Revitalize the Heart

Today, too, some elderly people with coronary heart disease, invalided by chest pain, can benefit from surgery to bypass a clogged coronary artery and bring more blood and nutrition to the heart muscle.

Such surgery, called revascularization, is being used increasingly for younger people, and there is evidence that some of the elderly can be helped by it.

A great deal of progress has been made in a short period of time. When blood supply to the heart muscle is impaired by atherosclerosis, or clogging, of the coronary arteries, angina may develop and the way may be paved for heart attack (see chapter 9).

Modern surgical efforts to provide added blood supply under such circumstances began in 1945 when Dr. Arthur Vineberg of the Royal Victoria Hospital, Montreal, thought of making use of the internal mammary artery as a new channel for the ailing heart. The internal mammary runs down behind the chest wall and supplies some chest areas with blood, but so do other arteries, and the internal mammary can be spared.

Vineberg freed the internal mammary from its attachments to the chest wall, brought it over to the heart muscle, dug a little tunnel in the muscle, and implanted the end of the artery there. The hope was that it would in time give rise to small branches that would search out and become hooked up with unblocked coronary artery branches, thus establishing a new network.

After years of experimenting with animals, Vineberg went to human patients, all with serious heart trouble. Of the first 150 patients, two-thirds had already suffered one heart attack. Seventy percent of the patients appeared to benefit; they felt better and could be more active. Vineberg and others improved the operation.

But one drawback was that time was needed after surgery, in some cases as long as six months, before new circulation pathways were established. Until then, the patient did not benefit and he might not be able to survive that long.

More recently, hoping for quicker results, surgeons tried other techniques. In one, endarterotomy, fatty deposits clogging a local area of coronary artery were left intact, but the artery wall in that area was cut open and a patch of vein or other material was sewn to the wall to enlarge the bore of the vessel so more blood could get through. In another technique, endarterectomy, a blocked artery was opened, the clogging material stripped away with a circular knife to widen the channel, and the artery was closed again.

A still newer version of endarterectomy uses gas rather than a knife. A jet of carbon dioxide is injected into a blocked artery and the high pressure jet separates the obstructing material from the artery wall so it can be removed. Gas endarterectomy requires less time. It has been used successfully to overcome obstructions in blood vessels of the neck, abdomen, and legs, and there is hope that it may be more effective in coronary artery disease than conventional knife endarterectomy. Still, endarterotomy and endarterectomy have limitations in that they can be used only for those patients who have only small lengths of artery clogged by deposits.

Bypassing now has become the most used method of bringing new blood supply to the heart muscle.

One method of bypassing a blocked coronary artery segment is to connect the internal mammary artery directly to the coronary artery beyond the diseased area. Blood then moves from the internal mammary into the healthy section of coronary artery and on to feed the heart muscle.

Another method is to use a length of saphenous vein taken from the patient's leg. The saphenous vein is the large vessel running the length of the leg. It can be spared because other veins can take over its work—and, in fact, this is the vein commonly removed in varicose vein surgery.

For a saphenous vein bypass, one end of the vein is inserted into the aorta and the other into a coronary artery beyond the point of obstruction. Thus, some of the blood coming directly out of the heart, fresh from the lungs, and entering the aorta moves directly through the saphenous vein to the coronary artery to feed the heart muscle.

Saphenous vein bypasses are being used not only for single coronary arteries but for both coronary arteries in many patients. And, when necessary, when the patient has had a heart attack and has been left with a dead section of heart muscle, the surgeon may remove that section during the bypass operation.

This, of course, is major surgery.

Before a patient is considered for it, X-ray movies of the coronary arteries are taken. They reveal what is going on within the arteries, where there are points of obstruction. A well-defined surgical plan is drawn up before the patient enters the operating room.

The surgeon is aided by a well-trained team that includes assisting surgeons, anesthesiologists, two or more nurses, a heart-lung machine technician, and a technician for the electronic equipment used to monitor the patient throughout surgery.

An incision is made in a leg to remove a length of saphenous vein from groin to knee. At the same time, the patient's chest is opened. The vein is thoroughly tested for leaks and if any are found they are sewn up.

The patient is then connected to the heart-lung machine. With a brief touch of electrodes to the heart, the surgeon can stop its forceful beating, making it just quiver so he has a quieter field to work in. A tiny slit is made in a coronary artery and one end of the saphenous vein is sewn in place with suture material as fine as hair. The other end of the vein is stitched to a slit in the aorta. The procedure is repeated for other bypasses if necessary. The heart-lung machine is disconnected, the patient's heart is started beating again, and often improvement is immediately obvious. The heart muscle is getting more blood.

The operation is long. It may last up to six hours or even more. Afterward the patient goes to a recovery room and remains there, constantly monitored, for several days.

Bypass is usually used only for seriously ill patients who do not respond to medical measures. At one medical center, for example, 68 percent of patients undergoing bypass surgery had had one to six heart attacks. In the first several hundred operations, the death rate was 14 percent. With refinements, it was reduced to 7 percent, still higher than anybody would like. It is being brought down farther. For early in the development of any surgical procedure, when it still must be regarded as experimental, it usually is employed only in the most severe and even terminal cases. Later, with proof of efficacy, it may be used for patients in earlier stages of disease and the likelihood of success is greatly increased.

Can the elderly stand up to such a procedure? Actually, at the medical center just mentioned, one of every six of the patients ranged in age from sixty to seventy-two. More recently, San Francisco surgeons have reported on results in one hundred patients aged sixty-five and older. Seventy-eight underwent bypasses and the remainder had removal of dead sections of heart muscle alone or in combination with bypasses. Some of the patients had other diseases unconnected with the heart yet these did not significantly affect the death or sickness rate after surgery. The elderly patients, in fact, did almost as well as younger ones undergoing such surgery. There were six early deaths, four later ones. Eighty-three of the remaining ninety patients could be followed up for extended periods, and seventy-seven of the eighty-three, or 93 percent, showed significant continued improvement.

Surgery for Cancer

Advanced age is no reason that a woman with breast cancer cannot benefit from cancer surgery. In fact, women over age sixty are usually good operative risks for breast removal—and with surgery they have a far better survival experience than those who are not treated or who receive only palliative treatment.

Investigators studying two groups of women over sixty with breast cancer found that those treated by operation had a fourfold better survival rate than did the others—a rate, in fact, very much like that for younger women with breast cancer.

Is surgery of use for elderly patients with lung cancer? One study covered eighty-one patients over age sixty-five, many of them in their seventies, who underwent surgery for lung cancer. Now, more than four years later, thirty-two, or 40 percent, are alive and happy. In comparison, of patients over sixty-five not undergoing surgery, only 2.7 percent survive more than two years.

When Physicians Give up Too Easily

When a sixty-three-year-old man was hospitalized because of progressive weight loss, weakness, and coughing, a chest X-ray showed a four-centimeter (about 1½ inch) dense area in a lung. He was a heavy smoker. It seemed he had lung cancer. And when he quickly developed headaches, papilledema (swelling of the optic disk usually associated with increased brain pressure), and paralysis of one side of the body, it was assumed that the lung cancer had spread to the brain. No tissue examination was done; no further tests made; he was allowed to die.

Yet, at autopsy, the shadow in his lung was found to be due to a lung abscess, not cancer, and he had a solitary well-encapsulated abscess in the brain. He might well have been saved, and given many years of useful life, by surgery.

But there is this tendency among some physicians to overlook the possibilities for helping elderly patients, especially those with past histories of incurable diseases that appear on the surface to be responsible for current problems.

The tendency may stem from failure to determine the accuracy of an original diagnosis, to carry out tests to confirm clinical impressions, to make use of expert consultation, and to keep up to date with advances in treatment.

A seventy-two-year-old man had had a melanoma, a malignant tumor, removed from his chest wall several years before. Now, when he developed paralysis of one side of the body and X-rays showed what seemed to be a lung mass and a lesion in the brain, the presumptive diagnosis was that the melanoma had spread. His doctor, thoughtfully but erroneously, advised against any further investigation and treatment; they would be useless.

The man died. But at autopsy, the lung mass was found to be a benign mass of lymph nodes and the brain lesion proved to be only a superficial hematoma, a mass produced by clotting of blood which may follow even a minor injury, which could have been removed through a single burr hole. His death was needless.

On the other hand, when an eighty-two-year-old man developed paralysis of the right side of the body and had difficulty in talking and understanding speech, no assumptions were permitted. Careful studies indicated a hematoma. And, despite considerable discussion among several physicians about the wisdom of surgery in a patient of such advanced age, the hematoma was removed surgically and without great difficulty. The patient promptly recovered—completely—and more than two years later is enjoying life and engaging happily in his favorite hobbies of gardening and gunsmithing.

Similarly, defeatism was expressed but not allowed to prevail when a seventy-two-year-old man "passed out" late one evening while watching television and was brought to a hospital comatose, breathing with great difficulty, his neck rigid. A diagnosis of massive stroke was made and the recommendation at first was for transfer to a nursing home, with little to be done in any case and particularly because of the man's age and the fact that he also had chronic emphysema and now was paralyzed on one side.

But tests were carried out. They showed blood in the spinal fluid coming from the brain. Special X-ray studies revealed a large aneurysm, or ballooning out, of a brain artery. By tying off the artery in the neck region where it was accessible, thus cutting off blood flow through the vessel, the bleeding could be stopped. In six weeks, the patient recovered. The paralysis was gone. Six years later he is still well. Age, per se, even in the face of emphysema, was no real contraindication to treating a ruptured brain artery aneurysm.

At one hospital, a sixty-five-year-old man was admitted with massive vomiting of blood. He had been losing weight and complained of abdominal pains. Nine months before, surgery had been performed for cancer of the colon. Now, too, he had an enlarged liver and anemia. The admission diagnosis was recurrence of the cancer and some of the hospital doctors favored letting the man die "with dignity" of hemorrhage. Fortunately, an operation was performed to make certain of the diagnosis. It was wrong. He had a bleeding stomach ulcer which was removed with part of the stomach. The enlarged liver was found to be due to heart failure which could be treated. There was no cancer recurrence. The patient recovered and lived in good health for many years.

Another recent case involved an elderly woman with severe parkinsonism, or shaking palsy, and mental dullness. Her family had been told she would have to get along as well as she could. Fortunately, the family insisted upon consultation, and thorough neurological studies indicated a brain tumor. The tumor was removed successfully and the parkinsonism immediately disappeared. So, not long afterward, did the mental dullness. Rehabilitation was complete.

Surgery is certainly not the answer to all problems of the aged. But when surgery can be helpful, age should not stand in the way. Among the surgical procedures applied routinely to younger people but which could benefit afflicted elderly people too are the stripping of varicose veins to restore adequate blood circulation and avoid unyielding leg ulcers; the removal of hemorrhoids; the repair of dropped wombs, bladders, and rectal tissue; the repair of hernias and removal of enlarged prostates; and those we've covered, such as the nailing of hips and other broken bones; the reattachment of detached retinas and treatment of glaucoma and cataract; and the reversal, sometimes possible, of progressive hearing loss.

Concern for allowing elderly people to die with dignity when death is inevitable should not obscure the possibility that many can live with dignity if treated aggressively and hopefully with available measures, including surgical ones.

11

TOO OLD TO BE ACTIVE, VIGOROUS? NONSENSE!

In the United States Senate on December 29, 1970, Senator Jennings Randolph reported, not without some awe, on a demonstration he had witnessed in Charleston, West Virginia, while conducting a hearing for the Senate Committee on Aging.

He had watched a group of older people go through vigorous calisthenics. They ranged in age from sixty-five to eighty-five. All were suffering from chronic conditions or recovering from acute physical disabilities which had made them almost completely immobile. But that was before they began participating in a program of Physical Fitness for Senior Citizens developed by the Lawrence Frankel Foundation.

Only six months after beginning a series of carefully supervised, individualized calisthenics classes, they had become able to participate in community activities and have social contacts instead of watching from the sidelines in loneliness and depression, as Randolph noted. The program was a pilot project on which a statewide plan for physical fitness programs for the elderly might be based. And it seemed to Randolph, he told the Senate, that if such a program could benefit older people with physical disabilities and ailments, it might well be a preventive measure for others, helping to avoid physical decline in old age.

Among those in the group the senator was talking about was Carrie Minotti, seventy-two, who had broken both legs shortly after her husband had died in 1950 and had been told by doctors that she would never be able to bend one knee and perhaps never walk again, and who had spent the previous three years languishing in a residence home, doing little but reading, viewing TV, and watching others like herself sit in limbo. She now moves around freely.

Another, Claude L. Board, eighty-one, two years before had been totally incapacitated after a spinal operation; he now walks unassisted.

A third, Barbara Lawson, sixty-nine, had been sick with heart disease a year before, had suffered from spinal arthritis and a nerve ailment, and had required sleeping pills nightly. Now she does sit-ups and strength exercises, balances on a balance beam, and hasn't needed a sleeping pill since starting in the program.

Across the country in California, Clarence Dayton, a Huntington Park business man, had suffered through much of his adult life with agonizing migraine headaches. Nothing had seemed to deaden the pain. At the age of sixty-seven, six weeks after starting on a program of prescribed exercises, the headaches vanished. In his whole life he hardly ever worked up a good sweat. But the routine he follows today makes him feel so good he exercises out of doors even when it's raining.

In California, too, William Kinsey, eighty-seven-year-old retired president of the Union Theological Seminary in the Phillipines, carries out a jogging routine three times a week and observes that it "has made a much younger man out of me."

The two men are among 150 older people taking part in a long-range study being conducted by the University of Southern

California's Gerontology Center, which is providing evidence that people in their sixties and seventies and even beyond can retain, with carefully planned exercise, much of the vigor of their forties.

In Grenoble, France, sports-club members work out in a gym at least once a week and many, in addition, regularly hike, bowl, ride bikes, or swim while others ski cross-country. There is nothing remarkable about this except for one fact: the sports men and women are all at least sixty-two years old and some are more than ninety.

The club, set up in 1965, has attracted worldwide attention from behavioral scientists and others interested in the emotional as well as physical well-being of the aged. It is part of a Grenoble Office of Aged Persons conceived by a physician, Robert Hugonot and a philosopher, Michel Philibert. The goal of the program, in the words of the founders, is "integration of the third age"—to help retired citizens, members of the third age, to rejoin those of the first and second ages, students and working people. Additionally, it seeks to reclaim older people in the fourth age—the dependent and handicapped—by making them independent again.

The emphasis is on stimulating the elderly to make their own lives more vigorous and happy. "Old people," declares Dr. Hugonot, "often believe themselves pushed aside, forgotten. But they do it to themselves. Sitting makes you atrophy physically and watching TV soap operas does nothing much to exercise your brain. That can atrophy, too. The less you move around in the world and use your brain, the less you communicate with other human beings, and the more you're alone. You think you've been losing your memory lately? Try exercising your lungs along with the rest of your body. Go out into a forest and breathe deeply. You'll find your memory returning, your handwriting becoming steadier."

What is being proved in Charleston, in California, in Grenoble, and elsewhere is the falsity of a whole series of assumptions: that aging must inevitably bring debilitating physical decline; that such decline can neither be prevented nor remedied; that the aged are inherently incapable of exertion; that exercise and activity not only are largely beyond their capacities but even are dangerous for them, harmful rather than beneficial. What is being proved, positively, is that the elderly can and need to be active; that they even have a special need for activity; and that proper activity can produce remarkable results in rehabilitation of some of the seemingly most hopeless cases of decline and invalidism.

The value of physical activity at any age has come in for earnest scientific attention only very recently, largely because of concern over the rising heart attack epidemic. But more and more attention is also being given to other values of physical activity beyond its usefulness in helping to combat heart disease—at any age, and even particularly for the very aged.

Exercise and the Heart

While heart disease, the Number One killer in the United States and all advanced countries, has been increasing, so has evidence that sedentary, physically inactive living may be a major factor in bringing on the disease and that exercise can be important in combatting it.

For one thing, throughout the world, every large population found to have a low incidence of heart disease has proved to be more physically active than American and Western populations.

An early study by Dr. J. N. Morris in Great Britain showed that drivers of London double-decker buses who sat still had one and a half times as many heart attacks as did conductors who had to run up and down steps to collect fares.

An American study of 120,000 railroad workers showed almost twice as many heart attacks among sedentary office workers as among men working in the yards.

Of 355 Harvard football lettermen followed over a long period, 34 developed coronary heart disease—but not one man who had kept up an exercise program since leaving college had become a victim.

A United States government study in Framingham, Massachusetts, that has followed more than 5,000 men and women there for twenty-five years has shown that the most sedentary had a death rate from heart disease five times that of the most active.

In a United States Air Force study, 15,146 men aged eighteen to sixty-two were placed in a progressive exercise program while 12,000 men of similar ages in a comparison group did not participate. Among the exercising men, there were no heart attacks and no deaths; among the nonexercising, there were nine heart attacks and two deaths.

The latest British study by Dr. J. N. Morris covered 16,882 business executives aged 40 to 64. Heart attacks occurred in 232. Those who exercised vigorously had only one-third the risk of heart disease compared with those who did not exercise.

Moreover, if a heart attack does occur, the chances of surviving it appear to be increased by exercise. A study in New York covering 110,000 people showed not only that heart attacks were less likely among those who were physically active; also, among those who experienced attacks, the chances of surviving were five times greater among the physically active.

Exercise and the Aging Process

The evidence now is that exercise is important at all ages and that, in addition to lowering the risk of heart attack, it may do much to retard aging and the effects of aging.

According to the American Medical Association's Committee on Aging, continued physical activity often makes the difference between the fine figure of a man healthy and enjoying life at seventy and a man burdened by aches, pains, and boredom at the same age—if, in fact, the chair-bound man reaches age seventy.

At the University of Southern California, ninety-six volunteers aged sixty to eighty-seven took part in a test program. Starting very slowly and easily, they exercised three times a week, no more than an hour at a time. Even at the end of six weeks, they showed significant benefits, including a 6 percent drop in blood pressure and a gain of 9 percent in a measurement called "maximum oxygen uptake," which is considered to be a prime indicator of fitness.

At Michigan State University, Dr. Henry Montoye has found that regular exercise of proper intensity and duration increases not only physical capacity in the elderly but also their interest in other people and the world about them, their energy for doing mental work, and in general their vigor for carrying out everyday activities.

Dr. Ernst Jokl of the University of Kentucky, who urges exercise as "preventive medicine" to help prevent degenerative disease and slow down the physical deterioration that accompanies aging, is emphatic that "those who maintain activity have better performance records, less degenerative diseases, and probably a longer life expectancy than the general population. There is little doubt but that proper physical activity as part of a way of life can significantly delay the aging process."

The body systems most susceptible to alteration with aging are the skeletal, muscular, arterial, and nervous systems. Exercise helps because it sets up a whole series of interactions that supply energy, remove waste, and promote rest so tissues can maintain their functions longer. And not only can light-to-moderate physical activity in middle age help avoid deterioration, but even if symptoms produced by inactivity in the aging begin to appear, they usually disappear after systematic exercise and training.

A Special Need of Older People

Physical activity for the aged may have profound psychological value.

All of us start out, as children, relishing movement. Almost invariably, children enjoy movement just for the sake of moving. When they discover some new pattern of motion, they get pleasure out of performing it—in play, sports, dancing, and other activities—to the point of satiation.

But for sedentary elderly people, pleasure derived from movement is steadily reduced and eventually they may become reluctant to move at all. Not only does such inactivity lead to muscular degeneration. It also leads to definite psychological changes.

And an important psychological change is distortion of body image. Physically inactive people over fifty perceive their bodies to be heavier and broader than they actually are and, as a consequence of this distorted perception, they come to consider bodily movements increasingly strenuous.

Then ensues a vicious cycle: finding movements to be more and more strenuous, the elderly make less and less effort to move, and the restriction of activity only adds further to the distortion of body image, which then leads to greater clumsiness and greater fear of physical activity.

Moreover, with no physical outlet for the discharge of energy, internal tension in the elderly increases. And this increase is piled on top of internal tension caused by pent-up aggression.

Aggressive tendencies are not, of course, confined to the

elderly. The young have them and, whereas to some extent the young must restrain them, they have more opportunities to release their energies, to direct their aggressive tendencies outward, through bodily movements.

Older people, on the other hand, find the expression of aggression more difficult as the result of introversion, intellectualization, social status. Society, with its stereotypes for "proper" behavior in old age, also tends to immobilize people as they grow older. An elderly person is not expected to dance rock and roll or even to ride a bicycle. Rather, the older person is expected to be "dignified," which seems to be synonymous with confining oneself to restrained movement.

The buildup of tension in the elderly can produce such symptoms as insomnia, fretfulness, and restlessness. And the elderly often turn inward upon themselves their unreleased aggressive tendencies; these become a self-destructive force, leading to depression which, in turn, may increase tendencies toward psychosomatic diseases or lead to sudden outbursts of rage.

Regular bodily exercise, according to Drs. Hans and Sulomic Kreitler, can provide emotional satisfaction; it can break the vicious cycle in which body image distortions caused by inactivity lead to more inactivity and further distortions; it can use up energies that need to be used up and prevent internalization of aggression.

If aging cannot be avoided, people can learn to accept and live with it—and keeping active or becoming active again can contribute significantly to accepting and living with it most satisfactorily.

Better than a Tranquilizer

A recent American study compared the effects of a tranquilizer drug with those of exercise. The subjects, six women and four men aged fifty-two to seventy, were chosen because they exhibited one or more symptoms of anxiety: difficulty in sleeping, persistent feelings of tension or strain, irritability, unremitting worry, restlessness, inability to concentrate, and, in some cases, feelings of panic in everyday-life situations.

To make the study objective—avoiding subjective reports from patients on how they felt or didn't feel, since these do not lend themselves to accurate measurement—muscle tension was used as the criterion. Muscle tension, in fact, is commonly used in the evaluation of drug effects in anxiety states.

Each subject came to the laboratory every other day at the same time of day. Muscle tension was measured with an instrument called an electromyograph through electrodes applied to an arm and wrist. Measurements were made before and after each of a series of experimental treatments. In one experiment, patients were asked to simply sit comfortably and read for fifteen minutes; in another, to walk at various paces for fifteen minutes; in a third to take a tranquilizer; and in a fourth to take an identical-looking but inert preparation.

The study showed clearly that muscle tension could be reduced by large doses of tranquilizer—but it also could be reduced just as much by moderate walking for fifteen minutes.

And moderate exercise does not have the side effects of tranquilizers: it does not impair motor coordination or slow reaction time and impair automobile driving or other performance.

Prescriptions for Safe, Effective Exercise

Exercise, if it is sudden, violent, far beyond the capacity of the individual, can be dangerous for both the elderly and the young. But, generally, exercise begun very slowly and easily in a long-sedentary person and gradually intensified over a period of time is both effective and safe.

Moreover, authorities, including the Committee on Exercise of the American Heart Association, have been developing specific guidelines physicians can use in prescribing exercises as rationally as they can prescribe medication when needed. Until now physicians, who usually have had little training in exercise physiology, have had little concrete advice to offer.

Heart rate can be an important guide. There are standards for what the heart rate should be in various age groups. Physicians can use such standards to help assure that exercise is beneficial without causing excessive strain.

Older people can be taught to take their own heart rate, by taking their pulse at an artery in the wrist or at the side of the neck. By taking the pulse for fifteen seconds immediately after finishing an exercise, a reasonably valid estimate of heart rate attained during the exercise can be made. If this is recorded by the patient at each exercise session, the record can be of value to the physician for his follow-up prescription of exercise intensity and duration.

Various types of calisthenics and other exercises can be used. For all but very well-conditioned older men, for example, vigorous enough walking to raise the heart rate to 100 to 120 beats a minute for 30 to 60 minutes a day provides enough stimulus to bring about improvement in heart condition and breathing.

In one study carried out with a group of almost 100 men ranging up to 87 years of age and with an average age of 72, the men did one hour of calisthenics three times a week and, additionally, ran and walked for progressively increasing time periods. The study lasted 42 weeks and, on the average, body fat decreased by 4.8 percent, blood pressure was lowered by 6 percent, arm strength increased by 7.2 percent, and maximum oxygen consumption—considered the best single measure of vigor—increased by 9.2 percent.

One of the most striking changes resulting from the exercise program was a marked drop in nervous tension.

Exercise as Therapy

Exercise is being used today in a wide variety of conditions. Hospital bed rest has become almost obsolete. Soon after hernia, appendicitis, and other operations, and even the setting of bone fractures, patients are urged to get up and be ambulatory. This practice is based on evidence that inactivity may foster lung clots and other complications and that activity can help reduce their likelihood.

Emphysema is treated with exercise. In diabetes, exercise burns up excess blood sugar and may reduce the need for insulin. Exercise is often a key element now in the treatment of arthritis, back pain, and physical deformities and dysfunctions from accidents.

A group at the Frankel Foundation comes to its gym three times a week and for an hour each session engages in a variety of planned exercise programs. For a second group, living in a housing project, a general purpose utility room is utilized. People in this group bring their own rugs or carpets plus a fourteen-inch length of broom handle, and with this limited equipment, plus use of tape-recorded background music, activities similar to those of the first group are performed twice a week.

The third group includes residents of a home for the elderly. They are less ambulatory than the others; some are confined to wheelchairs, some to straight chairs or couches, and some use walkers. For this group, exercises are designed so that they can be carried out in any position the individual finds most comfortable—in a chair, on a couch, or on a carpeted floor. The calisthenics are done slowly and rhythmically to music.

The results have been striking. Included in the third group are people mentioned earlier in this chapter: the eighty-one-year-old man incapacitated after spinal surgery who, within a few weeks, could get about confidently even without a cane, and the seventy-two-year-old woman with broken legs who had become lethargic and depressed and now has a new outlook, performs well and gracefully in all activities, and leads her group in dance routines.

Such activity programs could help vast numbers of people whose socioeconomic, cultural, and educational backgrounds precluded any opportunity in their lives when young to participate in organized sport or recreation and who now, hopeless and dispirited, see ahead of them only stark years of old age.

Sex and the Aged

In any consideration of aging and the problems of the aged, sex deserves, yet rarely gets, serious attention. Sexuality, no monopoly of the young, is present all through life, and sexual relationships can and should have as deep meanings for the elderly as for the young.

Sexual activity, indeed, often can be therapeutic for an older person, helping to reduce psychological tension, to maintain morale through a sense of satisfaction at the retention of masculinity or femininity, and possibly even, some evidence suggests, helping to ease pain and improve mobility for arthritics through its stimulating effect on adrenal gland output of hormones such as cortisone. Alert physicians today also are concerned with encouraging and guiding the return to sexual activity of patients after heart attacks at any age, and there are some who believe sexual activity may possibly have some value in reducing the risk of heart attack.

Yet in our culture a notion persists that by the time anyone is in his or her seventies—and even sixties—sex is not necessary, often is not possible, and in any case is neither normal nor nice. That notion can do, and too often is doing, incalculable harm.

Modern scientific studies show that capability for sexual activity persists into advanced age. Women's ovaries stop functioning at menopause but this has little influence on libido. And in men the cells that produce sperm diminish with age as do those that produce the male hormone testosterone, yet these events need not interfere significantly with potency.

Kinsey, Masters and Johnson, and other investigators of sexual behavior have found that a satisfying sex life is possible in the seventies, eighties, and even beyond. At Duke University's Center for the Study of Aging, where researchers have been following sexuality continuously in aging people over periods of many years, a notable finding has been that 15 percent of the men and women in the study show a steadily *increasing* rate of sexual interest and activity as they get older.

Each year there are some 3,500 marriages among the twenty million Americans over the age of sixty-five, and sexual activity is cited along with companionship as one reason for these late unions.

Moreover, in the last census, more than 18,000 couples over sixty-five listed themselves as unmarried and living together, and the actual number is undoubtedly far greater. In Sun City, Florida, and in other places across the nation, it has become apparent that elderly people in growing numbers are having emotionally close, long-term affairs. Rather than marry, many pair off in what sometimes are called "unmarriages of convenience"—relationships for companionship and sex which are never formalized because the couples, if married, would receive less income from Social Security and other retirement benefits than they do by remaining single.

Even the proprietors of some nursing homes have begun to realize that sexual interest and capacity can persist in the elderly. Up to a few years ago, an old couple admitted to a home were separated and their sex life ended. Now more and more they are being allowed to live together. Some institutions also have become more tolerant of sexual contact between unmarried residents.

But many of the elderly—the married as well as widowed, the noninstitutionalized as well as the institutionalized—lead sex-impoverished lives. Brought up to believe mistakenly that sexual capacity must decline and even disappear with age or that sexual activity is dangerous to their health, many give up sex to a great extent or even completely.

Some, aware of continuing sexual interest and urges, feel guilty about having them and try to shut them out. Some fear being ridiculed by their children if they evince any interest in sex. Many whose sexual performance has fallen off or failed worry about it, yet, out of shame, seek no help. And too often, when help is sought, doctors dismiss the problem with a "There, there; that's to be expected, and it's nothing to be concerned about."

We need an end to a nonsensical social deprecation of sexuality in the aged, a silly and harmful carryover of sexual puritanism which, if it is now less pervasive in terms of sex for the young, considers sex associated with wrinkles to be less than acceptable and even ludicrous.

And we need positive efforts to help older people express and enjoy and profit from their natural sexuality.

Often, anxiety can be relieved when older people are given to understand some of the basic physiological facts. As he ages, a man's responses may slow; he may take longer to achieve erection and orgasm and a second erection takes longer. Although such slowing in itself need not interfere with pleasure, if misinterpreted it can arouse anxiety over possible oncoming impotency, and the anxiety can lead to impotency.

Similarly, some elderly women experience vaginal changes—such as decreases in elasticity and lubrication—which may make the sexual act irritating and may even cause orgasm to become painful. But such problems can be overcome in many cases with hormonal treatment.

Doctors can and should do much else to help elderly people who have or believe they have sexual problems. Older people with heart conditions, both men and women, often fear that the sex act may lead to a heart attack. But the fact is that this is extremely rare. Nor need angina pectoris, the chest pain associated with coronary heart disease, interfere. Many patients who use nitroglycerin to terminate angina attacks and even to head them off when they occur under other circumstances are advised by their physicians to use the drug just before intercourse.

There is some possibility, as we have noted, that arthritics may benefit from sex activity. And for those crippled by arthritis, a knowledgeable physician can provide specific suggestions, depending upon the individual patient, for intercourse positions that allow freer participation.

12

NUTRITION AND THE ELDERLY

To what extent may diseases and discomforts of the aged be due to malnutrition?

Nobody knows, but there is substantial evidence that malnutrition is frequently involved and is sometimes a major factor. And there are striking examples of improvement of health, both physical and mental, when nutritional deficiencies are detected and overcome.

A Subject of National Concern

Once relegated to grade school "health" classes and touched

on there only briefly and superfically, nutrition—or, more accurately, the extent of *inadequate* nutrition—has become a subject of national concern and controversy.

The aged are particularly affected. Malnutrition is also common among the poor. But it is far from being all a matter of money.

We are not only a nation of nutritional illiterates; we even believe that nutritional ignorance and consequent malnutrition are vices only of the poor.

A full pocket does not mean a nourished gut. Of 83,000 people in ten states, one-fourth of those living below the poverty level were outrightly anemic for lack of sufficient iron in their diets; 8 percent were deficient in vitamin C and 17 percent in vitamin B_2. But similar deficiencies existed also among people living above the poverty level. And people over sixty in all income levels and ethnic groups had signs of general undernutrition.

Regardless of income level, many Americans' intake for several vital nutrients—calcium, iron, vitamin B_6, and magnesium—is below recommended levels. Yet research funds that might have helped put the rather shaky science of nutrition on a firmer basis have been all but eliminated by the federal government in recent years.

As a consequence, an ignorant public has been left at the mercy of the food industry and a growing army of faddists, diet concocters, vitamin hawkers, and self-styled nutritionists.

For many Americans, food choices are not nutritional choices but instead are directed by an interminable advertising barrage and the need of supermarket turnover.

In a typical supermarket, the shopper faces a dazzling array of goodies with little or no nutritive value, and the American diet relies increasingly on prepared foods, preconcocted meals, and synthetic imitations, many with a list of artificial ingredients that might well "make a chemist's tongue curl."

With about half of the food dollar going for processed foods, many people have difficulty knowing what they are getting. In processing, some nutrients are destroyed or lost and not all are replaced when the finished product is "enriched." For example, when whole wheat is milled into white flour, more than half of each of fourteen essential vitamins and minerals is lost; but white bread is usually "enriched" with only four of them.

The Special Influences in the Aged

For many reasons, nutritional problems in the general population may be magnified in the elderly.

The low or marginal income of many of the aged is only one reason.

Lack of interest in eating because of loneliness is not uncommon, particularly in elderly people who live alone.

Food faddism is an important determinant of the diet of many older people. In searching for relief for ailments that have not been eliminated by medical treatment, many old people grasp at the promises of the panacea merchants. Arthritis sufferers, for example, are commonly the prey of quacks. To the elderly, too, is directed much propaganda for youth elixirs, "natural" foods, wonder diets. Expenditures for such items may leave little in a limited budget for a varied diet.

Malnutrition may accentuate the lack of appetite in the elderly. By making the older person feel sick and weak, malnutrition not only may perpetuate but even accelerate itself.

Moreover, aging, insofar as it is accompanied by a decline in physical activity, brings with it a decrease in overall need for food—but not for food values. Actually, the elderly should have more food value per unit of food than younger people, who have larger food intakes. In what they do eat, older people should have a greater density of such vital elements as proteins, minerals, and vitamins. But often they do not.

Some Specific Findings in the Elderly

It has often been noted that when they are hospitalized and particular attention is paid to diet, chronically emaciated persons frequently respond not only with rapid gains of up to 15 percent in body weight but also with improvement in general health and the disappearance of varied aches, pains, and other symptoms that evidently were due to nutritional deficiencies.

A noted New York medical nutrition specialist found very often among the aged a condition which he and his colleagues named nicotinic acid deficiency encephalopathy, a brain disease brought on by a lack of this B complex vitamin. Insidious in onset, it produces early, vague symptoms such as fatigue, irritability, nervousness, and depression. Later, if undetected and uncorrected, it leads to intellectual impairment, which may be followed still later by stupor and coma.

Recently, folic acid deficiency has been discovered in many elderly people, sometimes associated with mental and neurologic changes. (Folic acid, one of the principal vitamins, is found mainly in fresh green leafy vegetables and fruit, organ meats, liver, and dried yeast.)

Upon examining patients—many of them elderly and malnourished—with neurologic complaints of various kinds, investigators in Toronto found some with very low blood levels of folic acid. In addition to suffering from irritability, sleeplessness, forgetfulness, and other such neurologic problems, some showed definite anemia from folic acid deficiency.

Because other investigators, in England and Scotland, had reported finding markedly reduced levels of folic acid in residents in old people's homes, the Toronto physicians studied 598 elderly patients admitted to hospitals from homes for the aged and a geriatric center, another 51 admitted from their own homes, and a third group (for comparison) of 100 younger, healthy subjects. They found very low folic acid levels in 24 percent of the patients from institutions for the aged, in 7.8 percent of those admitted from their own homes, and even (the more surprisingly) in 5 percent of the younger, healthy group. Studies are now under way to determine exactly how much disability results from folic acid deficiency and the extent to which the disability can be overcome by folic acid treatment.

Striking Recoveries with Treatment

When nutritional disorders are pinpointed in the aged, the results of treatment may be dramatic.

When a sixty-six-year-old man was hospitalized, it was because of a whole series of disturbances, progressively more worrisome and puzzling. Eighteen months before, he had first begun to experience a feeling of numbness in his hands. There ensued a gradual deterioration of his personality. First came memory disturbance, then mental apathy, then a confusional state. Four months prior to admission, he began to have difficulty talking. One month before admission, he developed an unsteady gait and weakness of the legs.

With thorough study, he was found to have a marked vitamin B_{12} deficiency. After two months of treatment with the vitamin, the mental changes were gone. After another four months of treatment, the numbness of his hands and weakness of his legs disappeared and subsequently his gait improved.

A sixty-five-year-old woman who had experienced increasing weakness of the legs over a four-year period was totally free of the weakness after a year of B_{12} treatment. After a similar course of treatment, a sixty-five-year-old man was relieved of unsteady gait, soreness of the calves, and numbness of the feet.

Many other disturbances traced to other vitamin deficiencies have also responded.

An eighty-three-year-old woman was hospitalized because of a confusional state. Soon after admission she was found to have bronchopneumonia which responded to treatment, but she remained confused. The confusion cleared completely with vitamin B complex treatment, and within three weeks she could be discharged home as a mentally normal person.

An eighty-nine-year-old woman who lived with her daughter was hospitalized on the recommendation of her physician because of an abdominal mass, puzzling anemia, and confusion. The abdominal mass proved to be a distended bladder and when she was catheterized to release the retained urine, the mass disappeared completely.

Tests showed that her anemia was of the iron-deficiency type and yet her blood level of iron was high. It seemed that she was not utilizing iron properly. When she was treated with vitamin B complex and folic acid plus iron, her anemia disappeared and her mental state became normal.

A seventy-two-year-old woman who lived alone was admitted to a hospital because of confusion and a variety of physical symptoms for which various medications prescribed by her physician had been of no help. It soon became evident that she had been grossly undernourished and was suffering in particular from pellagra, a deficiency disease caused by lack of a vitamin, niacin. When she was treated with niacin and fed on regular hospital food, she quickly improved and, when discharged home, was normal.

When an eighty-four-year-old woman who lived alone was hospitalized, it was because of an acute exacerbation of chronic bronchitis. While that was being successfully treated, she was also found to be suffering from slight confusion and from bone tenderness and multiple bruises over her body. Tests showed marked vitamin C deficiency. On one gram of vitamin C daily, she could be discharged in two weeks, free of confusion, bruises, and bone tenderness.

A seventy-year-old woman who lived with her husband was hospitalized with a heart murmur, fever, anemia, lethargy, and confusion. Not long before, she had spent some time in a psychiatric hospital because of attempted suicide. She was treated for six weeks with penicillin for endocarditis, an inflammation of the lining of the heart. The inflammation cleared. But she still complained of lethargy, depression, painful legs (actually, bone tenderness). Scattered bruises over her body raised the possibility of vitamin C deficiency; a test confirmed the deficiency; and after a gram of vitamin C daily for three weeks, she could go home free of all symptoms.

Not Just a Matter of Vitamins

Dietary deficiencies especially prevalent among elderly patients are not limited to inadequate vitamin intake.

In the late years, maintaining an adequate level of calcium, for example, is important in helping to prevent osteoporosis, the thinning of bone structure that leads to so much pain and disability through fractures and collapse of vertebrae. Yet few older people consume milk, and, if they do, it may be in the form of cottage cheese, from which some of the calcium has been removed during manufacture.

Calcium is essential not only early in life for bone growth but also all through life to prevent a negative balance in which the material is transferred from bone into the bloodstream, weakening the bone structure. Investigators have found that patients with osteoporosis absorb and retain calcium avidly when fed diets high in the mineral. Symptoms of osteoporosis then may be relieved.

Similarly, calcium is essential in the bony structure around tooth sockets. Periodontal disease, which leads to weakening of that bony structure, is a major cause of tooth loss. Evidence that dietary supplements of calcium may help comes from a recent Cornell University study with eighty adults having periodontal disease. When treated for up to twelve months with any one of three forms of calcium in a dosage of 1 gram a day—fat-free dried milk, dicalcium phosphate, or calcium gluconolactate-calcium carbonate—they showed marked increases in density of jaw bone.

New Elements Enter the Picture

An Air Force officer was about to receive a medical discharge because of severe artery hardening. He had had a heart attack several years before and had recovered from that. But now he had attacks of severe chest pain. His leg arteries also had been affected by arteriosclerosis to the point where he could walk no more than a block without having to stop because of leg pain. He complained, too, of failing memory; arteriosclerosis was affecting brain arteries.

Instead of a discharge, he was placed in a group of men with severe artery hardening who were receiving zinc sulfate capsules as an experimental treatment. Like most of the others, he showed marked improvement. Within two months, he was able to walk well enough to carry out regular duties. His memory improved and his chest pain disappeared.

Zinc, as noted earlier, has been found to help many people with taste disturbances. And some children suffering from retarded growth have low zinc levels; when given small amounts their appetites improve and in some there is a significant increase in growth.

Zinc is what is known as a trace element. One of the most fascinating and promising new areas of medical research today has to do with trace elements, which include copper, chromium, magnesium, and others. Only recently have they begun to be recognized as essential for normal body functioning. They seem to work at the most basic level of metabolism, influencing the activity of body enzymes and perhaps protein structure.

Even the best diet provides only small quantities of trace elements. The body has low capacity for storing most of them. And even though they are required in amounts as low as twenty parts per billion, a deficiency can result from any upset in the delicate balance between intake, absorption, and use.

Investigators are looking into the unhealthful effects not only of deficiencies but of excesses, and they are also examining interrelationships: how a little more or less of one trace element may affect need for others. It's a complex field, but already some practical values are emerging and many more are likely to in the future.

In addition to its promise in combatting the effects of artery hardening, retarded growth, and taste disturbances, zinc can speed the healing of wounds, including surgical incisions. And some schizophrenic patients fed zinc supplements seem to be showing improvement in mental state; investigators think it is because an abnormal blood protein found in these patients may contain copper when it should contain zinc. Possibly the zinc supplements displace the copper.

Chromium may favorably affect diabetes and artery disease. In early trials, chromium supplements have helped some diabetic patients. One reason seems to be that the metal, which declines in body tissues with age, is an essential part of a natural body material called "glucose tolerance factor" which potentiates insulin; activity of the factor declines with decrease in chromium, and, as a result, the effectiveness of insulin may also diminish. Investigators also have found, first in animals and recently in early human trials, that small supplements of chromium may help in artery disease by reducing cholesterol levels in the blood.

Fluorine is another trace element. Early studies in animals suggest that a deficiency of it reduces reproductive ability and impairs growth. And research at the Mayo Clinic suggests that fluorine may stimulate bone formation and may, in combination with calcium and vitamin D, help patients with osteoporosis.

Cadmium is also under study. People with high blood pressure appear to have an excess of it. There is some suspicion that an excess also may be involved in kidney disorders.

Although no role in human health has been determined at this early stage in trace-element research for selenium, manganese, molybdenum, and other elements, some have been found to be essential in animals and may well turn out to be so for man. For example, manganese-deficient animals show growth retardation, seizures, and impaired lactation. And molybdenum deficiency in animals has been found to be associated with growth failure and early death.

Practical Values

As of now, in a few specific instances, trace-element treatment may be prescribed: for example, zinc to speed wound healing and correct taste disorders; chromium as a possible help for diabetes; fluorine as a hopeful aid in osteoporosis.

But beyond this, trace-element research underscores even more than ever before the need for a balanced diet. The elements, which can be properly called micronutrients, are to be found in many foods. Some foods may contain relatively little; some much more. More of one element than another may be found in particular foods.

Until there are more detailed studies of precise requirements for the elements and much more detailed knowledge of interactions between elements, a balanced diet and a varied one—heavily weighted with unprocessed foods: fruits, vegetables, animal products, and these in variety rather than always the same ones—is the best source of the micronutrients, making it unlikely that there will be deficiencies or excesses.

Other New Research on Diet and Diet Therapy

Several new investigations are worth noting here. They are in early stages, not yet definitive, subject to more extensive verification. But they suggest some of the potentialities for diet and diet therapy.

Can diet possibly help overcome hearing loss and vertigo associated with inner ear disorder? So the work of one physician, an ear specialist, suggests. Himself a victim of progressive hearing loss and episodes of vertigo for five years, he decided to go on a low-carbohydrate, low-cholesterol diet for a different reason: to lower the high blood levels of cholesterol and fats found during a routine checkup. On the diet, he lost more than twenty pounds, and blood cholesterol and fat levels also dropped. Much to his surprise, within three months he also regained 87 percent of his lost hearing.

Checking on 444 patients with inner ear problems, he found that 46.6 percent had marked elevations of blood fats and another 10.3 percent had borderline elevations. Although follow-up studies are not yet complete, many patients with clear or borderline elevations who have been following a low-carbohydrate, low-cholesterol diet have been showing improvement of hearing.

Because high blood-cholesterol levels are associated with clogging of arteries of the heart and brain, among others, many physicians hope that keeping the levels low by diet and, when necessary, by drugs, may retard and possibly prevent the clogging. But can such measures reverse already-present disease?

Hope that the latter may be possible comes from studies at the University of Chicago. Investigators fed monkeys on high cholesterol diets for eighteen months and when, at the end of this period, some of the animals were autopsied, extensive artery clogging was found. Of the remaining animals who had not been sacrificed but would be expected to have the same clogging, some were put on a low fat diet while others were continued on high fat foods. Later, when the animals were autopsied, those switched to low fat diets had significantly fewer clogging deposits than those continued on high fat intake. To some degree, the investigators believe, even advanced stages of artery disease may be reversed if sufficiently low blood-cholesterol levels are sustained for a long period of time.

Many misconceptions abound about diet and migraine. Some victims have sought to avoid repeated migraine attacks by living primarily on such things as bananas and onions. Yet some dietary measures can be helpful in many cases. Certain foods do have an effect on blood vessels that may trigger migraine in some people. Such foods include aged or strong cheese, particularly cheddar; pickled herring; chicken livers; pods or broad beans; canned figs; and red wines and champagne—and avoidance of these benefits some migraine patients. For some, cured meats, such as frankfurters, bacon, ham, and salami may be culprits, and a trial of avoiding them may be useful. It is also important for migraine victims to avoid low blood sugar; for this reason they should eat three well-balanced meals a day and avoid excessive amounts of carbohydrates—sugars and starches—at any one meal.

Eating raw vegetables, it now appears, may be an important factor in avoiding stomach cancer. When 160 men and 68 women with stomach cancer were compared with other men and women without cancer or other gastrointestinal disease, with both groups matched in terms of age, country of birth, nationality of parents and grandparents, only one substantial difference between them was found. The healthy people ate far more raw vegetables than did the cancer patients. And low risk of stomach cancer seemed to be associated particularly with the eating of raw lettuce, tomatoes, carrots, cole slaw, and red cabbage.

In modern society, with heavy emphasis on refined foods, there is very little roughage in the diet of many people. Some investigators now are studying the possibility that the lack of roughage may be responsible in advanced countries for diverticulitis and other gastrointestinal problems that are relatively rare in less advanced nations where diets contain much roughage.

Can roughage—in the form of a diet high in plant fiber or even in the form of a bran supplement—help people with constipation problems on the one hand and others with nonspecific diarrhea? Researchers have measured intestinal transit time—the time needed for food to move through the intestinal tract—in a group of patients on their usual diet (a conventional refined diet with low content of plant fiber) and then again after four weeks on either a high-fiber diet or the usual diet supplemented with about thirty grams of unprocessed bran daily. On either the changed diet or the bran supplement, transit time in those in whom it originally was slow was reduced from a mean of 3.8 days to 2.4 days, a change helpful in overcoming constipation. In contrast, transit time in those in whom it was fast originally was lengthened from a mean of 1 day to a mean of 1.72 days, a change helpful in overcoming diarrhea.

What Do the Elderly Really Need?

Except under unusual medical circumstances, the elderly do not necessarily need the same total quantities, only the same types of foods that younger people need.

But there has been great unnecessary confusion even about the essential types of foods for the population in general.

Although foods can properly be divided into seven groups, as we'll shortly see, what has long been promoted is a "Basic Four" grouping. People have been exhorted to use daily foods selected from each of the four groups: meat (for protein); milk (for calcium); fruits and vegetables (for vitamins and minerals); and breads and cereals (for energy).

But there are shortcomings to such an oversimplified set of groups. Are all fruits and vegetables much alike? Hardly. Consider vitamin A content. While a mango contains 8000 international units of the vitamin and an apricot contains 5000, a banana has 400, an orange 290, and an apple only 120. As for vitamin C, an orange, with 75 milligrams of C, is fine, and a mango has a useful 55 milligrams, but an apricot, an apple, and a banana hardly have enough to help the eater avoid an acute case of scurvy.

The "protein group" idea misleads many people into thinking that cereals furnish no protein when, in fact, they are the major source throughout the world. And the "energy group" distinction has been criticized because it suggests to many people that all foods in it are much like sugar in contributing calories and very little if anything more.

The recommendation of many authorities now is that the elderly—and the general population—use a seven-group daily food guide. Amounts considered desirable vary somewhat between child, teen-ager, adult, and aging adult—for the elderly the amounts are somewhat lower—but choices from each group each day are considered essential.

Here is the grouping along with quantities for elderly people:

GROUP	DAILY AMOUNT FOR THE ELDERLY
Milk or milk products	2 or more cups
Meat, fish, poultry, eggs	2 or more servings*
Green and yellow vegetables	At least 1 serving
Citrus fruits and tomatoes	1 to 2 servings
Potatoes, other fruits and vegetables	1 serving
Bread, cereals, and pasta	2 to 3 servings
Butter or margarine	1 to 2 servings

Milk or milk products include cottage cheese, yogurt, cheeses, and ice cream, and contribute calcium, vitamins B_2, B_{12}, and A, many minerals (but not iron), and protein. Low-fat milk can be substituted for whole milk.

Meat, fish, poultry, and eggs contain large quantities of protein. Fish and poultry have less fat than most meats. Eggs contain virtually all vitamins and minerals but large amounts of cholesterol. Liver is rich in iron and vitamin A, but also cholesterol.

Green and yellow vegetables—excellent sources of minerals and A, B, and E vitamins—include spinach, kale, Swiss chard, watercress, collard, mustard and turnip (the greens), and carrots, pumpkin, squash of various types, and yams (the yellows).

Citrus fruits and tomatoes contribute vitamin C. Lettuce, cabbage, and other raw salad greens also can be included in this group and provide vitamin C but not as much of it as tomatoes, oranges, grapefruit, tangerines, and other citrus fruits.

Potatoes, other vegetables, and fruits include broccoli, Brussels sprouts, green peppers, and cauliflower, berries, cher-

*A meat, meat substitute, or vegetable serving is often considered to be 3½ ounces.

ries, melons, and peaches. They contribute vitamin C, minerals, some protein, and energy.

Bread, cereals, and pasta provide proteins, iron, and B vitamins as well as carbohydrates. They help fill energy requirements. Enriched flour and cornmeal offer vitamins B_1 and B_2, niacin, and iron. And whole-grain flour, bread, and brown rice contain other B vitamins, minerals, and desirable roughage.

Butter and fortified margarine provide vitamin A as well as calories. Margarine may be substituted for butter by people who have elevated cholesterol levels.

Nutrition and diet may once have been considered matters not warranting serious medical concern. But physicians today are viewing American eating patterns in general as disastrous, leading to overfeeding but undernourishment—and the more alert among them are increasingly aware that helping elderly patients to establish good eating patterns can be a vital element in keeping them healthy and, not infrequently, in restoring their health.

13

MEDICATION AND THE ELDERLY

The patient was an elderly man in a distraught state. The physician was alert and knowledgeable. When the patient told him that he felt he was losing his mind, could not concentrate, and feared for his very existence, one of the first things the physician checked was the man's use of medications.

Among the drugs he was using was phenobarbital—and, knowing that phenobarbital, which produces few adverse effects in younger people, sometimes can cause confusion, excitement, fear, and anxiety in the elderly, the physician immediately stopped the man's use of the sedative. That was all that was needed.

More than 7,000 drugs are now available and the number is being added to every year. While modern medicines can be valuable and quite often lifesaving, they can also be a source of trouble. It has been estimated that 1,500,000 hospital admissions a year are the result of adverse drug reactions. A survey in one hospital recently showed that over 30 percent of the inpatients were there because of drug-induced ailments.

There are problems of side effects and of special sensitivities of individual patients; problems of undesirable interactions between two or more drugs; problems of improper dosage. In the elderly, impairment of drug metabolism may sometimes add to the difficulties.

If you're concerned about an elderly parent and there has been no recent—and thorough—consideration of medicines being used and whether they conceivably may be causing trouble, you may want to seek answers from the physician to a number of questions:

Is each medicine in use really necessary? What is its nature and what does it do? Does it have possible undesirable side effects? What are those side effects so they can be recognized for what they are if they occur? Is it possible that if several prescribed drugs are being used, they may interact with each other detrimentally? And could nonprescription drugs that are being used interact with one another and/or with the prescribed drugs in detrimental fashion? Is it possible that any drug being used could be a factor in inducing malnutrition, and, if so, could this be compensated for?

Side Effects

In a recent study of patients taking prescribed drugs at home, over 83 percent were found to be in possible danger because they knew so little about the drugs. The study established that the greatest lack of knowledge was in the area of side effects. Almost three-fourths of the patients did not know *any* symptoms at all which might indicate harmful side effects of their medicines.

Here are a few examples of some of the side effects of frequently used—and valuable—drugs:

For a penicillin preparation: hives, skin rash, itching, diarrhea, nausea, and vomiting.

For an adrenocortical steroid, or cortisonelike drug, sometimes employed in the treatment of arthritis and severe skin and allergic diseases: moon face, excess hair, aggravation of diabetes, activation and complication of peptic ulcer, sweating, vertigo, weakness, headache, nausea, aggravation of infection, increased blood pressure, facial reddening.

For an agent used in the treatment of high blood pressure and psychiatric disorders: nausea, vomiting, loss of appetite, diarrhea, aggravation of peptic ulcer, itching, skin rash, dryness of mouth, nose bleed, nasal congestion, weight gain, impotence, increased susceptibility to colds, muscular aches.

These are *very* valuable drugs—and not unusual in producing side effects on occasion. Almost any drug may do so, as may almost anything taken into the human body under certain conditions.

People have varying sensitivities. While most people, for example, can eat eggs with impunity—as many and as often as they choose—others suffer upsets after eating a single egg.

Sensitivity also can change. Some people can go right on being exposed repeatedly to ragweed pollen or poison ivy, or can take aspirin over a lifetime, without any undesirable reaction. Others, however, may do so for prolonged periods but then comes a time when suddenly they react strongly—with hay fever, skin rash, or aspirin-induced gastritis.

A major reason for drug side effects is that no medication is 100 percent specific, that is, striking only the target at which it is aimed. Any drug is to some degree scattershot, with effects other than those desired.

For example, an antibiotic may sometimes successfully overcome a serious infection yet produce gastrointestinal upsets—cramps, diarrhea, rectal itching. The upsets stem from disturbance of body ecology, of natural germ balance. Always in the gastrointestinal tract there are many harmless bacteria; some, in fact, are essential, aiding in digestion and even helping to produce needed vitamins. When a powerful antibiotic with a broad range of action against disease organisms is introduced, it may also decimate normal bacterial populations, leading to gastrointestinal upsets. But this doesn't always happen. Individual sensitivity apparently plays a role here, too.

Side effects from drugs may occur for patients of any age. Generally, they occur in only a small percentage of patients, five percent or even less.

But undesirable reactions may be more frequent in the aged who have impairments of drug metabolism and whose bodies as a consequence do not break down and eliminate some drugs as do the bodies of other people.

Gastrointestinal disorders, for example, are a common complaint among the elderly. But some of the drugs most frequently used to quell gastrointestinal spasm and quiet the intestinal tract may cause varied problems in some of the elderly. Among those drugs are atropine-like ones that are valuable but in overdoses may produce mental confusion for any patient regardless of age. In some of the aging, even a proper therapeutic dose may cause extreme distress. And various other drugs in addition to the atropine-like ones may cause confusion, leading to excitement, mental disorientation, visual hallucinations, and sometimes even convulsions, which may persist until medication is stopped and for as long as twenty-four hours afterward.

In some of the elderly with weakened bladder tone, urinary retention may occur with use of such drugs for gastrointestinal disturbances, or with use of others such as some antiparkinsonism agents, certain antidepressants, and even minor tranquilizers.

The use of any potent modern drug involves a calculated risk and, ideally, should also involve alertness. The decision for use should be based on the likelihood that a drug may do so much good that any risks that may be involved are justified. And, given alertness on the part of patient and physician, any risks can be minimized when, at the earliest indications of undesirable effects, they are overcome by change of dosage, switch of medication, addition of other medication, or, if necessary, discontinuance of treatment.

However, a physician may hesitate to alert a patient to possible side effects on the grounds that to do so would make the patient anxious and might nullify treatment. If the patient is under very close medical supervision, the physician, of course, can watch for undesirable effects. But often the patient is not under such supervision.

It can sometimes be a tough, time-consuming task to help a patient to understand that, just as crossing a street carries risk, so does medication; that that possible risk should not prevent crossing the street if getting to the other side is necessary. It should be made clear that a risk might not of itself prevent using medication when the medication can do good; that watching for side effects is like watching for traffic that may be around a bend in the road; that there may be no side effects just as there may be no hazardous traffic, in which case, fine; or there may be side effects as there may be hazardous traffic and then, too, fine—if note is taken before any real harm is done.

However difficult it may be to achieve in some cases, such understanding can be vital. And if sometimes it cannot be achieved with a particular elderly patient, it may be with a member of the patient's family, who should alert the physician at the slightest sign of trouble with a medication.

Drug Interactions

Ten days after being released from a hospital, recovered from a heart attack, a patient developed an alarming new condition. While in the hospital, as part of treatment, he had received an anticoagulant drug to prevent potentially dangerous blood clotting. At home, he continued to take the drug as directed. But now it was thinning his blood far too much, putting him in danger of fatal hemorrhaging. Something had changed.

In the hospital, the patient had received phenobarbital before retiring. The sedative, during its activity in the body, had stimulated certain liver enzymes. These enzymes had broken down quickly an anticoagulant he was also taking. At home, without the phenobarbital, the anticoagulant activity was more potent, longer lasting. Without the sedative, what had been a proper dose of anticoagulant had become an overdose, which might have thinned his blood too much with danger of resulting hemorrhage. Once this was understood, the anticoagulant dosage could be quickly adjusted.

The effect of one drug upon another—their interaction —has become a matter of growing medical concern. The need has become essential to recognize that two or more drugs taken at the same time or in close sequence may act independently or may interact to increase or reduce the intended effect of one or both drugs or produce a new and undesired reaction.

Only recently have many important drug interactions been observed, and the list is growing rapidly.

For example, aspirin or an aspirinlike compound (salicylate) is sold not only in tablets but is an ingredient of other nonprescription remedies for headaches and other aches and pains, and for colds and fever. It is also found in some over-the-counter sleeping tablets and other readily available combinations. Aspirin and other salicylates can interact with anticoagulant drugs to increase the anticoagulant or anticlotting effect, bringing on bleeding. Aspirin and other salicylates can also decrease the effectiveness of drugs taken for gout.

Many nonprescription nose drops and sprays, decongestant medicines for coughs, sinusitis, and colds, and prescription drugs used to suppress appetite contain chemicals called sympathomimetic amines. These can counteract the effect of drugs used to lower high blood pressure. They can also produce a dangerous rise in blood pressure in people taking certain antidepressant drugs, especially those known as "MAO inhibitors," which include Parnate, Marplan, and Nardil. These and other MAO inhibitors, such as the antibiotic furazolidone (Furoxone) and the antihypertensive drug pargyline (Eutonyl) interact similarly with tyramine, a compound found in aged cheeses and Chianti wines.

Nose drops and related medications may tend to cause irregular heartbeats and, when they are taken together with digitalis, heartbeat irregularity is much more likely.

Alcohol adds to or changes the effects of many drugs. It is especially dangerous to drink when taking sedatives, sleeping pills, and other drugs which, like alcohol, depress the central nervous system.

Many prescription medicines interact adversely with anticoagulant drugs. A number of antibiotics and also the drug clofibrate (Atromid-S) used to lower blood cholesterol increase the effect of anticlotting agents. On the other hand, barbiturates and the sleeping medicine glutethimide (Doriden) decrease the anticlotting effect of anticoagulants.

The blood-sugar-lowering effect of antidiabetes drugs is increased, sometimes too much, by MAO inhibitors and salicylates.

Overdosage and Underdosage

One problem in connection with the use of potent modern drugs is the hangover of an old idea still shared by many people: If a little is good, more must be better.

With potent agents, excessive dosage can lead to serious

trouble. Instructed to take a prescribed dose of an anticoagulant—a drug that thins the blood and helps prevent clot formation—a man had to be hospitalized a few days later because of severe nosebleeds and vomiting of blood. He had doubled the dose and induced hemorrhaging.

An asthma patient had to be hospitalized because of heart palpitations after she had used a medication for her asthma at almost hourly intervals instead of just a few times a day as prescribed by her physician.

Patients who have taken more than prescribed doses of steroids, or cortisonelike drugs, have induced in themselves alarming changes in personality, marked fluid retention and weight gains, and other effects.

Underdosage, too, can cause problems. Not only may inadequate doses of a drug fail to help a patient when proper doses would help; the inadequate doses may allow the disease to advance and may even lead to resistance to treatment. When, for example, an antibiotic is used to fight an infection and the patient discontinues it prematurely, as soon as he or she begins to feel better, the infection may flare again and now the newly multiplying organisms may be resistant to the drug.

Almost invariably when studies are made of the compliance of patients with physicians' prescriptions, investigators are astonished at the high incidence of lack of compliance.

One example: the use of penicillin in patients with rheumatic fever when they develop strep throats. A strep infection may produce rheumatic fever to begin with and the joints are affected temporarily. But with repeated uncontrolled strep infections leading to repeated bouts of rheumatic fever, the great risk is that the heart will be damaged. New rheumatic fever bouts can be virtually eliminated if, at the first indication of strep throat, a ten-day course of pencillin is used. Yet investigators have found that 56 percent of patients stop taking the penicillin by the third day, 71 percent by the sixth day, and 82 percent by the ninth day.

Digitalis is an invaluable drug for congestive heart failure. Yet, a University of California study shows that the average outpatient has a 95 percent probability of taking anywhere between 40 percent and 140 percent of a prescribed regimen of digitalis, and half of outpatients take less than 70 percent.

In a study in Rochester of 101 patients on digitalis treatment, thirty-four acknowledged that they had missed at least one dose during a six-month period. Thirteen blamed forgetfulness, six said they could not afford refills, eight blamed adverse reactions to the drug, four were afraid of taking "too much medication," three didn't think they needed it, two were confused, and seven gave no reason (the total is more than thirty-four because some gave more than one reason).

The 101 patients' blood was tested to determine the level of digitalis. The mean concentration of the medication was twice as high in those who had followed directions as in those who had not.

Many physicians may be ignoring compliance in considering patient responses to treatment. They would do well to spend more time discussing drug regimens with patients and finding out whether they understand what is necessary and why, and are actually taking medications as prescribed. It was notable that in the Rochester study, one physician had seven patients represented, every one of them compliant. This physician made it a rule at each visit to inquire about how his patients were taking their medications, to point out any errors, and to discuss with them the purpose of each drug and its possible adverse effects.

Outdated Medicines

At each of three New York hospitals, physicians were mystified by patients who were admitted with nausea and vomiting along with symptoms like those of diabetes. When the physicians compared notes, they determined that in every case the patient had used an antibiotic, a tetracycline, long left over in the home medicine cabinet. The symptoms had been caused by chemical deterioration of the antibiotic.

Some drugs lose potency with time; some gain potency; some undergo marked chemical changes that can make them dangerous. Many prescription drugs carry on their original containers an expiration date beyond which they should not be used, but the patient does not see this. It might be well if all packaging in which patients receive medication carried such a date and a warning not to use the medication thereafter.

The use of outdated drugs can be particularly risky for elderly people who may have some loss of kidney function or other problems which do not allow elimination of harmful substances as readily as in younger people. It is much safer to throw out a drug when its regular use has been discontinued.

Self-prescribed Drugs

Nonprescription medicines—variously known as "patent," "proprietary," "over-the-counter" ("OTC")—have their uses. Often they ease minor afflictions and discomforts. They are generally milder than prescription drugs and have fairly broad safety margins.

Yet, they, too, can produce undesirable effects in some people.

For many of the elderly, a couple of aspirins at bedtime to head off minor discomfort or sleeplessness becomes a nightly habit. In some people, especially on an empty stomach, aspirin can produce gastritis and even gastrointestinal hemorrhage. Excessive aspirin also can lead to occult or hidden bleeding and anemia.

It's advisable always to take aspirin with food or with an antacid.

An elderly person's tendency to constipation and improper use of cathartics can lead to severe gastrointestinal irritation, with spastic colon and even further constipation forming a vicious cycle. Often this need not happen if a physician explains to the patient the advantages of various bowel aids such as milk of magnesia and the need to stop use of cathartics and to adopt a simple anticonstipation regimen. Even in a chronic gastrointestinal complainer, such measures often work wonders.

Because they are advertised on TV, sold without prescription, and consumed by hundreds of thousands of people, over-the-counter sleeping pills are generally considered to be safe and are consumed by many who wouldn't think of using barbiturates. Yet, with overuse, some nonprescription sleeping pills may trigger mental confusion, excitement, hallucinations, even schizophrenic behavior. Out of a group of patients at a Washington, D.C., emergency room, one-fourth had been taking nonprescription sleeping pills.

Excessive use of vitamins may cause trouble. For example, vitamin A intoxication, due to excessive intake, can produce a remarkable variety of problems: aching joints, falling hair, headaches, blurred vision, ringing in the ears, sleep disturbances, among them.

When elderly people take nonprescription drugs routinely, as many do, those drugs may have to be considered as possible causes of symptoms that otherwise may seem either mysterious or attributable to "aging." Also, nonprescription drugs must be considered, just as are prescription drugs, in terms of drug interactions and their undesirable effects.

Drugs as a Cause of Malnutrition

Only recently it has become evident that long-term use of some valuable drugs can cause bad nutrition.

Some curb appetite at the risk of insufficient nutrition. Others induce malabsorption, interfering with the absorption of nutrients in the small intestine.

Among drugs found to damage the intestinal lining and thus interfere with nutrient absorption are phenolphthalein, a common laxative; methotrexate, sometimes used to control severe psoriasis; colchicine, used to treat gout.

Cholestyramine, an agent used to control high blood-cholesterol, acts to absorb bile acids so that they are excreted in the feces. Because bile acids are required for intestinal absorption of fats and fat-soluble vitamins, prolonged high dosages of cholestyramine may lead to excessive losses of fats and deficiencies or decreased levels of vitamins A, K, and D.

Some oral antidiabetic agents may interfere with absorption of vitamin B_{12}. High intakes of either the antituberculosis agent, isoniazid, or L-dopa, a valuable drug for controlling the symptoms of shaking palsy, may cause vitamin B_6 deficiency.

Some drugs such as methotrexate can cause deficiency of the vitamin folic acid, leading to an anemia in which both red and white blood cells are abnormal. Other drugs can set off vitamin deficiencies by greatly increasing requirements for certain nutrients. For example, phenobarbital and a related compound, primidone, and the antiepilepsy compound diphenylhydantoin, seem to increase the turnover of vitamin D so that more is needed to fill normal requirements, and, if more is not provided, a deficiency results, leading to osteomalacia, a softening of bone in adults that is similar to rickets in children. As the bones soften, they become bent, flattened, or otherwise deformed.

Despite the complexities of drug effects on nutrition, drug-caused deficiencies can be prevented. If one or more drugs must be used for control of chronic disease over long periods, a knowledgeable and responsible physician can see to it that the patient receives additional vitamins or other nutrients in the diet or as dietary supplements.

Making Medicine More Effective—and Less Harmful

Although most people are beneficiaries of the treasure chest of modern medications, too many have unhappy experiences. Much can be done to minimize or even eliminate the latter.

In just the past few years, among knowledgeable physicians there has been a decided shift in emphasis in taking a patient's history. Where once the major effort was to elicit a description of symptoms and obtain an understanding of signs of disease, now a good portion of the history consists of identifying which drugs—both prescription and over-the-counter—the patient is taking. This is as it should be.

In the case of any patient—and especially an elderly patient who is more likely than a younger one to be taking a considerable number of preparations—a good hard look at intake is desirable.

The physician needs to evaluate the intake, considering how much good each drug may be doing and whether it is really necessary. He needs to consider whether a drug in itself may be producing symptoms, whether it may be doing so by interacting with another drug or even with a food, whether it may be a cause of nutritional deficiency. And he needs to act on the evaluation, eliminating any medications that aren't really necessary, compensating for any unwanted effects of others that are necessary by changes of dosage or other means, including dietary supplements.

Patients must learn—and in the case of some elderly patients it may be necessery for their families to share the burden—to follow medical directions exactly, to be aware of possible side effects and to be alert for them and to report them without delay so that they have no chance to do major harm. They need to learn—because of the possibilities of interaction—to add no new drugs on their own without consulting with the physician first.

They need to learn not to save leftover drugs for long periods because of the likelihood that outdated drugs at best will do no good and at worst may cause harm.

They need to understand, too, that many underlying diseases and disorders may share many of the same symptoms, and that because a well-meaning but not well-informed friend or neighbor highly recommends some remedy for this or that symptom doesn't mean that the remedy is transferable. It may or may not help the symptom and even if it does, it may be of no value for the underlying condition; such a remedy may do harm by masking the condition temporarily, and may cause additional trouble through interaction.

14

NURSING HOMES AND ALTERNATIVES

As long as they can lead independent lives in their own homes, older people are unquestionably better off. But there are times when, because of increasing infirmity or severe chronic illness, the decision to send an aging parent to a nursing home may have to be made.

Possible Alternatives

Depending upon the individual circumstances, there may be feasible alternatives to institutionalized care.

In many communities, varied services are available to aid the feeble or ill elderly in their homes. They include homemaker programs to assist with household chores; visiting nurse programs; "meals on wheels" programs that provide at least one nourishing meal a day brought to the home; special transportation programs; shopping services; accessible outpatient clinics; telephone reassurance programs.

An idea that has only begun to spread in the last five years is the day-care center for the elderly. Such a center can have value in many situations. One, for example, would be in the case of a couple, both of whom work, who have an elderly parent unable to prepare his meals, take medication on schedule, or tend to his sanitary needs. Usually, in such a situation, the choices have been limited: the wife might give up working to become a full-time nurse-companion; or a nurse-companion could be hired, but often at a cost the family cannot afford; or the elderly parent might be institutionalized even though not really needing full-time care.

A day-care center provides an attractive other choice. The patient arrives there in the morning, stays all day, and returns home at night. Meals and snacks and sometimes transportation are provided. The environment is usually pleasant and safe. Skilled medical care is available when needed; required medication is administered. Additionally, a center may offer physical therapy, group recreational activities, and training in self-care, including physical and mental coordination, memory improvement, dressing, and grooming. A good day-care center can help overcome the loneliness that troubles so many of the aged, providing social contacts and varied activities.

There is no standard fee. At one center, for example, the charge is thirteen dollars a day, including transportation. But the charge may vary considerably from place to place, though always, of course, it is much less than for twenty-four-hour care.

It is estimated that more than fifty centers are in operation across the country, most of them run in conjunction with hospitals or nursing homes supported by public or charitable funds, but operators of proprietary hospitals and nursing homes are becoming interested. The best way to find such a center is to check with your local health or welfare department or with a state agency concerned with programs for the aged.

Categories and Costs of Nursing Homes

In terms of care provided, there are two basic types of nursing homes.

A *residential* or *intermediate-care* home can be suitable for an elderly person who is not capable of completely independent living but who is not seriously ill and needs only light medical treatment, some nursing supervision, and help with grooming and other personal care.

A *skilled* nursing home may be needed if your parent requires continuous twenty-four-hour nursing attention and therapy.

In some cases, a single home may provide both types of care.

Homes are operated under three kinds of sponsorship. A very, very few facilities are run by city or state governments. There are voluntary or nonprofit homes run by religious, fraternal, or union groups. And there are proprietary, or profit-making, privately owned facilities, which constitute the great majority. In New York City, for example, 70 percent of the nursing home beds are privately owned, with almost all the rest voluntary.

Generally, professional opinion favors voluntary homes, but there is no across-the-board rule. The attitudes of nursing-home administration and staff toward patients are, of course, important and there is some feeling that such attitudes and the overall quality of care delivered are likely to be more favorable in a voluntary home. In many cases, a fuller range of programs and services is available in voluntary institutions, and often voluntaries give preference to those unable to afford private care whereas proprietaries may need a high proportion of paying patients to make a profit. However, even in proprietary homes, Medicaid patients often make up a large proportion of the population.

The cost of nursing-home care varies widely from area to area and often from institution to institution within an area. The cost varies, too, of course, with the degree of care. Generally, the cost runs from $300 to $700 a month or higher.

Some portion of the cost may be covered by health insurance. Several bills introduced into Congress would broaden such coverage. Medicare may pay at least a part, sometimes a considerable part, of the cost for skilled nursing-home care for specific services for up to one hundred days after a hospital stay. Medicaid may pay costs for those without financial resources in either skilled or intermediate-care homes. Medicare and Medicaid payments apply only to homes certified by these agencies.

Nursing-Home Standards

Many homes do a good job, but abuses in institutional care of the elderly abound. And it is important to be aware of the abuses as an aid in choosing a home that can be expected to do a good job.

Bad homes can be extremely bad. There have been reports of homes in which patients are locked in their rooms or tied to chairs, of less than one dollar a day being spent on food for each patient, of many being kept on drugs often dispensed without prescription.

In 1973, the Senate Select Committee on Nutrition and Human Needs investigated nursing homes in ten states over a six-month period and found that "poor food is the most current abuse in today's nursing homes." Dietary departments in more than 50 percent of the facilities visited "demonstrated an attitude toward therapeutic diets which often approached a disregard for the patient's health." In many homes patients who should have been on restricted diets were given the same meals as other residents, and often all residents were subjected to high starch-content meals. The Senate Committee estimated that 86 percent of the homes surveyed served too many starchy foods, with many patients receiving approximately three times the amount of calories necessary.

The Committee recommended stricter requirements for dietary management in nursing homes, a full-time dietician or person with comparable experience in every home, a monthly review of each patient's diet made by a physician or a nutritionist, intensified in-service training in dietary management for physicians and nursing-home personnel, and unannounced nursing-home inspections to catch unsanitary food practices.

In 1973, too, a crash survey by state health inspectors of 104 profit-making nursing homes in New York City found accumulations of dirt and garbage, overcrowding, improper infection control, or other "serious operating deficiencies" in nearly two-thirds of the facilities. Among the "other serious operating deficiencies" were lack of isolation quarters for patients with contagious illnesses, no separation of clean and soiled linens, improper dietary services, lack of rules and regulations for the staff, and lack of training for the staff.

Lower-echelon staff in nursing homes, particularly nurse's aides and orderlies, who have closest contact with the elderly, are rarely paid above federal minimum wage standards; their turnover is high; many receive little if any training.

A key to good nursing-home operation is the administrator who, with some imagination and compassion and skill, can help materially to make a nursing home a more pleasant place to live. But only 10 percent of nursing-home administrators have any sort of training for their work; only one-third have college degrees.

Not all abuses are flagrant. There are sometimes more subtle ones. One woman, who spent eight months looking for a nursing home for her eighty-one-year-old mother, observes: "You go in the front door and the furnishings knock you over. But then you watch the patients sitting, doing nothing all day long. Good care doesn't mean good carpeting. It means compassion."

In some homes, the elderly are treated like children rather than like adults who are ill or aging. Patronized, they may tend to deteriorate into childishness and real helplessness.

Most nursing institutions are not "snake pits," but too many have sterile environments with few features or programs to stimulate their elderly patients and, for the lack of them, they inadvertently encourage, or at least allow, loss of competence as the patients go downhill mentally and physically.

There are many ways nursing homes can provide stimulation for their residents—simply and inexpensively. Dr. Arthur N. Schwartz, who heads a model nursing home education project at the University of Southern California Gerontology Center, which provides training for administrators of nursing homes, points to some of them:

Why not allow pets and provide plants for residents to take an interest in and care for? Why not make the environment stimulating by painting walls and ceilings bright colors instead of sickly institutional green? Why not provide environmental cues, such as clocks, calendars, signs, and other markings that help keep older people oriented as to time and space? And, urges Dr.

Schwartz, with the proven mutual benefits of association between very young and very old, why not design nursing homes near nursery schools?

Also important could be small changes in policy away from hard and fast practices that subtly tend to deprive residents of their options and to an extent dehumanize them. Some homes require that staff members go out and buy clothing for residents, but why not find a way to let each person choose his own attire? Many homes don't allow women patients to have their purses with them, yet purses to women are very personal symbols of self-identity throughout life; why can't they have their purses and cosmetics so they can continue their interest in making themselves up?

Administrators taking the USC training program are given opportunities to experience personally some of the losses that aged people are up against. At one point, they are required to stare up at a ceiling for a protracted period; they learn quickly what it must be like for a bedridden person who has only that kind of stimulation twelve or fourteen hours a day. At another point, the administrators are blindfolded, cotton is placed in their ears and they are seated in a wheelchair alone and isolated for a period; they quickly realize the grim monotony some old people must live through.

The training appears to be impressing adminstrators who take it, and improvements in their institutions are being noted. As more of them are reached by such programs and carry the message back to their staffs, there could be notable progress in care for the aged. What's really involved, of course, is something very simple: just treating humans like humans.

Choosing a Home

Your first move is to consult your physician about the type of care your parent needs. What should you look for—a residential or intermediate-care facility or a skilled nursing home?

Once you determine the type, your physician may have recommendations for one or more homes you can check. Local medical societies, hospital and nursing-home associations, religious organizations, and the district Social Security office may also be helpful.

At the least, a nursing home and its administrator should be state licensed. Look also for a Joint Commission on Accreditation of Hospitals certificate. JCAH standards are perhaps the toughest. They are supported by the American Hospital Association, the American Medical Association, and the two major national nursing-home associations—the American Nursing Home Association, representing principally proprietary homes, and the American Association of Homes for the Aging, representing the nonprofit homes. Participation in the JCAH's inspection and evaluation program is one good indication that a nursing home has nothing to hide. Such participation is voluntary; less than 10 percent of the nursing homes in the United States have asked for and met standards for JCAH accreditation.

Be sure to check the home in person. You can make an appointment in advance with the administrator or another staff member and be shown around. But one of the best ways to discover what a home is really like is to make an unannounced visit. Usually, good homes have open visiting hours.

You should be able to get a feel for the home when you visit it. Inspect the dining area, look over the menus, and if possible sample the food. Look at recreation facilities and check the activities program. Look into individual rooms and check for cleanliness and comfort.

Consider the medical program. A home should employ a qualified physician or at least have one available on call. Specialists such as dentists, ophthalmologists and rehabilitative therapists should be available when needed.

If your parent needs extensive medical attention, find out whether the home has one or more full-time registered nurses and whether coverage extends around the clock. Look at the scheduled number of hours per week that registered and licensed practical nurses and aides are on duty.

There are many other things, too, you can look for.

Is the home cheerful and bright? Do residents evidence concern for their appearance? Are they encouraged to be independent, to come and go as much as physically able? Do they have any voice in running the home? Are there places a patient can go to be alone? Is there a lawn or garden where residents can go for fresh air, and is it accessible, perhaps by ramp, to wheelchair patients?

Do you find residents talking to each other, and are you permitted to talk freely to them? Are there signs of normal, noninstitutional life such as coffee pots, flowers, newspapers? Is the recreational program varied, with more activities than just cards, bingo, and television? Does it include perhaps trips to museums and parks, arts and crafts, social functions? Is there a relationship with the outside community and perhaps community volunteers helping with activities programs and other projects in the home?

Notice how the staff address residents. Is it in condescending fashion, or are residents addressed as adults?

Is there a definite arrangement with a nearby hospital for quick admission of residents who become acutely ill—and is emergency transportation readily available? It can be worthwhile to double-check with the hospital about these arrangements.

It's not likely that any one home will fulfill all such criteria. The chances are that you will have to compromise and choose a home that is something less than 100 percent ideal. If possible, when you have narrowed you choice to one or two homes, spend a day there, following the activities and talking to residents. If possible, your parent should approve of the home you finally select and should see it at least once and preferably twice before moving in.

To make an informed and wise choice of a nursing home is a painstaking business. Nor does the matter end once the selection is made. In addition to visiting your parent as often as you can—something vital to his or her morale and even physical and mental health—you can and should take the opportunity during visits to check repeatedly on specific aspects of the care.

15

CURRENT RESEARCH IN AGING

Aging is probably the most universal and least understood of all biological phenomena. The causes remain shrouded in mystery.

Of theories and working hypotheses about aging, there is no shortage. Gerontology—the study of aging—seems at first glance to be a morass of theories and speculation. For many years, numerous concepts of what is involved in aging have been offered almost wholesale, often with little in the way of scientific experimental evidence to buttress them.

But scientists working in the field today can point to some indications of progress.

In the past, aging research was criticized because experiments were neither well thought out nor precisely designed, and could not be expected, however much work and time went into them, to produce meaningful results. The quality of research has improved. There is less interest in chasing after theories having little plausibility. There is growing maturity in the field with recognition that aging is complex rather than simple, and no one mechanism is likely to explain all of aging.

With the growing numbers of the aged, public awareness of the need for and desirability of gerontological research has begun to increase. Federal support has increased somewhat. Over a period of eight years, the National Institutes of Health have increased the aging-research budget from three million dollars yearly to upward of eleven million dollars, and the Atomic Energy Commission and Veterans Administration have provided support to a lesser extent.

The funds are not munificent. But aging research is not confined to the United States. And some gerontologists are becoming sanguine.

"Some day," says Dr. Bernard Strehler of the University of Southern California, "we may live almost indefinitely." More immediately, Dr. Alex Comfort, director of research in gerontology at University College, London, sees a prospect of being able, within the next four to five years, to interfere with human aging—not to stop the process but to slow it down.

A Discarded Theory

Largely negativistic though it was, for a time a "watch-spring" theory of aging had a vogue. It held that much in the manner of a watch spring, the human body gradually ran out of energy and had to stop functioning. Most scientists now consider the theory naive, even absurd. Any evidence that body energy is exhausted in time is lacking.

The Underfeeding Theory

In the early 1930s, in one of the pioneering experiments in aging research, Dr. Clive M. McCay of Cornell University demonstrated that curtailing food intake could have a significant effect on longevity.

McCay fed rats a diet sharply reduced in calories and found that some lived as long as 1450 days while rats fed conventional diets seldom lived beyond 965 days. In one series of experiments, rats fed unlimited calories usually were dead within 730 days, while those restricted to a diet of essential protein, minerals, and vitamins, with insufficient calories even to maintain growth, remained in the pre-adolescent state for 1,000 days. When they then received a normal diet allowing them to grow, they matured sexually and lived longer than usual, even as long as 1465 days, about the equivalent of a 130- to 140-year life-span in man.

More recently, Dr. Roy Walford of the UCLA School of Medicine has shown that cutting the food intake of mice not only lengthens life-span but reduces susceptibility to cancer. Some of his low-calorie mice have lived to double normal life-span and have had a markedly lower incidence of cancer than normally fed mice.

Other investigations have shown that underfeeding also increases longevity of rotifers, silkworms, fruit flies, bees, chickens, and other animals.

In other studies, a synthetic diet lacking in a single protein building block, tryptophan, has stopped the maturing process in mice and chickens. After nine months when tryptophan was restored in the diet, the animals started to grow again and lived to twice-normal life-span.

Still other studies have indicated an influence of diet on both aging and cancer, but it appears that however reduced intake may work, diet must be so limited that growth is retarded and must be kept limited for long periods, which would not make it attractive to humans.

The Temperature Theory

Evidence that body temperature has an influence on the aging process has been accumulating. Dr. Walford has doubled the life-span of some fish by lowering water temperature by five to six degrees Centigrade. At Rockefeller Institute, fruit flies, which are also cold-blooded organisms, lived twice as long as usual when kept at nineteen degrees Centigrade instead of the normal twenty-five degrees.

At the National Institutes of Health, Dr. Charles H. Barrows, Jr., first increased the life-span of rotifers from eighteen to thirty-four days by reducing temperature from thirty-five to twenty-five degrees. When the rotifers, in addition, received only half the usual amount of food, they lived for fifty-five days. Barrows has found that at least in rotifers, the reduced food intake extends the fertile, egg-producing period of youth, and the reduced tempterature extends the later stages of life.

Dr. Strehler, mentioned earlier, has, by cooling, kept alive and well some mice to the advanced age of eight years, a species that ordinarily live two to three years. Strehler believes that the principle that lower body temperature favors longevity may apply to man. There is some thought, in fact, that long-lived people may be long-lived because they have slightly lower-than-average temperatures, and that a thorough investigation of this possibility is called for.

Strehler and others have studied hibernating rodents, including bats, and have determined that for every increase of seven to eight degrees Centigrade, their rate of aging doubles whereas, on the other hand, with equivalent reduction of temperature life-span doubles.

If man should react in the same way, Strehler and others suggest, a two-degree Centigrade reduction might add fifteen to twenty-five years of healthy, useful life. Strehler believes that drugs may be found that can achieve such a reduction, though thus far no ideal one is known. At the Institute of Experimental Gerontology in Basel, Switzerland, Dr. Fritz Verzer has tried novocaine, a local anesthetic, and found that it does reduce animal body temperature but is not satisfactory because increasing doses are needed to maintain the temperature-lowering effect.

On the other hand, some scientists fear that lowering human body temperature by two or three degrees Centigrade for prolonged periods might not be practical and might even be dangerous, possibly reducing body metabolism to the point of inducing sluggishness and impairment of mental processes along with chills, shivering, and discomfort.

The Clock in the Cells

It has long been accepted that longevity or the lack of it runs in families. In one extensive study, Dr. Lissy F. Jarvik of UCLA checked on two thousand sets of twins over the age of sixty and found that identical twins have a significantly greater similarity in life-spans than do nonidentical twins.

The familial pattern coupled with another fact—that most species of organisms seem to have a more or less definitie life-span limitation (40 days for fruit flies, 3 years for mice, 110 years for man)—suggests to some investigators that there may be a kind of genetic clock built into body cells that determines when old age sets in.

Some evidence to support the concept was turned up more or less by accident a decade ago by Dr. Leonard Hayflick, now at the Stanford University School of Medicine. Until then, it had been assumed that if animal cells were properly nurtured in tissue culture, they would be immortal. The famed studies of Dr. Alexis Carrel, Nobel Prize winner, in the 1930s had indicated that cells from the embryonic hearts of chickens could be kept alive indefinitely in tissue culture. But it was to turn out from Hayflick's work that Carrel had been misled; that his results stemmed from unknowing addition daily of new embryonic cells to the chicken embryo extract he used as a nutrient in his tissue culture work.

Hayflick was surprised when, working with cells cultured from the lung tissue of a human embryo, he found that each cell population went on doubling for about fifty times, but then stopped and died. He found that if he took cell colonies after about twenty doublings and put them in the deep freeze and later thawed them, they "remembered" after thawing how many times they had already doubled and how many doublings they had left, and then proceeded to stop after thirty more doublings. When Hayflick took cells from the lung tissue of a twenty-year-old man, he found that they underwent an average of only twenty doublings.

Hayflick proposed that cells stop dividing and die not because of external forces but rather because of factors inherent in the cells themselves. Still, despite his work, which lends support to the concept of a built-in cellular clock, Hayflick doubts that human beings age because their cells just stop doubling. For one thing, a human doesn't live long enough to have the cell population double the apparently maximum fifty times. It seems more likely to Hayflick that aging involves changes—structural, biochemical, and perhaps others—in the cell that take place before division stops. Conceivably, however, the genetic clock that stops the division of cells may have some role in inducing these changes.

The Gene Theories

Two theories have been proposed about how genes, the units of heredity, may affect aging processes.

One holds that the genes age: that the program laid down at conception in the DNA, the genetic material, simply runs out; it plays out its message and once it has done so, cell function stops.

A second theory holds that as a person grows older, the DNA gradually becomes impaired and deterioration sets in as errors occur in the course of the repeated copying of the genetic message. Such errors could lead to production of defective proteins that do not allow the body to carry out its normal functions and therefore contribute to the destructive processes of aging.

Recently, Dr. Hayflick has begun an ingenious series of experiments. He wants to learn whether cell doubling is determined by the DNA in the cell nucleus or by RNA, a material that carries out DNA instructions, or possibly even by other chemical processes within the cell but outside the cell nucleus. He removes nuclei from some cells and "fuses" them with other whole cells, combining cells of long-lived and shorter-lived species and young cells with old. If an old cell were to keep doubling beyond its normal limit following fusion with young cytoplasm (the material in the cell outside the nucleus), it would suggest that genetic control for division resides outside the nucleus—which could have important implications for therapy, since the cytoplasm of a cell is an easier target for drugs or chemicals to control aging than is the nucleus.

Enzyme Errors

Aging might be due to certain errors that do not necessarily have anything to do with the genes and defects in DNA or RNA. They may be errors in any of the intermediary materials involved in protein production.

A decade ago Dr. Leslie E. Orgel of Cambridge University, England, proposed that damage is done by cumulative errors in synthesis of the special proteins known as enzymes. Some of these enzymes serve as "tools" for the production of other proteins and, if the tools become defective, so may the proteins produced with them, leading to an "error catastrophe."

The idea has been pursued by Drs. Robin Holliday and G. M. Tarrant of the National Institute for Medical Research,

London. Working on the principle that when enzymes are defective, they are more sensitive to inactivation by heat, Holliday and Tarrant have found that heat-sensitive enzymes in human cells increase rapidly with age.

Hormones

Also under study as a possible factor behind at least some symptoms of aging is the body's complex system of messenger chemicals, or hormones. Although the ability to produce hormones generally does not decline with age, the action of the hormones does become less efficient. A possible reason may be that the "receptors" on which the hormones act become less receptive.

At Temple University Medical School, Philadelphia, Dr. Richard C. Adelman has used rats to study the effect of aging on ability to process glucose, a sugar. In man, this process tends to deteriorate with age, leading to diabetes. When glucose is administered to a rat, its pancreas is stimulated to release the hormone insulin. The hormone then causes the liver to turn out glucokinase, an enzyme that helps the body process the glucose.

The efficiency of the system can be checked by determining how much anti-insulin is required to turn it off. The amount declines steadily, beginning at about two months after birth. By twenty-four months, the anti-insulin check shows that glucokinase synthesis is halved. Several possible reasons for this need study. The pancreas may have less insulin with age, or the insulin delivery system may become less efficient, or the quality of insulin may be poorer, or it could be that the liver becomes less sensitive to insulin stimulation.

The Immune System

There is a theory that the body's immune system, which ordinarily protects us from disease, may undergo changes that make it a cause of aging.

The antibodies and special white blood cells produced by the immune system have the job of recognizing and attacking invading viruses, bacteria, and other foreign agents. Additionally, evidence is growing that they are responsible for detecting and destroying incipient cancer cells arising in the body.

Sir Macfarlane Burnet, of the University of Melbourne, and

other scientists have shown that the body also can produce antibodies that, instead of attacking invaders, attack natural body tissues. Such autoantibodies, as they are called, are believed to account for certain diseases, including rheumatoid arthritis, which have been labeled autoimmune diseases.

And, according to the immune theory of aging, as a person gets older, his immune system becomes less able to distinguish normal body materials from foreign materials and destroys the normal materials.

Dr. Walford has reported finding that with age the production of disease-fighting antibodies declines but the level of autoantibodies goes up. In investigating why this may happen, he has worked with mice, giving them low-calorie diets, and has shown that underfeeding not only retards general development but also development of the immune system. When the immune system does mature, it gradually weakens in typical fashion with time, but the weakening is deferred and the immune system remains relatively strong to a later age.

At the National Institutes of Health, Dr. Takashi Makinodan and his associates have been able to measure how drastically immunologic efficiency can decline with age, and their work suggests a possible approach to correcting immune defects.

When the investigators exposed mice to controlled doses of disease organisms in order to stimulate immune system defense, they found that the response in old mice was only 10 percent of the response in young mice; the old animals had one-tenth the capacity of the young to fight off infection. In man that may mean that a seventy-year-old is ten times as open to disease as a teen-ager.

The problem may lie with the two types of cells that produce antibodies. These are T cells formed in the thymus gland and B cells formed in the bone marrow. When a foreign agent enters the body, one T cell and as many as eight B cells join to form an immunocompetent unit, and it is this combined unit that produces antibodies. Makinodan and his group have found that in old age, the T and B cells do not diminish in numbers but are not as efficient in recognizing invaders, form as few as 20 percent of the normal number of immunocompetent units, each of which turns out only half as many antibodies as in youth.

Promisingly, however, when old and young cells are mixed together, the old cells become able to make antibodies at the same rate as the young cells. The NIH researchers infected young mice with disease bacteria to stimulate their immune systems, then extracted some of their T and B cells, froze them for several months and, after thawing, injected them into old mice. Long after receiving the injections, the old mice were infected with disease organisms lethal to other unprotected old mice—and resisted infection.

Could humans deposit T and B cells in frozen storage during youth and use them in old age to revitalize their immune systems? Possibly. First, however, researchers will have to determine if they can successfully freeze and restore live human cells.

Cross-Linking

Leather and rubber—and human skin and blood vessel walls as well—lose elasticity as they age. This appears to be the result of a cross-linking process. Original elasticity comes from long fibers of a material called collagen. With time, chemical cross links are formed between the fibers, reducing their elasticity.

One theory being explored is that aging may be the result of a gradual chemical cross-linking in all cells of the body. Actually, cross-linkages are always being formed, and most of the time no harm is done because body enzymes break the linkages as fast as they are formed. But a certain percentage of cross-linkages may be formed in a way that prevents enzymes from splitting them, and, as more and more such linkages are formed with time, normal cell functioning may deteriorate.

The effect can be compared to what would occur in a large factory employing several thousand workers when, at first, a few workers somehow become handcuffed together. These few, of course, no longer can work efficiently. If the handcuffing spreads to other workers even slowly, the entire operation will eventually come to a stop unless some way is found to uncuff the workers as fast as they became cuffed.

Some scientists believe that, in the human body, as cross-linking increases and prevents some protein molecules from being metabolized properly by enzymes, the proteins begin to accumulate in cells as "frozen metabolic pools" which can clog and ultimately destroy the cells.

If this is indeed true, it may be possible to find enzymes capable of breaking down any cross-linkages not broken by natural body enzymes. One source for such enzymes could be soil bacteria. It seems to some investigators that soil bacteria must contain suitable enzymes for the purpose, otherwise the earth would be covered with the undecomposed bodies of animals.

There is even a proposed method of approach for finding and growing suitable bacteria. It involves breaking down cross-linked protein from old animals as far as possible with known enzymes, then using what is left as a food source in laboratory cultures of many types of soil microorganisms. Before long, only organisms capable of breaking down the cross-linked material to get materials they need for survival would remain alive. Possibly, such bacteria then could be grown in quantity and their enzymes extracted for use.

Free Radicals

The possibility that aging may be influenced by a class of substances known as free radicals is under study.

Free radicals are fragments of molecules that have come unstuck. Eagerly looking to recombine, to find new molecular homes, they may react with anything nearby. Such free radical reactions or recombinations, called oxidative reactions, are the basis for many natural decay processes—such as the rancidification of butter and even some industrial processes such as the drying of oil paint. To counter the effects of free radical reactions and help preserve foods, antioxidant materials are often used and include vitamin E and BHT, a material employed as a preserver in breakfast foods.

Free radicals are present in the body, and some scientists believe they may be involved in aging within body cells. Dr. Denham Harman of the University of Nebraska School of Medicine has found that free radicals have a role in the formation of amyloid, a fibrous protein that can be seen in increasing amounts with age in blood vessels in the brain and in areas of cell degeneration in brain tissue. Conceivably, free radicals could have a role in producing senility by damaging brain cells and vessels—and, by damaging other body cells and vessels, a part in general aging.

In laboratory studies, Dr. Harman has fed mice on vitamin E and BHT. In some strains, such feeding has increased average life-span as much as 50 percent, encouraging further research with the hope that eventually the findings may be applicable to humans.

The Emergence of Thymosin

Among the latest studies is one suggesting that a hormone produced by the thymus gland, a long-mysterious organ behind the upper part of the breastbone extending into the neck, may be directly related to the process of aging.

In 1973, Dr. Allan Goldstein and other researchers at the University of Texas Medical Branch, Galveston, reported that the hormone, thymosin, only recently purified, declines with age and that lowered thymosin levels may contribute to aging by retarding the ability of the immune system to function effectively.

A significant fall in thymosin levels in the blood of normal people between the ages of twenty-five and forty-five was noted. Moreover, thymosin blood levels in patients with specific immunodeficiency disorders are lower than those in normal people. Goldstein and his co-workers hope to find a way to increase a patient's immunological response to disease by manipulating the amount of thymosin in the blood. Having established that injections of thymosin in mice increase their immunity, they believe there is good reason to suppose such injections will do the same in man.

The Rejuvenation Therapists

While basic research into aging continues, there is no shortage—nor has there ever been—of "we-can-do-it-right-now" rejuvenationists.

As far back as recorded history goes, there have been those who thought they had found ways to prolong life or recapture youth. Sleeping with young virgins as a means of absorbing "revitalizing" emanations was practiced by King David. Achilles is reputed to have eaten the marrow of young bears in order to increase his vigor.

Modern rejuvenation practitioners do a thriving business.

For example, cell therapy is currently very much in vogue in Europe. Devised by the late Dr. Paul Niehans of Switzerland, it involves taking tissue extracts from fetal lambs and injecting them in the belief that they provide a general body revitalizing effect and even can reestablish function of failing organs. Reports that Niehans treated many celebrities, including the Duke and Duchess of Windsor, Winston Churchill, Pope Pius XII, Bernard Baruch, Charles Chaplin, Gloria Swanson, and a large number of "jet-setters" have made cell therapy fashionable. Since Niehan's death, his clinic, La Prairie, a mansion at Lake Geneva, continues to function in high gear, using fetal cells from some five hundred specially bred black sheep. Patients pay two thousand dollars for a course of eight injections over an eight-day period. It's estimated that Europe has more than five thousand practitioners of cell therapy.

Cell therapists claim cures of an almost endless variety of problems, ranging from mental retardation to emphysema, as well as dramatic revitalizing effects on the bodies and minds of older people. But for lack of scientifically controlled studies to support their claims, scientists generally discount them.

Gerovital, a drug developed more than twenty years ago by Dr. Ana Aslan of Bucharest, currently is receiving serious scientific attention in this country.

Gerovital has been reputed to be effective in treating arthritis, arteriosclerosis, and the general debilities of old age. To Dr. Aslan's clinic have come not only Rumanians but some fifty thousand others, mostly Italian, French, and German, plus a growing number of Americans. Nikita Khrushchev, Konrad Adenauer, Charles de Gaulle, King Ibn Saud of Arabia, and movie stars Lillian Gish, Kirk Douglas, and Marlene Dietrich are among the celebrated reputed to have been Aslan patients.

Gerovital is mainly procaine, a standard anesthetic agent best known to Americans under the trade name of Novocain. Efforts by physicians to duplicate claimed results have largely failed in the past. A few investigators did, however, report as far back as a dozen years ago that procaine appeared to be useful in relieving depression.

Generally, Gerovital has been dismissed for lack of controlled scientific studies that support Dr. Aslan's claims for it. To this, Dr. Aslan has long replied that others were not using the same drug and the same methods she employed. There are substantial differences between Gerovital and standard 2 percent solutions of procaine, she has pointed out. Gerovital is chemically buffered; its action, too, she indicates, is potentiated by additional compounds such as benzoic acid and potassium metabisulfite.

At the University of Chicago in the mid sixties, one group of investigators did find that the additives in Gerovital are apparently responsible for significant differences in biologic action, and reported greater improvement in nerve conduction and psychological and other functioning in subjects treated with imported Gerovital than in a matched group treated with procaine products in this country.

More recently, the United States Food and Drug Administration decided to license trials of Gerovital in this country for its possible effects on depression in aged patients. In large part, this is due to the work of Drs. Josef P. Hrachovec and M. David MacFarlane of the University of Southern California, who reported, in 1972, on what appears to be the mechanism by which Gerovital apparently retards some of the mental and physical deterioration of aging.

Using experimental animals and also working with isolated living tissue, the two scientists found that Gerovital inhibits the activity of an enzyme, monoamine oxidase (MAO), in liver and brain tissue. MAO is needed to regulate certain chemicals in the brain, nerves, and other tissues of the body. But after age forty-five, the levels of MAO increase and apparently decrease the quantities of the chemicals to excessively low levels. The reduced concentrations of the chemicals may be linked to depression in the aged. Gerovital, the USC researchers have suggested, may alleviate depression by inhibiting the activity of elevated MAO levels in the elderly.

Currently, Dr. Nathan S. Kline of Rockland State Hospital, Orangeburg, New York, is testing Gerovital in elderly depressed patients. Studies are also under way at Hillside Hospital on Long Island, New York, and at Duke University Center for the Study of Aging and Human Development.

While they have high hopes for a rational approach to inhibiting aging in the future, perhaps even in the relatively near future, researchers in gerontology generally agree that as yet no treatment for the purpose can be recommended on the basis of valid experimental evidence.

Social and Psychological Influences

While much of the emphasis of research has been on trying to understand what happens physically to induce aging and what may be done physically to retard the process, the influence of social and psychological forces has not escaped attention.

That social and psychological factors may influence life-span is indicated by data obtained at the Duke University Center during a thirteen-year study by Dr. Erdman B. Palmore. The study found that when such factors are taken into account, the accuracy of longevity predictions can be improved upon by about a third over similar predictions based on actuarial tables.

Participating in the study were 270 volunteers between 60 and 94 years of age. Each of them underwent a series of tests designed to reveal social, mental, and physical factors most influential in adjustment to aging.

From hundreds of answers supplied during two days of testing, thirty-eight variables were selected for correlation with a longevity quotient (LQ). LQ is the number of years an individual survived after the initial study divided by the expected number of years given by actuarial tables based on age and sex alone.

An LQ of 1.0 means that an individual lived exactly as long as expected actuarially.

Of the thirty-eight different variables, which included intelligence, hobbies, education, and community and leisure activity, four proved to be most important. One was work satisfaction, derived from a questionnaire designed to measure satisfaction with various areas of life. The second was happiness rating designed to show attitudes toward life in general. The third was a physical functioning rating gauging how well an individual functions despite any physical limitations. The fourth was use of tobacco.

Surprisingly, the factors that might be expected logically to play a paramount role in determining longevity—physical functioning and smoking—were less important than the work satisfaction and happiness ratings.

If an individual's work satisfaction was high, his life-span was predicted to be longer, and the prediction usually proved true.

As an example, an eighty-one-year-old man in the study had an actuarial life expectancy of another 5.6 years. His health was average but his work satisfaction rating was the highest possible. According to prediction based on LQ, he was expected to survive 9.5 years, though he actually lived another 11.6 years, more than double the actuarial prediction and reasonably close to that of the LQ.

Generally, among all taking part in the study, those who professed satisfaction with their work (whether paid employment or household activities) and displayed an optimistic attitude lived longer than those who were unhappy with their work and pessimistic.

It has been recognized, of course, for some time that the mind can affect the body in various ways. The Duke study provides further evidence of a relationship between mental state and physical condition, and even between mental state and longevity.

The study also serves to underscore the importance of social influences that impinge on the mental state of the elderly.

To a large extent, the elderly have been detached from modern society. Once, when the extended family was the rule instead of the exception as it tends to be now, older people remained functional members of the family. Now relatively few remain so.

"If a person is forced to retire, if he feels useless and his income drops, then his health, his interest in taking care of himself and his urge to live longer may also suffer," declares Dr. Palmore. "His decline may have nothing whatever to do with his chronological age or genetic make-up."

It appears that those who live longest and most vigorously are those who, despite the inhibitions of society, refuse to give in. The decision to have an active mental, physical, and social life is really the important decision.

16

ENVOI

However bright the future may be, the present could be brighter.

If we are really to appreciate what often can and should be done for the elderly right now, we must appreciate what old age can and should be today.

There is a common notion that the late years must inevitably be years of rapid decline, dullness, and apathy—and any notable exceptions only prove the rule.

To be sure, the argument runs, an Andres Segovia, grandee

of the classic guitar, may perform with great vitality at age eighty, playing fifty recitals in a season and traveling the country to do so. Yes, P. G. Wodehouse publishes a new Jeeves novel at ninety. And, of course, Goethe finished *Faust* at eighty-two, Verdi composed his *Requiem Mass* at eighty-seven, Sophocles was in his eighties when he wrote *Oedipus*, and Isocrates was ninety-four when he wrote *Panathenaicus*. But such rare examples of undiminished vigor are to be found only among the exceptionally gifted, the argument would have it.

Except that there are many more examples, and they are to be found among so-called "ordinary" people.

Not long ago, a *New York Times* report told of a man selling lubricants to the petroleum industry in Alaska, of another who was enthusiastic about "closing a honey of a deal" he had been negotiating for eleven years, of a third who puts in a full eight-hour day traveling all over Arkansas and returning to his Little Rock home every night, and a fourth in Ohio who is sure he is just getting started and has at least thirty more good years before he "calls it quits." The first man is 72; the second, 83; the third, 78; the fourth, 67—and they are among some 350 salesmen, all over 65, working for a Texas company which has a policy (how rare!) of emphasizing the hiring of older men.

Recently, the United Steelworkers newspaper hailed Basco Vasquez, a ninety-three-year-old worker in a Bethlehem Steel rod mill in San Francisco. "Last month," the newspaper noted, "he handled a record 8,600 bars in an eight-hour shift."

Loma Linda University recently documented the fact that Mrs. Hulda Crooks, at seventy-five, not only was still working full time as a research assistant in the School of Health but had just finished her tenth annual week-long, seventy-mile pack trip through the High Sierra mountain range of California and her tenth 10½-mile hike to the top of 14,495-foot Mt. Whitney, highest mountain in the continental United States. Mrs. Crooks is five feet one inch tall.

In Niagara Falls, New York, at age 100, Edwin R. Larter, M.D., shovels snow, gets his own meals, does push-ups every night, and keeps up with his medical practice. He likes to observe that "doctors today have become too conservative with their strengths and abilities. They suffer from the same malady as our society—they sit too much, eat too much, and think treating a patient in his home is a crime." About his own health, Dr. Larter comments: "About the only physical problem I've had is an occasional sore toe from tight shoes—but that's the price we pay for wanting to look fashionable." The only thing he deplores is inactivity. "I just can't stand it when things get dull."

Many things are true about old age: responses may slow somewhat, physical changes do occur, and the correlation between old age and illness is high.

But what is *not* true is that it is expectable, inevitable—and all right—for old people to be sick.

The need is to separate out how much is old from how much is sick—and, vigorously, to treat the sick.

Certainly, we should have more—much more—research about aging: why and how it takes place, how it may be postponed, how perhaps life may be extended, and how—possibly even more desirable—the latter years and any extended years can be made more rewarding.

We have committed relatively little to aging research. Perhaps, all told, annual expenditures for such research amount to fourteen million dollars at most. That is scandalously low—equal to one twenty-fifth the cost of a fighter bomber, or about eight cents per person per year.

But we need urgently to apply right now what is already known.

Not all the elderly can be expected to benefit dramatically, any more than can all the young, to vigorous use of available medical knowledge and tools.

But many of the elderly will respond dramatically, and many others will benefit, if less dramatically, to a significantly worthwhile extent.

When they are not labeled, indifferently and indiscriminately, as hopelessly senile victims of unalterable hardening of the brain arteries, many of the elderly are far from hopeless and, surprisingly often, they are not victims at all of brain artery disease.

When their emotional problems are recognized—when the very fact that they can *have* emotional problems is taken into account—those problems, which are not very much, if at all, different from the emotional problems of younger people, often respond as well as do those of younger people to suitable treatment.

When the same diagnostic acumen that would be applied in puzzling conditions in the young is applied, as vigorously and hopefully, to puzzling conditions in the aged, many of those conditions prove to be understandable and treatable.

And when the aged have serious physical problems and even combinations of them—heart, lung, and others—they are not inevitably beyond help simply because they are old. Nor are they, simply because of age, beyond surgical help.

There are hopeful signs of growing awareness within medicine of what can be done for the aged. Many medical schools have begun stock-taking and are setting up programs to give future physicians training in geriatrics. A National Advisory Council on Geriatric Medical Programs has been organized to stimulate the development of geriatric medical training. Mount Sinai School of Medicine in New York City has established at an affiliated hospital a program offering fellowships in geriatric medicine.

The Veterans Administration wants to improve geriatric medical training. Hopefully, a modest starting proposal to set up geriatric centers at five of its hospitals at a total cost of three million dollars, which was not carried out because of federal cutbacks in medical funding, will be revived. Public support is needed for its revival and also for enactment of a bill (Senate 764) proposed by Senator Frank Moss of Utah to provide for funding of up to half a dozen medical schools with up to $500,000 each for developing physician-training programs in geriatrics.

Significantly, in December 1973, *Prism*, an American Medical Association publication for physicians, carried a hard-hitting report titled "We're Doing a Third-Rate Job for the Aged" in which Dr. Theodore R. Reiff, chief of the Division of Geriatric Medicine at the University of North Dakota School of Medicine, pointed to lack of research funds, insufficient medical training, and plain indifference.

Much of what has been achieved (and noted earlier in these pages) by many physicians who have approached the problems of the aged hopefully and aggressively could just as well be achieved by others.

It is up to you. Effective treatment will be applied to the aged if people know there is such treatment, and demand it, and go looking for it.

NOTES

Chapter 1. But Are They Really Beyond Help? Now? Today?

Page

1–2 Editorial, "A Curable Form of Dementia," *Canadian Medical Association Journal,* vol. 97, p. 1358. *Medical World News,* June 4, 1971, p. 42 I. See also references, chapter 4.

Page

2 *Journal of the American Geriatrics Society,* vol. 19, p. 240.
Canadian Medical Association Journal, vol. 106, p. 1289.
GP, vol. 39, no. 4, p. 90.

3 *West Virginia Medical Association Journal,* vol. 61, p. 334.

3–4 Dr. Raymond Harris, Albany Medical College, Albany, N.Y.

4 *Journal of the American Medical Association,* vol. 204, p. 17. See also references, chapter 12.

5–6 Editorial, *British Medical Journal,* May 27, 1972. See also references, chapter 10.

6 *Journal of the American Medical Association,* vol. 218, p. 95.

7–8 *Enterprise Science News,* October 2, 1972.

8–9 R. A. Kalish, *Mental Hygiene,* vol. 55, no. 1, p. 51.

9 R. Keyes, *Modern Maturity,* April/May 1973, p. 43.

Chapter 2. Condescension Medicine

10–11 Alex Comfort, "A Vote for Humanity: Withhold Care from the Aged? Nonsense." *Medical Opinion & Review,* February 1971, p. 28.

11–12, 16 B. B. Moss, *Roche Medical Image,* August 1966.
M. A. Falk, *Psychosomatics,* vol. 9, sec. 2, July/August 1968, p. 36.

13–14 *Journal of the American Geriatrics Society,* vol. 16, p. 186.

14–15 B. L. Kutner, "How the Nation Fails to Serve Its Elders," *Centerscope,* Boston University Medical Center, November/December 1972.

15 *The New York Times,* editorial section, April 23, 1972, p. 7.

15–16 J. Deitrick, Seminar: "Geriatrics and the Medical School Curriculum," *Journal of the American Geriatrics Society,* vol. 17, no. 3.

16–17 *Canadian Medical Association Journal,* vol. 93, p. 797.

17–19 L. Cammer, "The Case of the Balky Patient," *Roche Image of Medicine and Research,* January 24, 1973, p. 22.

Chapter 3. Myths, Misconceptions, and Realities

Page

20 *Journal of the Canadian Dental Association,* vol. 36, no. 2.

21–22 P. M. Dreyfuss, University of Southern California School of Medicine.

B. F. Miller and Lawrence Galton, *Freedom from Heart Attacks* (New York: Simon & Schuster, 1972).

Lawrence Galton, *The Silent Disease* (New York: Crown, 1973).

26 *Working with Older People: A Guide to Practice,* vol. 3, *The Aging Person: Needs and Services,* United States Department of Health, Education, and Welfare, 1970.

Science News, vol. 102, p. 412.

Physician's Panorama, October 1967.

Journal of the American Geriatrics Society, vol. 19, p. 871.

Editorial, "The Decreased Adversity of Age," *Medical Tribune,* February 24, 1971.

Aging: Prospects & Issues, University of Southern California, 1973.

26–28 *Scientific American,* vol. 229, no. 3, p. 44.

Hospital Practice, October 1973, p. 75.

28–29 *Human Aging II,* Department of Health, Education, and Welfare Publication No. (HSM) 71-9037, 1971, p. 61.

29–31 Dr. James L. Birren, in *Aging: Prospects & Issues,* University of Southern California, 1973.

31–32 *Personnel Journal,* vol. 47, p. 786.

32–33 R. N. Butler, in *Clinical Geriatrics,* ed. I. Rossman (Philadelphia and New York: Lippincott, 1970).

Chapter 4. New Hope for the Senile (the Falsely Senile and the Truly Senile)

34–35 *Time* Magazine, August 4, 1967, p. 45.

36–40 *California Medicine,* vol. 109, p. 273.

36–39 *Journal of the American Geriatrics Society,* vol. 19, p. 172.

39–43 *New England Journal of Medicine,* vol. 273, p. 117.

Hospital Practice, August 1973, p. 53.

Page

	Editorial, *Canadian Medical Association Journal,* vol. 97, p. 1358.
	Journal of the American Medical Association, vol. 223, p. 409; vol. 225, p. 1486.
43–45	*Enterprise Science News,* October 2, 1972.
	Geriatrics Special Issue, *Medical World News,* 1971.
46–50	*Modern Medicine,* June 17, 1968, p. 52.
	Journal of the American Medical Association, vol. 204, p. 17; vol. 220, p. 1065.
50–51	*Journal of the American Geriatrics Society,* vol. 20, p. 127.
	International Congress of Gerontology, 1969.
	Journal of the American Geriatrics Society, vol. 19, p. 208.
51–52	*Metabolism,* vol. 18, p. 635.
52–57	*American Family Physician,* vol. 6, no. 3, p. 74.
	Hospital Practice, April 1970, 5/68.
	West Virginia Medical Association Journal, vol. 63, p. 345.
57–58	See references, chapter 12.
	R. K. Henkin, National Heart and Lung Institute, Bethesda, Md., in report to Cleveland General Hospital Symposium, 1972.
58–59	See references, chapter 9.
59–61	See references, chapter 7.
61–62	*Journal of Rehabilitation,* November/December 1970.
62–63	*Mental Hygiene,* vol. 53, p. 381.
63–64	*Archives of Otolaryngology,* vol. 93, p. 183.
	Personal letter, June 1, 1970.
	Journal of the American Medical Association, vol. 211, p. 31.
65–66	*Medical World News,* January 31, 1969, p. 42.

Chapter 5. The Great Masquerader

67–71	J. Cowen, "Depression or Disappointment?" *American Family Physician,* vol. 102, p. 99.
	"Masked Depression," *New York State Journal of Medicine,* February 15, 1968.
	A. J. Krakowski, "The Many Faces of Depression," *New York State Journal of Medicine,* February 1, 1971, p. 325.
	F. J. Braceland, "Depression," *New York State Journal*

Page

of Medicine, February 15, 1972, p. 1825.
"The Great Pretender," *Emergency Medicine,* August 1971, p. 21.

71–72 S. Cohen, *The Physician's Panorama.* September 1965, p. 13.

72–74 D. H. Smith, *West Virginia Medical Journal,* vol. 61, p. 334.

74–76 N. S. Kline, *Journal of the American Medical Association,* vol. 227, p. 1158.

75–77 *Learning about Depressive Illnesses,* National Institute of Mental Health, DHEW Publication No. (HSM) 72–9110.
Facts about Electroshock Therapy, National Institute of Mental Health, DHEW Publication No. (HSM) 72–9152.

77–78 *Medical World News,* April 20, 1973, p. 42.
"Coping with Depression," *Newsweek,* January 8, 1973, p. 51.
M. B. Bowers, "Clinical Aspects of Depression in a Home for the Aged," *Journal of the American Geriatrics Society,* vol. 17, p. 469.

Chapter 6. Other Problems for Which Psychiatry—Often Quick Psychiatry—Can Be Effective in the Aged

79 E. Merrick, Geriatric Rejects, Scientific Exhibit, American Medical Association Annual Meeting, June 20–24, 1971.

80 S. L. Safirstein, *New York State Journal of Medicine,* November 15, 1972.

80–81 V. A. Kral, *Canadian Medical Association Journal,* vol. 93, p. 292.

81–82 Symposium, Psychiatry for the Non-Psychiatrist, *Modern Medicine,* May 29, 1972, p. 70.
E. W. Busse, "Psychologic, Psychiatric, and Sociologic Aspects of Aging," *Sandoz Panorama,* May/June 1969.

82–83 R. B. Taylor, *The Practical Art of Medicine* (New York: Harper & Row, 1972).
F. J. Braceland, *Modern Medicine,* May 29, 1972, p. 73.
J. P. Sapira, *The New Physician,* May 1967, p. A-11.

Page

83 H. A. Rusk, *Medical World News,* March 14, 1969, p. 69.

J. N. Kaufman, *Medical Tribune,* June 27, 1973, p. 5.

P. Castelnuovo-Tedesco, "Brief Psychotherapy: Current Status," *California Medicine,* vol. 107, p. 263.

85–87 S. L. Safirstein, *New York State Journal of Medicine,* November 15, 1972.

Chapter 7. An Errant Gland and Its Bewildering Faces

89–90, 94–95 P. C. Whybrow, et al., "Mental Changes Accompanying Thyroid Gland Dysfunction," *Archives of General Psychiatry,* vol. 20, p. 48.

93–94 J. M. Tsao and B. Catz, "Disguised Thyroid Disorders," *California Medicine,* vol. 103, p. 91.

93–95, 96 G. M. Cremer et al., *Neurology,* vol. 19, p. 37.

93–96 A. J. Prange, Jr., et al., *American Journal of Psychiatry,* vol. 126, p. 457.

93–97 J. P. Duruisseau and E. Laurendeau, *Union Medicale du Canada,* vol. 94, p. 51.

97–100 B. O. and C. W. Barnes, *Heart Attack Rareness in Thyroid-Treated Patients* (Springfield, Ill.: Charles C. Thomas, 1972).

100–102 J. C. Wren, *Journal of the American Geriatrics Society,* vol. 19, p. 7.

Chapter 8. A Common, Overlooked—and Easily Remediable—Disease of the Elderly

103–104 *Medical World News,* March 3, 1967.

104–105 E. R. Dickson, et al., "Systemic Giant-Cell Arteritis with Polymyalgia Rheumatica," *Journal of the American Medical Association,* vol. 224, p. 1496.

105–107 L. A. Healey, Jr., "Giant-Cell Arteritis: A Common Disease of the Elderly," *GP,* vol. 34, no. 4, p. 90.

K. R. Wilske, "Giant-Cell Arteritis May Be Relatively Common," *Journal of the American Medical Association,* vol. 217, p. 1036.

Chapter 9. Other Significant Diseases of the Elderly—Combating Them, Not Automatically Giving Up to Them

Page

109–110 L. J. Nostro, *Journal of the American Geriatrics Society,* vol. 18, p. 62.

110–112 *Primer on Rheumatic Diseases,* 1973, American Rheumatism Association.

112–113, 114–115 J. S. Paolino, *Journal of the American Geriatrics Society,* vol. 19, p. 240.

115–117 *Arthritis News,* The Arthritis Foundation, 1972.

117–119 J. A. Lynch, "Early Experiences with Total Knee Replacement," Interim Scientific Session, American Rheumatism Association, December 8, 1972.

119–121 *Surgery for Arthritis of the Hip,* Bulletin of the Rheumatic Diseases, vol. 22, no. 7, The Arthritis Foundation.
Medical World News, December 21, 1973, p. 34.

119–121 *Medical World News,* June 25, 1971, p. 32.

122–124 *American Family Physician,* vol. 7, no. 4, p. 83; vol. 8, no. 2, p. 84.

124–127 *Medical Tribune,* April 11, 1973, p. 5.
Medical World News, July 14, 1972, p. 20.
Research & Demonstrations, vol. 5, no. 5, Dept. of Health, Education, and Welfare.
Canadian Medical Association Journal, vol. 106, p. 1289.

128–135 W. Likoff et al., *Your Heart: Complete Information for the Family* (Philadelphia and New York: Lippincott, 1972). B. F. Miller and Lawrence Galton, *Freedom from Heart Attacks* (New York: Simon & Schuster, 1972).

135–137 Lawrence Galton, *The Silent Disease: Hypertension* (New York: Crown, 1973).
Intelligence and blood pressure in the aged, *Science,* vol. 172, p. 9595.
Adequate therapy of hypertension improves survival, *Medical Tribune,* January 3, 1973, p. 1.

138–141 D. M. Gordan, *Physicians Panorama,* vol. 7, no. 1, 1969.
D. Paton, *American Family Physician,* vol. 7, no. 1, p. 122.

141–143 A. A. Scheer, *Medical Science,* August 1965.

143–145 A. Grieder et al., *Journal of the American Geriatric Society,* vol. 19, p. 68.

Page

Editorial, *Journal of the American Medical Association,* vol. 224, p. 622.

Chapter 10. Too Old for Surgery? Nonsense!

146–147 T. C. Case, "One-Stage Multiple Surgical Procedures in a Ninety-one-year-old Male," *Journal of the American Geriatrics Society,* vol. 19, p. 360.

147–148 J. L. Ponka and B. E. Brush, "Groin Hernia Repair Can Improve Quality of Life for Elderly," *Medical Tribune,* vol. 14, no. 34, p. 10.

147–148 G. N. Weiss, The remarkable ability of the aged to tolerate extensive procedures, Release from the American Society of Abdominal Surgeons.

E. Malan, "Surgery in the Elderly, Surgical Notes," *Medical Tribune,* February 21, 1973.

148–149 W. F. Mitty, Jr., et al., "Surgical Management of Diverticulitis in the Elderly," *American Family Physician,* vol. 3, no. 2, p. 94.

150–151 W. Burnett et al., "Surgical Procedures in the Elderly," *Surgery, Gynecology, & Obstetrics,* vol. 134, p. 221.

151–153 "Heart Pacemakers Stir Medical Revolution," *New York Times,* July 22, 1973, p. 30B.

Editorial, *Chest,* August 1971.

W. Likoff et al., *Your Heart: Complete Information for the Family* (Philadelphia and New York: Lippincott, 1972).

152–154 B. J. Messmer, G. L. Hallman, and D. A. Cooley, "Geriatric Open Heart Surgery: Experience with 292 Patients over 60 Years of Age," *Journal of Cardiovascular Surgery,* vol. 11, supplement to no. 3, p. 29.

157 *Surgery,* vol. 107, p. 30.

157–158 *Archives of Surgery,* vol. 99, p. 649.

Thorax, January 1973, p. 86.

American Journal of Surgery, February 1973, p. 181.

158–160 M. J. Levine, "The Chance to Live with Dignity," *Journal of the American Medical Association,* vol. 226, p. 672.

R. Raskin et al., "To Remain Alive with Dignity," *Journal of the American Geriatrics Society,* vol. 20, p. 170.

Chapter 11. Too Old to Be Active, Vigorous? Nonsense!

Page

161–162 Jennings Randolph, "You Are Never Too Old to Feel Young," *Congressional Record,* vol. 116, no. 210, December 30, 1970.

162–163 "The Third Age," *Time* magazine, May 7, 1973, p. 93.

163–165 W. Likoff et al., *Your Heart: Complete Information for the Family* (Philadelphia and New York: Lippincott, 1972).
B. F. Miller and Lawrence Galton, *Freedom from Heart Attacks* (New York: Simon & Schuster, 1972).

165–166 *Exercise and Health,* Bureau of Health Education of the American Medical Association, 535 N. Dearborn, Chicago 60610.
L. A. Larson and H. Michelman, *International Guide to Fitness and Health* (New York: Crown Publishers, 1973).

166–167 H. and S. Kreitler, in *Physical Activity and Aging,* eds. D. Brunner and E. Jokl (Baltimore: University Park Press, 1970).

167–168 H. A. De Vries and G. M. Adams, "Electromyographic Comparison of Single Doses of Exercise and Meprobamate as to Effects on Muscular Relaxation," *American Journal of Physical Medicine,* vol. 51, p. 130.

168–169 *Exercise Testing and Training of Apparently Healthy Individuals: A Handbook for Physicians,* American Heart Association, New York, 1972.
H. A. De Vries, Prescription of exercise for older men from telemetered exercise heart rate data, *Geriatrics,* vol. 26, p. 102.

169–171 L. J. Frankel, personal letter, May 7, 1973.
L. J. Frankel and C. J. Roncaglione, Report to International Congress on Sports Medicine and Physical Fitness, in connection with the Games of the XXth Olympiad, Munich, Germany, August, 1972.

171–172 Alexander Leaf, "Getting Old," *Scientific American,* September 1973, p. 51.

171–172 Dr. Paul Glick, Senior Demographer, Population Division, United States Census Bureau.

171–172 *Time* magazine, June 4, 1973, p. 48.

Page

R. N. Butler and M. I. Lewis, as reported in "Sex and the Senior Citizen," by Norman M. Lobsenz, *New York Times Magazine,* January 20, 1974.

Chapter 12. Nutrition and the Elderly

174–175 "Nutrition: One-Sixth of a Nation," *Time* magazine, January 31, 1969, p. 74.
"Significant Number of Persons Malnourished, Survey Shows," *West Virginia Medical Journal,* vol. 69, p. 22.
"Nutrition Is Now a National Controversy," *New York Times,* August 27, 1973, p. 1.

176–177 J. Mayer, *Overweight: Causes, Cost and Control* (Englewood Cliffs, New Jersey: Prentice-Hall, 1968).

177 *Journal of the American Geriatrics Society,* vol. 18, p. 317.

177–178 *Journal of the American Geriatrics Society,* vol. 18, p. 67; vol. 19, p. 536; vol. 20, pp. 93, 284.

178–179 *Journal of the American Geriatrics Society,* vol. 18, p. 67; vol. 19, p. 536.

179 George Christakis, *Roche Image of Medicine and Research,* March 28, 1973.

179–180 *Roche Image of Medicine & Research,* September, 1971.
S. J. Esposito et al., "Nutrition in the Aged: Review of the Literature," *Journal of the American Geriatrics Society,* vol. 17, p. 790.

180–182 B. F. Miller and Lawrence Galton, *The Family Book of Preventive Medicine* (New York: Simon & Schuster, 1971), p. 47.

181–182 *Medical World News,* vol. 15, no. 29, p. 7.

182–183 D. Vesselmovitch and R. W. Wissler, University of Chicago, Report to American Association of Pathologists & Bacteriologists, Washington, D.C., meeting, 1973.

183 *American Family Physician,* vol. 6, no. 6, p. 60.
Cancer, vol. 30, p. 927.

183–184 *Lancet* 1 (1973), p. 1278.

184–186 P. L. White, *Today's Health,* September 1973, p. 13.
J. Mayer, *Family Health,* December 1973, p. 40.

Chapter 13. Medication and the Elderly

Page

187–188 Editorial, *Journal of the American Medical Association,* vol. 199, p. 662.

188–189 *American Journal of Nursing,* June 1973.

188–189 H. F. Morrelli and K. L. Melmon, "The Clinician's Approach to Drug Interactions," *California Medicine,* vol. 109, p. 380.

J. R. DiPalma, "Drug Interactions," *American Family Physician,* vol. 7, no. 2, p. 140.

Editorial, "At Cross Purposes," *Journal of the American Medical Association,* vol. 204, p. 165.

"Interactions of Drugs," *The Medical Letter on Drugs and Therapeutics,* vol. 12, no. 23.

189–191 P. P. Lamy and M. E. Kitler, "Drugs and the Geriatric Patient," *Journal of the American Geriatrics Society,* vol. 19, p. 23.

192–198 B. F. Miller and Lawrence Galton, "A Special Word About Medicine Taking," in *The Family Book of Preventive Medicine* (New York: Simon & Schuster, 1971), p. 35–43.

193 L. Scheiner, Report to Annual Scientific Session, American College of Cardiology, San Francisco, 1973.

M. Weintraub, Report from the University of Rochester, April 20, 1973.

195–196 *Medical World News,* February 17, 1967, p. 43.

196–197 D. A. Roe, Vitamin Information Bureau Seminar, Washington, D.C., 1973; *Canadian Medical Association Journal,* vol. 103, p. 360.

Chapter 14. Nursing Homes and Alternatives

1–2 *American Geriatrics Society Newsletter,* November 1973.

Release, March 25, 1973, Social and Rehabilitation Service, United States Department of Health, Education, and Welfare.

U. S. News & World Report, March 5, 1973, p. 40.

202 "Perspectives in Long-Term Care," *American Medical Association,* vol. 5, no. 1, 1974.

Page

202–203 "Study of Nursing Homes Calls Two-Thirds Deficient," in *The New York Times,* November 1, 1973.
A. N. Schwartz, University of Southern California, Ethel Percy Andrus Gerontology Center, Release, June 4, 1973.

For answers to particular questions about nursing homes, you can contact your local welfare department or local Social Security district office.
In addition, you may wish to see some of the following informative United States government booklets; all available from the Superintendent of Documents, United States Government Printing Office, Washington, D.C. 20402, at prices indicated:

1. *Nursing-Home Care.* Stock number 1761–00032. Consumer Information Series #2, United States Department of Health, Education, and Welfare. 45c per copy.
2. *Let's End Isolation.* GPO: 1971 0–455–155, published by the Administration on Aging, Social and Rehabilitation Service, United States Department of Health, Education, and Welfare. 30c per copy.
3. *It Can't Be Home.* GPO: 1971 0–438–021, published by the Public Health Service, United States Department of Health, Education, and Welfare. 50c per copy.
4. *Medicare/Medicaid–Which Is Which?* GPO: 1970 0–388–551, published by the Medical Services Administration, Social and Rehabilitation Service, United States Department of Health, Education, and Welfare. 25c per copy.

Chapter 15. Current Research in Aging

207–218 "Special Report: Human Aging," *Chemical & Engineering News,* July 24, 1972, p. 13.
Medical World News, October 22, 1971, p. 46.
"Can Aging Be Cured?" *Newsweek,* April 16, 1973, p. 56.
"Aging: A Vision of Control," editorial, *Medical*

Page

	Tribune, September 18, 1969.
210	B. L. Strehler, testimony before Senate Special Committee on Aging, Washington, D.C., December 6, 1967.
211–212	H. J. Curtis, "Biological Mechanisms of Aging," symposium on medical chemistry, Laval University, Quebec, Canada, June 26, 1968.
212–213	L. Orgel, *Salk Institute Newsletter,* no. 5.
216	D. Harman, *Journal of the American Geriatrics Society,* vol. 17, p. 721; *American Journal of Clinical Nutrition,* vol. 25, p. 839.
218–220	*Medical World News,* May 11, 1973, p. 25; April 6, 1973, p. 6.
	J. P. Hrachovec and M. D. MacFarlane, report to Gerontological Society, San Juan, December 18, 1972. *Geriatric Focus,* February 1973.
219–221	Report from Duke University Information Services, May 31, 1970.

Chapter 16. Envoi

222–223	*New York Times,* February 21, 1973.
	Wall Street Journal, February 6, 1973, p. 1.
223–224	*Medical World News,* January 30, 1970, p. 26A.
223–225	*Medical World News,* April 7, 1972, p. 42.
	T. R. Reiff, "We're Doing a Third-Rate Job for the Aged," *Prism,* December 1973 (American Medical Association Publication).

INDEX